SPOT FIRES
AND
SLOP-OVERS

MEMOIR OF A FIREFIGHTER

BUCK WICKHAM

ISBN: 978-1-4834-9137-0 (sc)
ISBN: 978-1-4834-9138-7 (e)

Library of Congress Control Number: 2018911129

Because of the dynamic nature of the Internet, any web addresses or links contained in this book may have changed since publication and may no longer be valid. The views expressed in this work are solely those of the author and do not necessarily reflect the views of the publisher, and the publisher hereby disclaims any responsibility for them.

Any people depicted in stock imagery provided by Getty Images are models, and such images are being used for illustrative purposes only. Certain stock imagery © Getty Images.

Lulu Publishing Services rev. date: 09/26/2018

CONTENTS

INTRODUCTION

I started working for the forest service in 1971 when I was eighteen years old. I retired on November 11, 2011. My career was a great one, and it provided a substantial living for me and my family. It also allowed me to work with an amazing group of people. My career started in fire management, and I was there for ten years. Then I switched to range management and worked there for twenty years. Finally, I switched back to fire management for the final ten years of my career.

Looking back, I see the highlights of my career include the years that I was lucky enough to serve on fire teams—or incident management teams, as they are referred to now. I have served on incident management teams now for more than thirty years, and as a result, I have worked with some of the finest people in the world. Additionally, my involvement with these teams has taken me across our nation and exposed me to areas that I would have never been able to experience on my own. Moreover, I've encountered a host of wildfires in most areas within our great nation.

With little exception (two years as a safety officer), I was involved in the operations groups within the teams. I served many years as a division supervisor and also eventually worked as operations section chief. As a result of these experiences, I have had many good times … and some tragic instances too. Through it all, the strength of unity and companionship that the team atmosphere created was always near and dear to my heart.

The people in the incident management teams become your

extended family. You share the good times and the bad times together. You can count on the support of the team both in work endeavors and in home issues. All this ends with a group of folks you may not see except on fire assignments, but you share an undeniable bond, which is always a unique and heartwarming experience.

The operations groups that I have served with are composed of a unique group of folks. They are can-do people who accomplish their tasks in a professional manner in some of the worst working conditions possible. However, they can make the best of bad situations and still maintain great attitudes and accomplish incident goals. You don't want to let your guard down around a group of operations guys, or you may end up with a snake in your bedroll.

Two things acted as the catalyst for my writing this book. The first was a book titled *Leave It to Cowboys* that my friend Kenny Seidell wrote. It's about his life working on ranches in Northern Arizona. As I read his book, it reminded me of the people and things that I had all but forgotten. I admire him for capturing those times, and while I doubt it will make the best seller list, I still value his efforts to capture his memories. They have a value to him … and also to me.

The second reason comes from a conversation I shared while eating dinner on a fire assignment. I was eating with one of my fellow operations section chiefs during one cold evening. We shared a table with a few members of a hotshot crew. Our discussion drifted to the fires during which we had nearly frozen to death, and we also joked about how many of the old-issue paper sleeping bags we needed to survive. The hotshots finally spoke up and said they were not buying our story. They didn't think there was anyone stupid enough to go to a fire without a sleeping bag, and the story about paper sleeping bags clearly cinched it as unbelievable, in their minds. They knew we were trying to pull the wool over their eyes, and they refused to believe us. So I feel the need to capture some of my experiences for the good of the order and to provide those who now fight fires with a glimpse of how things were.

In the recent past, a guy who spent a summer working on one of the local hotshot crews wrote a few books about the happenings during the summer. He must have kept a diary, and in his writing he used everyone's name as he told his story. He called me prior to publishing the books, saying that he had used my name and he wanted me to sign a waiver that would give him permission to use my name in his book. My knee-jerk reaction and what I told him was that before I signed anything, I wanted to read the books. I was reluctant to allow anyone to use my name because some things were just better left untold, especially if you were still employed by the forest service. I never signed a waiver, but when I finally secured a copy of his book, I was relieved that I was spared some embarrassment. Many of the others mentioned in his book were alarmed by the rather embarrassing and perhaps incriminating stories about them. So as not to incriminate or embarrass anyone, I will attempt to leave the names of people out of this book. So all you guilty folks can relax.

I also would like to leave most of the bad words out of this work. I wouldn't want to upset anyone, and hopefully, I can tell most of the stories without many cuss words. If you know anyone who does fight wildfires, you are probably aware that most don't follow this model and some cuss like sailors. Cussing is more offensive the older you are. Some young folks also cuss like sailors. Male or female, it doesn't seem to matter. There are probably fewer kids getting backhanded for cussing these days. That was the way my father taught me not to cuss. You caught on pretty quick. My dear grandmother told me once, "If you can't express yourself without cussing, it shows you're not smart enough to do that," and she still cussed like a sailor. Of course, this has often proved to be a challenge, but I will try.

The use of acronyms for federal agencies has gotten completely out of hand. An understanding of all these acronyms is needed in order to make sense of the things we do. Instead of spelling out the departments, laws, or projects, almost everyone uses the acronyms, and that can leave someone who's not in a federal service wondering what the hell everyone is talking about.

For example, TU commonly refers to *tango uniform*. I believe this term was first coined by firefighters on the Mormon Lake Hotshots and was first used to refer to someone who was hurt and needed assistance. A person was then carried off the line on a litter with their "tits up." Hence, the term. The international phonetic alphabet term of *tango uniform* was used to prevent any sexual harassment or discrimination issues. I may add that I have been corrected in the past. People have said that it is actually "teats up," but you get my drift. As this term gained wider usage, it eventually started meaning anything that was broken or not working. Therefore, a pump may be tits up even if it doesn't have tits or teats. The term *tango uniform* is utilized to avoid offending anyone who may not like the reference to tits/teats.

A complete listing of all the acronyms used would make for a huge and boring portion of this book, so in order to not bore everyone, I will capture the ones I need to use by showing the acronym in parentheses after the term. Acronyms are necessary because government agencies often use complex names for things and institutions. For example, there's the Lake Tahoe Basin Management Unit (LTBMU), and I think we all know that WTF is not "welcome to Flagstaff."

The list of acronyms is not set in stone, and we are dreaming up new ones all the time. So one has to keep current in these references. I have been in many meetings when a new acronym was brought up that I didn't understand, and I always delighted in asking the stupid question about what the hell it actually meant. Most folks just act like they know what is going on and ask later to find out what the acronym meant.

So to follow the inspiration of my friend Kenny, who captured some of his own memories of my past, and to honor my fellow firefighters by documenting the many things that current firefighters may not believe about the old days, I will attempt to assemble a narrative about how things have changed and retell some fire stories that are hopefully entertaining.

CHAPTER 1
THE BEGINNINGS

Growing up, I would hear my father and his contemporaries talk about how things used to be. As a kid listening to these talks, I often wondered what the big deal was. The world as I knew it was just fine, and given the way it was now, it seemed better than the one they often talked about. I hadn't been around long enough to notice any changes, but I was aware that a lot of folks thought there were better days long before. I would ride my bike into town, go swimming at the public pool, get a Coke and candy bar for a dime, and ride my bike home, only spending a quarter in total. The older folks thought that was a little too much money. I would mow lawns in town for a buck to finance my swimming and snacks. Now you couldn't get a guy to flip you off for a buck.

I find myself having the same type of conversations with my friends about how much things have changed and how nice it would be if people—and life in general—had kept some of the good things of the past. The longer we live, the more change we see, and the more opinionated we grow as we see the changes, both good and bad, in our view. Like it or not, I find myself having the same kinds of talks with my friends and sounding a lot like my father.

My first summer working for the forest service is a far cry from the job today. I worked at a place called Buck Springs Guard Station. This place was about twenty miles of good gravel road from Blue Ridge Ranger Station, which was up on the Mogollon Rim in Northern Arizona, and it was quite a beautiful place. Buck Springs Guard Station consisted of a single-room log cabin with a covered porch, and it was all situated next to a large meadow. It was close to eight thousand feet in elevation and right at the vegetation change from ponderosa pine to mixed conifer. The guard station was originally one log cabin that was constructed in the 1923. Then in 1946 another larger log cabin was built and the older one was left abandoned.

One afternoon we returned to the guard station to find two eighty-year-old men standing out in front of the cabin. We parked the tanker and walked over to them to see whether they needed anything. These two guys told us that they had built the older cabin and had decided to get together and drive up to see what the old place looked like. Both of them had spent a few summers there working for the forest service in their younger years, and they thought it was time to return and remember those days.

As we visited with the guys, they started talking about fires, their horses, the people who lived in the area, and their experiences with them. They talked about how after a thunderstorm they would ride their horses to high points or to the trees they could climb and see whether any fires had started because of the storm. They would fish for trout in the beaver dam in the meadow that was in front of the cabins. The road system was not in place; however, trails and packhorses were the mode of transportation. While some roads followed ridgetops down from the General Crook Trail, there were no roads that crossed the many canyons in the area. The gentlemen told us how they had no radios and little contact other than with the local folks who made their living in the forest.

During this conversation one of the gentlemen was telling us that if you did see a fire, you rode over to it and lined it, and then you stacked up some green limbs on the fire to send a smoke signal that you had caught the fire and didn't need any help. I asked him what you did if you needed help, and he looked at me like the rookie I was and said, "Hell, son, if you lost the fire, it put up so much smoke that everyone knew you needed help." It was common in those days that the local loggers, cowboys, hunters, shepherds, or anyone who saw the smoke would come to help out. It was expected that everyone would fight a fire if they were needed. Wooden boxes of fire tools and canteens were cached around the forest just for this need.

We talked with these guys until they had to leave, and it was quite an enjoyable discussion for all of us. They had a wealth of knowledge about the area from long ago. We had found a very old log cabin in one of the draws off Leonard Canyon, and we wondered who'd built the place in such a remote canyon. They knew of the place and the guy who lived there. "That was old Whiskey Pete's cabin. He built it there because he was a bootlegger, and the remote draw and a nearby spring provided him everything he needed to practice his craft." A place called Holder Cienega had the old foundation of a cabin and part of an old corral, so we asked what the scoop was with that. "Well," one of them began, "that was old Gene Holder's place. He was a game warden and had a pack of lion hounds, and he was sure a good and fair guy." The day ended, and the old guys headed home. But they gave us an important history lesson of the era. As I said, this happened during my first season. If I were to run across these guys today, I could have talked for days about the way things were.

Thinking of this visit today, I see how lucky we were to have the afternoon to talk with these old guys about their adventures fifty years prior to our own. They were surprised at how much stuff we had—and how much things had changed—and so were we. We had no clue that the meadow had held a beaver dam large enough to fish in. After all, the beaver had long since left the area. Hopefully, with my writings, I can offer somewhat of a glimpse of how things have changed in my years fighting fires.

In retrospect, I find it heartwarming that these two old guys who worked fighting fire when they were young so many years ago were still friends, that through the years they kept in touch and kept the memories that they'd experienced so long ago.

Just as the forest service was a different place for the two old gentlemen who came by the guard station, it is different today from the way it was when I started. As I attempt to write down some of my memories, I am entering my forty-seventh year of fighting forest fires. I, too, find myself remembering my old days, and while I still look up to the folks whom I mentored in my career, I see that the new workforce thinks of me as an old-timer. Everyone is a product of his or her time, and the new workforce—before they know it—will be like me, getting old and remembering the way it was.

I started in a simpler and more straightforward place to work. And although the number of folks employed was fewer, I feel that about the same amount of work was accomplished. Right or wrong, I do feel there was more actual work done in the forest, as currently most of the *work* is done working through the minefield of environmental issues. Employees of the era wore many different hats and accomplished a wider variety of tasks. The focus of the district where I started was the logging industry. While national parks and monuments were established to protect the natural beauty of the areas they encompassed, the forest service was established to provide for the national need of resources that helped build this nation. The terms *multiple use* and *sustained yield* were the battle cries of the forest service in that day. The battle cry may not have changed; however, the means to get to that have become quite boggled up in a tangle of agency and public demands.

One issue that I should clear up prior to this discussion is that this is the way I remember things. It may have been different in different places or forests, but in the Coconino National Forest during my era, this is how it seemed to me. We should also discuss my education. I am not a *professional* but rather a *technician*, a term that is still as current today as it was when I was hired. Inside the forest service, that means I have no college degree. When I was reading a recent issue of the *Amigos* newsletter, which is a newsletter for southwestern forest service retirees, I saw there was a forest supervisor who refused to discuss anything with anyone under the GS-12 level because he felt they had nothing of value to say. This is a great example of the professional/technician mind-set, and I must say I'm glad I never worked for this guy. I did graduate from high school, and I actually did start to attend a university; however, my heart was not in it, and I wanted to pursue the cowboy life. So I quit college after one semester and secured a job on a ranch.

When I grew up, there were two issues of the time—the military draft and Vietnam. Call it a police action, war, or whatever, but all my contemporaries were exposed to the draft. And while there were many deferments that allowed some to not get drafted, being a cowboy was not one of them. A host of my high school classmates and I were immediately drafted when we turned eighteen years old. After finding out they had been drafted, a group of my friends joined the army on the buddy system. The buddy system was supposed to allow you all to go into and serve in the army together. This ended up being true to a point, as all four of them got to ride the bus to Albuquerque, New Mexico, together. Then they were scattered around the world, never to see each other until they were discharged.

The army's lack of commitment to my buddies did not give me much confidence in enlisting. As my report date approached, I decided to enlist in the navy. They had a 180-day delay from the time you enlisted to when you reported. This sounded good to me for a couple of reasons. The first was that I could continue my current job on the ranch. Second, there were rumors of peace negotiations that would end the Vietnam conflict, and hopefully, they'd be successful in the next 180 days. Like most folks in that era, I had friends who were killed in Vietnam, and understandably, I was apprehensive about being sent there. One of the reasons that I decided the navy was that the news reported so little about their involvement in the crisis. I felt I could fulfill my military obligation and avoid Vietnam. This may sound a little chicken shit, but it is truthfully how I felt at the time. I was working for a ranch when I received my draft notice and enlisted in the US Navy on a 180-day delay.

My father loved the mountains, and he was an avid hunter and fisherman. He had worked in the rim country as he grew up on ranches. In his time there were yet any subdivisions or the sprawl that we see today. It seemed there were fewer folks around, so pretty much everyone knew everyone. So too, we had woodstoves and fireplaces, which required firewood. This need and my father's desire to go to the mountains took us there quite often. I think he wanted to cut every dead alligator juniper tree on the rim and haul it home. While I always liked heading up to the hills, my love for cutting firewood was pretty much fulfilled at a very early age.

Another factor that probably helped out my career in fire

management is that I have always been awed by fire. I think it shouldn't come as much of a surprise that there's quite a few firefighters who may be closet pyromaniacs. When I was a kid, we had woodstoves, and we burned our trash in an old fifty-five gallon barrel, so there was a box of kitchen matches hanging on the wall just waiting to be struck. While I was very limited with what I was allowed to do with matches, I sometimes crossed the line. I was allowed to burn the trash, and this alone made it a chore that I would do. My father and the other folks who used the irrigation ditches every fall would band together and burn the weeds out of the ditches. This was pretty cool, and most of the time, I got to go along. That probably got me in the worst trouble. One day I actually decided that I should burn some weeds, and the fire got out of hand and had to be put out by grown-ups who were pretty pissed afterward.

Because we spent a lot of time up on the rim, I ended up finding my way around pretty well by the time I was in high school. A friend of my father's was the fire control officer (FCO) at Blue Ridge Ranger Station, and every time we ran into him, he told me that when I turned eighteen, he would give me a job working for the forest service. He liked the idea that I knew the lay of the land, and he also knew that I had outdoor experience, especially with cutting firewood.

When I got out of high school, I was only seventeen years old. The next day after my high school graduation, I went to work on a ranch, which had a large forest grazing permit. The ranch had cabled several thousand acres of pinyon/juniper woodlands, and it was all scheduled to be burned and seeded that summer. The ranch folks ignited the blocks from horseback using fuzees on bamboo poles daily, and the forest service had a few folks there to contain fire within the blocks. The folks from the ranch would be out there every morning for a few hours, waiting for the forest service guys to get there, and they would leave every afternoon a few hours before we did. The old eight-hour workday had not hit the ranch yet, and it still hasn't, I might add. The forest service guys even got a couple days off each week as they should. Working at the ranch was what I always wanted, so I was happy. As the summer passed, the fire control officer again said on a few occasions, "When you're eighteen come in, and I'll give you a job."

One afternoon the following spring, I was driving down Highway 87, and as I approached the ranger station, I started thinking of stopping in. I had just turned eighteen, and I thought I would stop in for a visit with the FCO, my dad's old friend. I went into the ranger station and walked back to his office and found him sitting in his chair, rubbing his belly, and smoking a cigar, which he was seldom without. Smoking was allowed in the offices at that time. I told him that I had turned eighteen over the winter and was following his request to stop in. He asked me if I wanted a job. I told him that I did but that I had enlisted in the navy and only had four or five months before I had to report. This didn't matter to him. He knew that my departure was to be expected. Most of the young folks had been drafted anyway. So he told me to go down to the crew quarters, throw my stuff in one, come back down to the office, and then fill out an application. This was how I started my career with the forest service. The hiring process is just a little more complex now, which comes as no surprise.

My official title was assistant tanker truck operator (ATTO), and my grade was a GS-3, which made me a seasonal employee. My duty station was Buck Spring Guard Station, but you still couldn't get into the high country because of deep snow, so I was to work out of Blue Ridge until the roads were open.

The district fire organization at the time I was hired consisted of three tankers—one at Blue Ridge Ranger Station, one at General Springs Guard Station, and the tanker at Buck Springs Guard Station. Each tanker was staffed with two people, and one worked during the other's days off. Additionally, at Blue Ridge, there was a small bulldozer, a nurse tanker, and the FCO. One guy actually served as the maintenance man for the ranger district, but he also served as the assistant to the FCO and the nurse tanker operator if one was needed. One married couple worked at Moqui Lookout, a fire lookout, and brought the total fire personnel up to eleven.

The timber shop had quite a few necessary employees as logging was one of the main tasks of the forest service then. Sawmills were common in most of the neighboring communities. There were mills in Winslow, Payson, Flagstaff, Williams, and Prescott, and many others served the Apache-Sitgreaves National Forest to our east. There was a timber staff officer, a presale forester, two timber sale administrators, a five-person timber-marking crew, and a timber stand improvement crew (TSI crew). This TSI crew consisted of six individuals, who for the most part thinned the forest to promote tree growth, but if needed, they would also respond to fires.

Loggers were common in the forest as it was common for several timber sales and logging companies to be active each year. Most logging companies had a host of employees who worked in the woods and the mills. There was a logging camp named "Happy Jack" across the highway from Happy Jack Ranger Station, where many of the loggers lived. Several years later the logging camp was moved to a new location near Clint's well and called Happy Jack Too. We got to know these folks well since we often ran into one another and shared the same workplace. So too, if a fire was active near their operations, they would provide help to suppress it as part of the timber sale contract. So it was not uncommon to have some of the loggers helping on a fire, especially if it started to get big. They would supply bulldozers and equipment as needed. Some of the best dozer operators I have seen were the guys who drove dozers for the logging companies. Most of them had worked for years for the outfit, and they'd helped out on several fires. They were accustomed to working on slopes and in timber. Such skilled dozer operators are hard to come by in current times.

Another function of the forest service was providing forage for livestock grazing. The range shop consisted of one individual who was responsible for administering the grazing permits within the district. This person also managed some wildlife and watershed responsibilities. This was a time when the range conservationist were classified as the range, wildlife, and watershed staff. In days before there were such specializations within the forest service, one person accomplished all these tasks within a shop.

Business administration was taken care of by three ladies who handled all the paperwork, keeping time, filing, typing letters, purchasing, and generally keeping all the other employees out of trouble. This was long before computers, and all the typing was done on typewriters. They used carbon paper to make copies, and everything needed copies. They also answered the phone. That's right—the phone. And there was only one radio phone for everyone.

The recreation staff consisted of one old Hopi man who took care of the campgrounds. He kept them maintained and hauled off all the trash. He did this without any supervision and with a smile on his face for decades.

The total employees on the district numbered thirty in the summer and dwindled to nine in the winter. Everyone lived at the ranger station either in duplexes for the staff and families or the crew quarters for the balance of the workforce. No one lived in town, and the subdivisions didn't exist at the time.

Life at the ranger station was similar to living in a small community. Secrets were hard to hide, and it seemed that everyone knew one another's business. We not only worked together but lived together too. While some disputes occasionally flared up, we all got along pretty well and put up with one another's kids and dogs. Everyone seemed to help one another whenever necessary.

If there was a large project or if one of the organizations needed help with something, everyone pitched in and got it done. We all worked for the forest service, and people went beyond their normal skills in order to get the various jobs done. One great example was fire suppression.

In those days everyone was expected to participate in putting out fires if there was a need. There is actually quite a bit to do in managing fires. As a result, people take on roles—keeping time, logistical support, or firefighting. All fire needs were taken care of by the dispatch office in Flagstaff, and the dispatcher would call in the personnel needed to suppress the fire. When a call was received by dispatch, it wasn't really a request but rather an assignment. Fire suppression was a duty. It was expected that forest service personnel as well as the loggers and others who worked in the forest to drop everything and do what was necessary. Often the local personnel for Arizona Game and Fish Department would set up a kitchen and cook meals for the firefighters.

This process has changed though. Now dispatch calls and offers a fire assignment and asks if you want to participate. This is quite a change, and while there are quite a few more employees, there is a huge number of folks who don't participate in fire suppression. This growing number of employees who choose not to work on putting out fires has resulted in a lack of qualified fire personnel. This lack of participation in fire suppression does not mean that some of these folks aren't experts in the many aspects of fire. It is amazing that this has occurred, but it has become common to deal with experts on fire who have worked on controlling few if any fires. One of the best incident commanders I've have had the pleasure of working with once said, "Regardless of popular opinion, it still takes ten years to get ten years of fire experience."

The general attitude of employees has also changed in my opinion. With the forest service, you could work as hard as you wanted or slack off as much as you wanted. The adage of "screw up and move up" is hard to refute. When I started—and maybe this was just how I felt about it—questioning someone who told you what to do was unacceptable. If you were told to go do something, you just did it. While some of the assignments were better than others, people weren't likely to debate if an unpleasant task should fall upon them.

I was visiting with a seasoned rancher who had managed a large ranch in Arizona for years. He said something that day that has stuck with me throughout my career. Looking back, I can see his logic, and only on a few things can I refute its truth. He told me, "The forest service will do something until it works. Then they will never do it again."

CHAPTER 2
THE EARLY YEARS

Buck Springs Guard Station was my duty station for my first several summers. The cabin had one room with two bunk beds, a sink, a few cupboards, a propane stove and refrigerator, a woodstove, and a resident population of chipmunks. We didn't have electricity, and we used Coleman lanterns for lighting. We didn't use the woodstove for much cooking, but we did use it to heat the cabin from time to time. The propane stove worked well enough, but the propane refrigerator worked better as a freezer as it tended to freeze its contents regardless of the setting. We did have a gravity-flow water system that delivered cold water to the cabin. We had no hot water, and we didn't have a shower or a bathtub. If you wanted hot water, you needed to heat it up on the stove.

We had little contact with anyone. The FCO would bring fifty-five gallon drums of gas, filled propane tanks, and radio batteries to us as we needed them. The nurse tanker would deliver a load of drinking water a few times during the summer. We would monitor the radio daily and respond to fires as they occurred. These usually consisted of small lightning fires. My first summer we had only three vehicles come by that weren't coming out to see us for one reason or another.

In the spring one of our main tasks was to cut trees out of the road system. Each winter there were inevitably ones that had fallen down and closed off the roads. The area had a huge road system that accommodated the logging activities in the area, and this task kept us busy for at least a month as the summer started. In this era there were few man-caused fires. People who camped in the forest during those days were fewer and more skilled in camping protocols. The fires we went to were almost always caused by lightning.

The monsoon in the summer months kept us busy as it was common to have several fires start on the same day. Most of these fires were held in check with some rain and the humidity that came with the monsoons. One of the biggest challenges was finding the fires when the lookouts reported them. We called this activity smoke-chasing, and it is one of my favorite things to do. Once located, most of the fires were easy to catch, and then it was off to another. I have many great memories of running around the rim country and looking for fires. My favorite time of year is the monsoon period, and the rim country is some of the prettiest land I have been on.

One instance during my first year has followed me throughout my career. One afternoon I was sitting around the guard station alone because it was the other guy's day off. It was the monsoon season, and the afternoon brought a huge buildup of thunderstorms. Lightning started really popping. A thunderstorm on the Mogollon Rim can be difficult to describe. Because of the lay of the land, the rim can really get pounded by lightning. This was one such afternoon. I loved to stand on the porch at Buck Springs and watch the show. It was so cool to watch the storms pound the area.

A few hours into the storm, a fire flash came in from Moqui Lookout. When the first lookouts saw a fire start up, they would call dispatch with a fire flash. This was music to any firefighter's ears as it was a call to take action. A fire flash would immediately get the adrenalin flowing. The smoke reported by Moqui Lookout was out on the rim in the area of Myrtle and Lost Lakes, which are two little natural lakes close to the edge of the Mogollon Rim.

In a few minutes, I got a call from the dispatcher, who then told me to head out to the new start. I eagerly jumped into the tanker and headed toward the smoke by myself. It was a common thing that that one of us was alone during the week as each of us usually got at least one day off. When I reached the general area where the smoke had been reported, the ground was covered with about six inches of hail. This was also a common occurrence on the rim as the thunderstorm cells in the area often deposited huge amounts of hail. I turned north onto a small road that went in between the two natural lakes and proceeded only about two hundred yards before I got the tanker stuck in the mud.

Getting stuck was just one of the unfortunate things that happened while you were working in the woods. I was well versed in what to do to get unstuck, so I started the process. First, I got out and locked in the hubs, but as I tried to free myself with the four-wheel drive, I just managed to get even more stuck. Now the tanker was bogged down to the frame in a large puddle in the middle of the road. Next I grabbed the high-lift jack that we all carried and start jacking the truck up and putting rocks and sticks under the wheels. I was kicking some rocks under the wheel of the tanker when a bolt of lightning hit a mature ponderosa pine that was located about three feet from the tanker. At the time the lightning hit, I was standing in the puddle, a shovel in my left hand and leaning on the bed of the tanker with my right.

I immediately felt the shock of my life. It felt like I was being shocked by a wall outlet but many times more powerful. I was knocked unconscious and landed on my back in the puddle. If I would have fallen facedown, I would have drown, which is a thought that has always haunted me. The next thing I remember was waking up and lying faceup in the puddle the tanker was stuck in. I was freezing cold because the ground was still covered with hail. In fact, the puddle I had fallen into was as cold as a glass of ice water. I lay there for a minute. I knew what had happened, but I was still a little fuzzy. I hurt all over, and it felt like every joint in my body was welded together. I also had a few burn injuries, but I was unaware of them at that time. My knee-jerk reaction was to climb into the tanker and call for help. When I tried to get up, I then realized that my right arm and leg didn't work. I was really scared then and still quite fuzzy about what was going on.

Lying in the cold water, I kept trying to get up and go back into the tanker. I finally did, and I thanked God the radio still worked. I called Moqui Lookout and reported that I had been struck by lightning and needed help. Of course, when the news hit the radio, it caused great concern, and everyone in that neck of the woods hauled ass to my location to help me. The district ranger was the first to arrive. He walked up and asked if I was all right. I told him that I wasn't and that I was hurting all over. He then grabbed my lunch box and walked back to his truck and called me on the radio and told me to come on over and get in. I told him I couldn't do that because my arm and leg wouldn't work, so he came over and helped me get into his truck.

The district ranger was old school, and he moved in slow motion. I was not really impressed with him prior to this accident and the entire time he worked on the district. However, as my career progressed, I became more and more appreciative of him, and eventually, I became a fan after working for many other rangers after him. After I got into his truck, he drove at a snail's pace to the district office. He wasn't much for talking, and this drive was not only slow but very quiet. I asked him to hurry because I was in a great deal of pain, and he said that he didn't want me to go into shock and that was why he was driving carefully. I felt like telling him that if I wasn't in shock after the lightning, I must have dodged the bullet, but it was my first year, so I just sat there and shivered all the way into the station.

When we got to the station, he went into the office to get the "paperwork for the hospital," as he said, and left me sitting in his truck. The district fire control officer walked out of the office and saw me sitting there alone, shivering and painfully waiting for the ranger, and he went ballistic. He ran back into the office and brought out the ranger, screaming at him to get me to a hospital now. He said that we'd worry about the paperwork later.

I was driven to the hospital in Winslow, and then I was admitted. They told me I was suffering electrical paralysis, which they said would go away in time. I had received burns where the rivets of my pants, the metal buttons of my shirt, and the eyes of my boots were. I also had a ruptured left eardrum, and I was still moderately hypothermic. Luckily, I was only eighteen years old, so I did heal quickly. The paralysis only lasted until the next day, and the burns healed quickly. I still have issues with my ear, but in a few days after the incident, I was released from the hospital and allowed to return to work.

To say that I recovered fully from this experience would be untruthful, and while the physical stuff other than my ear went away, it planted the fear of lightning in me forever. Instead of standing out on the front porch at Buck Springs and delighting in watching the storms of the rim country, I would sit inside the cabin in a wooden chair with each leg in a coffee cup, scared as hell. Because of my experience, I was called upon throughout my career to lead meetings about lightning safety when that subject was discussed.

I have amused my fellow firefighters with paranoia whenever they have been around me in a lightning storm. If you have ever taken care of a dog that was scared of lightning, thunder, or fireworks, then you can imagine how I was for several years after that. To this day, I flinch at the flash of lightning, which is still amusing to my friends and coworkers. Since this happened, I have been caught out in some horrible storms, and in those times, I feel like hiding under a couch, suffering alone while most of my friends laugh their asses off about my sissy behavior. As a result of my encounter with lightning, I started paying closer attention to religion, and I didn't cuss for a year and a half after this mishap just to be on the safe side.

Most people think I have been hit by lightning several times. When it happened, there were rumors that it had killed me, so I surprised a few folks by showing up alive and well. I am tall, so I've heard just about every joke about being a lightning rod. I have grown used to no one wanting to stand near me in a lightning storm. In the end, there are many better ways to get a reputation than getting struck by lightning.

The Coconino National Forest suffered a tragedy that summer. As the monsoon season approached, the forest was very dry from a lack of moisture. The forest was closed to camping, and loggers were also required to be out of the woods each day by the burning period in the middle of the day. When the monsoon started, the rim country received dry lightning, and more than ninety fires were reported on the southern portions of the forest. The following day the same dry lightning hit the northern portions of the forest. While flying the new starts in a small airplane on the northern portions of the forest, a plane crash took the lives of a district ranger and the pilot.

The dry lightning did produce some moisture, and the humidity helped more than the rain in a lot of areas; however, within a week all the fires were controlled. It was a busy week, and our tanker had six fires a day for six days straight. This happened during my first summer, and it was one thing that made me want to fight fires for a career.

After my experience with lightning, the summer went by without any additional trauma, and I was exposed to what eventually became my career. I loved living on the rim at Buck Springs, loved chasing smokes around on the rim, and generally enjoyed the summer before I was supposed to report to the navy. One afternoon we fought a fire out on Leonard Points, and when we were finished with it, we jumped into the dodge power wagon, which was our tanker, and found out it wouldn't start. We called Moqui Lookout to request some help. In a few minutes, they called back and said the FCO (my dad's old buddy) was headed out to give us a hand.

It was no secret that the FCO and the district ranger did not get along very well. They must have had a difference of opinion that day because when the FCO arrived, he was quite mad. He got out of his truck and asked if we had any drinking water. Of course we did, and he knew we did. We had a few canteens, so we got one and gave it to him. He then reached into his truck and pulled a quart of whiskey out and said, "Well good." We didn't really know what had happened, but we caught on really quick that a pull on the bottle could make things somewhat better. He took a big drink and passed the bottle to us. So we each had a drink or two of whiskey, and then we looked into the issue with the truck. After another drink or two, we decided that the problem was the voltage regulator, and after we jumped the truck, we had it running again. Then we took off for Buck Springs with the FCO following us to make sure we made it.

As we were headed back to Buck Springs, we passed through a little rain shower, and as we turned on the windshield wipers, the truck died again. We got out the jumper cables and the whiskey bottle, and we jumped the truck and had another pull on the bottle. Neither I nor the other guy on the tanker was old enough to legally drink, but that didn't seem to matter. So we were off again, headed to the guard station. One of us pushed in the cigarette lighter, and the truck stalled again. So we jumped the tanker again and shared another drink. After that, we caught on that we shouldn't try to turn anything else on as the truck would stall again, and we both had a pretty good buzz going because of the whiskey. We finally made it back to the guard station, which warranted one more pull on the bottle for our success, and then the FCO headed back to the ranger station.

In about thirty minutes, Moqui Lookout called us and said that the FCO needed us to come and give him a little help and that he was on the road by Yeager Canyon. This request caught us by surprise. He knew we didn't have any vehicles but our personal ones, but we said we would head down that way. We jumped in my pickup truck and drove down to Yeager Canyon. We found the FCO had run off the road on accident and couldn't get back on. Consequently, he wanted us to pull his truck back up on the road. We helped out without any issues. Then we had another pull on the whiskey bottle, ready to go our separate ways. The FCO suggested that the fewer people who knew what we were up to that afternoon, the better off we all would be. That seemed like the right thing to do, so we all kept our mouths shut and just let it go. This is the first time I've brought it up since then.

As mentioned, when I was initially hired on for the forest service, I had enlisted in the navy, and I worked until I was supposed to report for active duty. I didn't know it at the time, but this played well into my career. I entered the navy, and after boot camp, I was assigned to a marine group that was positioned on a helicopter carrier. I joined the navy on a 180-day delay because I hadn't heard of much naval involvement in Vietnam. That didn't work out very well as I found myself bobbing around just off the coast of Vietnam. We had a battalion of marines and a marine helicopter squadron on the ship I was assigned to the marines. If you're a navy guy assigned to the marines, you were called a squid, so I was a squid, like it or not. This is another story that I have chosen not to write about, but after serving my time, I was sent to Treasure Island in California to be discharged.

If you were a marine or you know one, you understand the phrase "high and tight." That refers to the hairstyle that was required of marines and squids. When I reported to Treasure Island, it had probably been two weeks since my last haircut. I went to the chow hall the first day. I got there, and the sergeant at arms working in the chow hall told me to get a haircut. He said that if I didn't, he would place me on report. The naval hair requirements were quite a bit more relaxed compared to the marines, but this dude didn't feel that way.

If he did put me on report, I would have to postpone my discharge in order to go to a captain's mast, which is the navy's equivalent of a trial that usually precedes disciplinary actions.

I must admit that I was sick of people telling me what to do, and I was eagerly awaiting my discharge so that I could get on with my life. As a result, I choose not to go to the chow hall. The barracks that I was staying in was filled with guys being discharged, most of which had just returned from Vietnam. They were sympathetic of my dilemma and made it a point to smuggle me food so that I wouldn't have to risk going to the chow hall again.

I'm sure that most veterans would agree with me that when you enlist in the service, they are eager to get you in as soon as they can, but the discharge process moves at a snail's pace. The days dragged on. We all just hung out all day long, waiting to be discharged. One day we were scheduled to talk with counselors to discuss how we felt and what our plans were after we went home. There was a big push at the time to hire veterans, and this discussion addressed that. I told the counselor that I had worked for the forest service before I had gone into the navy and that I hoped that I could return to that job. He told me that if I wanted to call and see if there was a job waiting for me when I returned, he could hurry my discharge along. I would have told this guy anything to get the process started. When I called Blue Ridge Ranger Station and talked with the district ranger, he confirmed that I could start work as soon as I returned. The ranger talked to the counselor to confirm my employment, and bingo bango bongo, I was discharged and headed home in two days.

I returned home in October, and I immediately went back to work for the forest service. The FCO had retired in my absence, and there was a new guy in his position, which had been renamed the fire management officer (FMO). I worked for a few weeks, and then I was laid off for the winter. On my last day of work, the new FMO told me that I needed a haircut if I wanted him to hire me in the spring.

It seemed there were two sides of the fence on hair length, and the dispute was often between what many referred to as rednecks and hippies. While men with long hair were being accepted in many areas of the country, this wasn't one of those areas. Any guy with long hair was generally thought of as a doper, draft dodger, sissy, and just generally someone who needed to have their asses kicked or their hair cut or both. Unfortunately, there were many hippies that were beat up, and some even had their hair cut for no reason other than the fact they had long hair. However, some rednecks found out that a few guys with long hair were pretty damn tough, and they were sometimes embarrassed when a hippie beat them up.

I fell into the redneck group in the local area. I had never had long hair and had worked on a few ranches. Generally speaking, cowboys fell into the redneck faction. I have known some really great cowboys, and thought I never considered myself one, I aspired to be one. But a true cowboy in my mind is someone that actively punches cows, and I wasn't. There is a hell of a lot more to being a cowboy than wearing a cowboy hat. Towns across the area had groups of guys who considered themselves cowboys and dressed the part but really weren't cowboys at all. Many of these guys were my friends, so I figured I had to a redneck. I knew that they weren't real cowboys, and I sometimes referred to them as town cowboys. So there were real cowboys ... and town cowboys.

When I reported to work the next spring, the FMO again told me that I needed to cut my hair or look for another job. I will admit that I probably did need a haircut by then, but it pissed me off that he was going to fire me if I didn't cut my hair. It turned into a big deal with me, and I decided that he could go to hell. I wasn't in the marines anymore, and I vowed to let my hair grow. To the FMO, I was little more than a traitor, a good redneck kid who'd gone to hell and turned into a hippie. He made fun of me and made my job a pain sometimes, but he never fired me. That year I succeeded in growing quite a head of hair. My dad felt the same way the FMO did, and he was generally pissed at me for letting my hair grow.

It is really weird how I was treated with long hair. People who had known me all my life no longer talked to me. The town cowboys especially felt that I was a real redneck traitor. I had been one of them, and now I looked like a damn hippie. About the only group of people who didn't treat me any different were the real cowboys. As I said earlier, I had quite a few friends that were true cowboys, and while they were amused by my hair length and didn't understand why I didn't cut it, they never treated me any different. One long-term ranch foreman would just shake his head and tell me I looked like George Armstrong Custer.

I commonly wore a cowboy hat, and this didn't change when my hair flourished. I had worn one since I was a kid, and I didn't see the need to change that. This was not accepted too well by the town cowboys, but for the most part, they put up with my decision. One year the forest service hired a new fire management officer. He was an ex-marine and a legendary firefighter, and the word was that he was just mean as hell. None of us had ever met him, and since we worked seventy miles from the supervisor's office all we knew of the guy were rumors, all of which had us all on edge. We were all told that we were to head into town one spring day to attend tanker training. This class was supposed to teach us about hydraulics and how to better utilize our tankers. Prior to the new fire management officer there was no training other than trial and error. So we all headed into town, and just as the class started, the new fire guy showed up. From the stories we had heard, we thought he would look like a middle linebacker, but we were surprised to see that he didn't really look that mean. The class started with this guy welcoming us. Then he looked at me, and in his marine voice, he said to the class that there were two things that he couldn't stand. One was long hair, and the other was forest service guys who wore cowboy hats. There was no doubt that I had gotten off on the wrong foot with this guy, and this would last for a few years before we were ever on the same page.

We also got into some trouble when we were returning from a fire assignment one time. By this time, I was in charge of a tanker, and in returning home, we ended up staying in a motel for the evening. At that time, we didn't have government credit cards to pay for the room, but we would pay on our own dime and settle up when we got home. There were three of us on the engine, and while two of us had the money to pay for a room, the other guy didn't. Of course, we told him not to worry about it. He could just stay in one of our rooms. After checking in, we had dinner at a place nearby and then bought some beer to take back to our rooms.

We were relaxing in my room, drinking a few beers, and watching TV when the guy who didn't have any money started telling us about his time working as a roadie for a rock-and-roll band. He went on and on about all the parties and all that happened on a tour with a rock band. This discussion turned to how the band would trash motel rooms. It was getting late, and the other guy and I had heard just about all the rock-and-roll stories we wanted to hear. We were not buying this guy's stories. The guy who had paid for the other room left and went to his room, leaving the rock-and-roll guy in my room. I told him that we should get some sleep since we were going to head out early the next morning. He wasn't ready to go to sleep, and he started to get a little rowdy. All the talk about the rock-and-roll tour must have gotten him worked up. He then said kind of calmly, "I'll just show you what I mean." He then walked over to the TV, tore it from the wall, and tossed it out of the closed window of my room.

Our rooms were on the third floor of the motel, so the TV crashed on the sidewalk three stories below. I freaked out, and while the guy was basking in how great it was to relive the tour antics, I grabbed him and threw his ass out of my room and into the hall. I then walked over and looked out of my broken window to see all the pieces of the TV on the sidewalk below. As I stood there and thought about how we all might be fired, I heard the door shut on my buddy's room next door. I ran out into the hall and knocked on his door to warn him that this idiot was up to no good. He opened the door, and I saw the other guy tear his TV out of the wall and toss it through his closed window again. Naturally, this made quite a bit of noise late in the evening.

We grabbed this guy and tossed him out into the hall and just stood there, dumbfounded about what had just happened. We knew we were in some serious trouble. There was no doubt about that. I walked over and looked out my friend's window and saw that his TV was three floors below, but his had crashed through the windshield of a state trooper's patrol car that was parked in the lot.

Our thought that we were in some serious trouble was spot on, but fortunately, we really only had to pay for all the damage. We dodged the bullet when it came to more serious charges, but that didn't happen without quite a bit of discussion and pleading. We spent some major cash that night. Of course, the rock-and-roller didn't because he was supposedly broke, but everyone wanted payment before we left for home.

However, word of our actions did make it back to the forest fire officer. Not long after we returned home, we got word that we were to head into Flagstaff for a meeting with this guy. It was a seventy-mile drive into Flagstaff from Blue Ridge, and all the way in, we just knew we were going to be fired. The supervisor's office at the time was located in downtown Flagstaff, and as we got there and checked in with the dispatch shop, we were told to head on down to the basement and wait there for the fire staff. The idiot who'd tossed the TVs spent this time trying to come up with a lie that would justify our actions and keep us out of trouble. The other guy and I just sat there and wondered where we could get another job after the fire staff fired us. We didn't see any way to avoid trouble, and we felt just guilty as hell.

For some unknown reason, the district ranger from Blue Ridge was in the supervisor's office that day, and he walked through the basement just as the fire staff got there. He asked the fire staff why some of his employees were here, and FCO just said he needed to talk with us and left it at that. This guy served in the marines and was no doubt well versed at chewing ass, so we just sat there, awaiting the worst. I always admired him for keeping this problem in his shop.

His opening comments are ones I remember to this day. I still find them to be the best way to open a good ass-chewing too. He said, "Okay, boys, this isn't a discussion." In other words, he was telling us to keep our mouths shut. The guy who had caused all the problems kept trying to justify our crimes, which really angered the fire staff. The other guy and I just sat there and took our licks, which ended up being the right thing to do. The rock-and-roller was fired, and we were informed that we each had a black mark on our forehead. We wouldn't be allowed to leave the forest on another fire assignment until we had sweated it off. He then told us that he had done stupid things too but that he had not been caught, which was of little comfort to us at the time.

To make the shift from a seasonal or temporary employee—at least if you were a forestry technician—to a full-time or career employee required one get on the civil service roster. The civil service roster was not open all the time, so you have to pay attention so that you heard when it opened up for additional applicants. I figured it only opened as the pool of applicants diminished, but who knew for sure? You could wait for an opening for a year or more without any luck, and it took a few years for me to get registered on the roster as well. So too, if your name came up on the roster, you were offered a job, and if you decided not to take it, you were taken off the roster altogether and had to reapply. Regardless of where it was based, refusing a job meant you might have to wait a long time until you were back on the roster and reconsidered for a career/conditional job.

My opportunity came when I was offered a position on a tanker with the Prescott National Forest. I was offered a career/conditional appointment with a crew located at Camp Wood on the Walnut Creek Ranger District. I was happy that they select me, but I had no knowledge really of the Prescott National Forest or Camp Wood. Because of all the issues with getting on the roster in those days, it was a common for a person to accept an appointment regardless of where it was. I did accept the appointment, and then I moved to Prescott, Arizona. Fire suppression on the Walnut Creek District was quite a bit different from what I was used to. While working on the Coconino National Forest we had multiple fires each summer and were allowed to go off forest on large fires, this was not really the focus on my new district. The district averaged seven starts per year, and we always had to find them quickly. Generally, they started because a single juniper tree was hit by lightning, and the fires would go out if one didn't discover them fast enough.

When I moved to the Prescott National Forest, I cut my hair off, and since no one there knew me, they didn't have any knowledge of my betrayal of my redneck amigos. At birth I was named Myron Gilmore Wickham, which is quite a handle and not one I would have preferred, but I wasn't consulted when my parents made the decision. When I was born, the doctor told my mother that I was a buck instead of a doe. Hence, I was given the nickname of Buck. As I grew up, though, everyone started to call me Bucky. No one ever called me Myron with exception to my mom or sister when they were mad at me. When I reported to the Prescott National Forest, I didn't tell them my nickname was Buck, so they called me Myron at my new job. I am pretty tall, and the new guy Myron with very short hair was considered quite the dork in my new district. It was kind of fun to play the dork, and I played the part well.

My new job had little to do with fires. There weren't many starts, and even when there was a new start, it wasn't a sure thing we would be sent to it. Our primary tasks consisted of building fences all over creation. We did get a break at times to build a trail on the newly declared Juniper Mesa Wilderness, but for the most part, we were a fence crew. There were no timber activities on the district. As a result, the main funding came from range management, and that was why we were tasked with the fence work. On more than one occasion, we'd be fencing, and someone would report a fire; however, resources from another district would be sent to fight the fire because we still needed to complete the fencing. This was a huge frustration to me and my crew. I worked at the Prescott National Forest for two years, and I never was sent off that forest to a fire. I applied for a job back at Blue Ridge Ranger Station. It was actually the one that I left, but they'd converted it to a career/conditional appointment. Fortunately, I was successful in getting it, so I moved back to the Coconino National Forest soon after that. I did gain an extensive knowledge of building fences, and I now had the same attraction to it that I had gained as a boy for cutting firewood.

CHAPTER 3
MOGOLLON STORIES

Some might feel that living at the ranger station would be boring, but we did manage to keep ourselves busy and make our own fun. This is no doubt true of any ranger station at the time because the folks who lived there dreamed up their own fun things to do when they weren't working. We played a lot of horseshoes. Almost everyone was a hunter or fisherman, so those activities were ongoing. Somehow, we managed to purchase a pool table kit, which required quite a bit of construction, but in the end, we had a quality pool table. We spent many evenings playing pool in the shop. We didn't get any television stations at that time, and in future years, we only got one channel, so there was no need for a TV guide. We just turn it on or turn it off. There was only the one phone at the office, so no one was distracted by any phone calls either.

I have no clue how a certain activity started, but flying little homemade airplanes was a hit for a few years. These airplanes were powered by glow plug engines and constructed of balsa wood, which was easy to repair after crashes. They were controlled by strings, which meant you just flew around in circles. This got to be quite popular. One could easily purchase a kit with the basics, but everyone was always trying to come up with a better and faster plane. Eventually, everyone got bored just flying around in circles, and someone thought it would be great to have dogfights with our little planes. It quickly was a hit, and a boneyard for lots of little airplanes. Someone came up with an even better idea. We discovered we could tie a piece of flagging of equal lengths on the tail of our airplanes. In the dogfight the objective was to chew off your opponent's flag with the propeller of your plane. If both planes made it through a full tank of gas and actually landed, the one with the longer flagging was the winner.

It was pretty common to repair your plane each week so that you could trash it in the dogfight that weekend. This resulted in scores of broken propellers as these little planes hit the dirt. We started nailing them above the doorway to the shop, and before long, we had quite a collection of them there. I made a quality airplane and painted it like a slurry bomber. I was actually quite proud of it. On its maiden flight, I was flying it around in circles and tearing holes in the sky. Going around and around, I became dizzy, wandered unknowingly outside of the circle where you had to stand, and flew my slurry bomber into the gas pump at full power. It was just another tragic end to one within the balsa wood fleet.

I really don't know when forest service employees were banned from packing guns. It happened prior to my first year. I figured that someone shot himself somewhere, and consequently, officials banned guns nationwide. That was usually the way things seemed to work. The FCO at the ranger station had a big belly on him, and he always wore Levi pants cuffed up on the bottom and square-toed cowboy boots with riding heels. If you saw him from behind, though, he was just a wedge of a guy. He could unload full fifty-five-gallon drums of gas alone. He wasn't much for walking, and he would always drive pretty much where he wanted to go in his two-wheel-drive forest service truck. If he couldn't drive there, he just didn't go.

When deer season came around, the "no gun" policy didn't seem to affect him and his travels around the district. Since he really didn't like to walk, if he shot a deer, he would always come over to the crew quarters and get one of us young guys to retrieve it for him. One day he drove up and waited until it was just me standing there with him. He told me that I should take a drive down Moqui Draw and look for a blue piece of flagging on the right side of the road. At the flagging there would be a buck lying beside a big alligator juniper tree about a hundred yards off the road. He gave me his deer tag and said that I should put this on the animal when I got there.

Living at the station, you had to put up with some cantankerous folks. We always tried to put up with everyone and their ways. One guy was pretty opinionated and often would tell you how he felt, whether you wanted to know or not. This rubbed many people the wrong way. I have always subscribed to the "what goes around comes around" way of thinking. Rather than working yourself into a fit and seeking revenge afterward, patience works out better most of the time. He was a prevention patrolman in the district when there were no gun-packing law enforcement officers as yet. This guy had the ability to write violations to visitors if they broke the law or if he saw fit. He took this to heart and wrote multiple tickets each year, and he would bask in the glory and stupidity of the visitors. This guy informed many visitors of the various rules found in the Code of Federal Regulations. This was all well and good, but sometimes this guy stretched the rules when it suited him. This didn't deter him from writing some visitors tickets for something that he would do on a regular basis.

We all loved to fish, and this guy did too. He was always ready and willing to go fishing. One year fishing for catfish was a popular deal. According to this guy, he was an expert when it came to fishing for catfish. He told us time and time again about his secret bait for landing monster cats, and by golly, he was going to prove his ability on the next fishing trip. He told us that he was going to get his famous *stink bait* going for the next trip to the lake and just kill the catfish. We asked him what the bait consisted of, but of course, it was top secret.

Soon we went down to Roosevelt Lake for the weekend. It was common for most of us to head down there in the spring. One of my buddies and I set up camp, and just as soon as we got set up, we saw the catfishing expert himself set up his camp next to ours on the shore of the lake. We were eager to get fishing, so as soon as we were set up and starting to leave in our boat, this guy produced the secret catfish bait. He hadn't shown his concoction to anyone yet, so we wanted to take a look. He produced a gallon milk jar that was full of this horrible-looking tan stuff that had various pieces of fish and shrimp suspended in the gore. It looked horrible, but he assured us that it was the catfish bait of the year. He produced five different fishing poles, even though it was only legal at the time to have one. We thought, *No wonder he catches so many catfish. With all those poles, his odds are bound to increase.* He wanted us to smell this stuff when he baited all his fishing poles up, so we hung around until he was ready.

In due time, he had hooks and sinkers tied on all his poles, and the time for baiting up arrived. He proudly grabbed his gallon milk jar of slime and popped the lid. When he opened up the milk jar, you could hear the air rushing out as he cracked the lid. The smell hit us and just about made us throw up. It was almost unbearable. He fished out five rotten shrimps from the soup and baited up all his hooks. It was very gross, and the smell was indescribable.

We'd had enough, so as he cast all his rods in the lake, we got into our boat and shoved off. We hadn't gotten but a few hundred yards from the shore when a game and fish boat pulled up and asked us for our fishing licenses. We produced our licenses, and the game and fish guy shoved us off, fired up his motor, and headed directly into our camp, obviously headed to check the license of our catfishing buddy. We had just watched him toss in his fishing poles, which were all baited with that nasty stuff, and now the game warden was headed directly at him. He was about to get caught right before our eyes. This guy smoked, and you could see him fire up a cigarette as the game and fish boat approached. He slowly walked by four of his five fishing rods, which were all propped up on sticks, burning off the lines with his cigarette. We hung out and acted like we were fishing, but in reality, we just wanted to see if he was going to get caught.

The game warden checked him out, and it appeared that he'd gotten away with it. After the man checked his license, he fired up his boat and headed out to patrol the lake. We did get a kick out of this because he had to fish out more shrimp out of that nasty jar and bait up again. With the show over, we headed out and fished for the rest of the day. Our catfishing buddy had dodged the bullet, and we joked about that for most of the day. As we pulled up in the boat on our return, the smell of our camp was nothing short of horrible. The stench of the catfish bait was so bad you could hardly stand it. Our buddy was sitting in a lawn chair and tending his five poles upwind from the camp. We commented about the smell of the place, and he informed us that his jar of stink bait had exploded. I don't really know if it was the change in elevation from the rim to the lake or the warm day at the lake that caused the explosion, but the smell was everywhere. It was hidden in our buddy's camping gear, and now it had spread its nasty contents all over his stuff. He did manage to avoid getting a citation, but man, the exploding stink bait was by far worse than the fine.

The same guy became interested in trapping. Some of the guys at work had started trapping more as a hobby than as a business. Of course, our friend was taken by the thought of running a trapline during the winter. He had stink bait down for sure, and he was informed that there was a place down in the Bradshaw Mountains that had varmints aplenty just waiting to step into a trap. He decided that during the winter layoff, he would head down to the Steller's Basin, where his buddies had told him of the great furbearer population. He went there and set up a tent camp and established his trapline. He was supposed to be gone for several weeks because his place was remote. Plus getting all those furs would take some time. He was gone for just a week and returned home. We saw him and asked what had interrupted his plans. He told us that one day after running his trapline, he returned to his tent camp and encountered a swarm of bees in his tent. He crafted a torch for his tent to smoke the swarm out, and he accidentally caught his tent on fire and burned down his camp.

Every week we would have a safety meeting, and all employees were required to attend. At one such meeting, the cat fisherman stood up and held in his hand some felling wedges. He informed everyone in the meeting that he was "working a case" because someone had been cutting green oak on the district. He went on to say that he felt he was getting close and asked all of us the keep our eyes open and to report to him if we saw anything. As soon as he quit talking, the pulp wood guy in timber said, "Those wedges are mine, and I'd like them back." He realized what he had said as soon as the words left his lips. Everyone heard it, and we all just stared at him, dumbfounded. The guilt was all over this guy's face. I don't think he ended up with a ticket, but this was not the kind of guy you wanted to do your taxes.

During one of those long winter nights with little to do, my roommate and I started joking around about starting a newsletter for the ranger station. We had quite a great time laughing and carrying on about what we could put in it. One beer led to another, and soon we were in production. We named our gossip column *The Blue Ridge Star,* which seemed both patriotic and catchy. I've always liked doodling, so I provided a quick sketch for the front page, and we started thinking of what seemed funny for us. We had a great time, but in reading what we'd dreamed up the next morning, we decided that we should tone it down if we were going public. We did, and we made the review on the morning after one of the rules. We had to live with all the subjects in our paper after all.

This all happened prior to computers and printers hitting the scene. We did have a new copy machine at the district office, but typing on typewriters and using rubber cement to stick everything together prior to making any copies was a requirement. All this work was accomplished in the dark of night. We successfully completed our first newsletter and just made a few copies and left them on the desks in the district office so that the folks who came in each had a copy. Everyone had a good laugh, and it became kind of a hit. At any rate, it was received well enough that future issues seemed in order.

We had several columns. We even had one for all the dog gossip called Fanny's Footnotes. If you have ever worked at a ranger district, you know that dogs are one of the common problems, and Fanny was my little sweetheart Aussie dog that never ever did anything wrong. I think kids and dogs caused more issues than anything else. In Fanny's Footnotes, all the problem dogs were highlighted. If anyone had something stolen or misplaced, the item would appear in the For Sale portion. One example of this was the camping gear that required "some cleaning" after the stink bait explosion I talked about earlier and a bee smoker that was "like new" and "only used once." If anyone did something stupid, it usually made the paper. We made a few issues, and they all were received well.

This predated not only computers but also the archaeological survey required prior to doing any project. This was new to all the district folks, and it was the first of many hoops we had to jump through to do our work. In the next issue, we wrote an article zinging archaeology in the supervisor's office, who was at the time the only archaeologist on the forest. What good is it to zing people in our little newspaper if they aren't able to see it. We smuggled a copy into the supervisor's office and hung it on the bulletin board in the break room. I still remember the last line on the portion dedicated to archaeology. It said, "We don't care. We don't have to. We're archaeology."

After a few hours of our cute little newsletter hanging in the break room, we learned that it would be the last issue. The supervisor had determined what we thought was humor was actually a crime, and by the end of that day, we were informed that we could even lose our jobs. A group was organized to investigate who had made the newsletter and determine if anyone had violated the rules in its production. Right off the bat, it was obviously a dead giveaway and a bad idea to name it the *Blue Ridge Star*. The investigation group immediately determined where the propaganda had originated. While we had never admitted that we were the culprits, we didn't want to see someone innocent gain all the glory, so we fessed up. The investigation group determined that government equipment and paper was used in the production, and this was a clear violation. All in all, we probably used two hundred sheets of paper, the typewriters, and all that government rubber cement. The threat of losing our jobs soon faded to a possible two-week suspension without pay, and eventually, it was just dismissed with a gag order that prevented us from future production of the the *Blue Ridge Star*.

General Springs Guard Station was the other guard station on the rim. Those guys were pretty much in the same boat we were at Buck Springs. They lived there and basically did the same stuff we did on a daily basis. One year one of the guys working there decided to get a pet snake. One afternoon while they were out driving around, they came upon a rattlesnake. There weren't a lot of rattlesnakes on top of the rim, but they did seem to like the area close to the rim.

Not to be drawn back by the fact they could lose their lives, it was decided that it would be way cool to catch it for a pet. The rattlesnake was what all the locals called a timber rattler, which was very black with faint yellow markings and a yellow belly. I think the actual name for this species is an Arizona black rattlesnake. As rattlesnakes went, these guys were usually pretty pissy and had a reputation that they were aggressive. They also have a higher than normal desire to inflict their terror on you than your common rattlesnake.

The quarters at General Springs Guard Station consisted of a single-wide house trailer, and it soon became the home for the newly acquired pet rattlesnake. A cheap ten-gallon fish tank with a window screen weighted down with a rock became his new abode. The new rattlesnake display was put on a bookshelf that was just a few old boards balanced on some cinderblocks. The whole setup was placed just inside the front door of the trailer.

Soon after they captured their new pet, they invited us over. Not really sure why we'd been invited, we accepted the invitation, and after work, we jumped in a truck to drive over and see what was going on. Snakes just scared the hell out of me. It doesn't have to be a rattlesnake either. All it takes is a garter snake slithering through the grass. I usually yell like a little girl when I see one, and I about turn inside out in my attempts to get away. Some have viewed this as me just being a big chicken, but I feel that it is a survival instinct that has evolved naturally with most Homo sapiens.

When we arrived, the General Springs crew was inside the trailer, and they hollered at us to come on in. I walked into the trailer, and to my horror, I heard the buzzing of a rattlesnake really close to me. In an instant, I exhibited the survival skills buried deep in my DNA and went into my usual spastic getaway and screaming ritual. Of course, the General Spring guys laughed out loud.

We listened to them tell us how cool they all thought their new houseguest was. I think they were somewhat spooked having it in their house too, but they were more determined to make us feel as uneasy as they could. They informed us they had named it Buzz, which did seem appropriate. As we got somewhat used to sitting as far away from Buzz as was possible in a single wide, they decided to turn up the volume a little. They wanted to feed Buzz, and they let us watch him gobble down a mouse.

Fortunately, these guard stations came with a resident population of mice and chipmunks. Each fire season the battle for turf began anew, and each winter the rodent population rebounded. This provided quite a bounty to sustain Buzz with a daily ration of little critters. One had actually been caught in a mousetrap and was earmarked as the main course for Buzz. They removed the rock, which caused Buzz to sound off and coil up, ready for action. They slid the screen over a little, and they dropped the dead mouse into the fish tank. They quickly returned the cover and rock afterward. This really got Buzz going, and he struck at the rock a few times just to show us that he meant business.

Buzz just ignored the mouse and hardly cast a glance that way. Either he just wasn't hungry, or he was as blind as a bat.

They determined that Buzz didn't want a dead mouse for dinner, and our anticipation of the process w was all for not. They then decided to fish the mouse out of the tank and warm it up in the oven in an effort to whet Buzz's appetite. The idea of fishing out the dead mouse and not getting bitten or allowing Buzz to escape got me pretty damn nervous, and all my pleading to just get another mouse fell on deaf ears. I wasn't really a chicken, but while the mouse retrieval process was underway, I waited outside just so someone could go for help if things went south.

The operation was a success, the mouse was retrieved, and Buzz was kept in custody. They put little mouse in the oven for a quick warm-up and the whole process started again. Buzz got just as worked up when they started to move the lid, and they tossed warm mouse into the corner of the tank. Buzz noticed it right away and immediately coiled up and struck at the mouse. Then he commenced with eating the poor little thing. I suppose that if you think snakes are cool, this would be something interesting to observe. If you have a snake phobia, however, this image won't help at all.

The summer progressed, and Buzz became quite a big deal for the General Springs guys. They derived countless hours of fun from killing little birds and chipmunks with a BB gun and warming them up for the Buzz buffet. We quit going over to visit because it just didn't seem natural to share your house with something that could kill you. They never missed a chance to joke with us about being little sissies who were afraid of snakes. After weeks of ridicule, we felt it was time to take some action and get even.

We put our plan in place one afternoon. The two guard stations had a secret message that we used when we wanted to get together. We would call Moqui Lookout and request some supplies from the ranger station. Our only contact with the outside world was our forest service radio, so we both monitored it constantly. This was not really a necessary item, but it served as a secret communication that we wanted to meet up for some unimportant reason. We had a spot to meet, and this usually involved sharing some gossip or playing with a Frisbee. One quiet afternoon we made the call to the lookout and hid out off the rim road, waiting for the General Springs guys to drive by en route to the meeting place. When they drove by without seeing us, we put our plan into action.

Our plan consisted of a three-pronged attack. Phase one was to lure them away from their single-wide trailer at General Springs. Phase two was to gain entry to the single-wide, catch Buzz, remove him from the fish tank, and return him to the wild. Phase three was to leave the lid off just a bit to make it look like Buzz had broken free. The General Springs guys would return home and think that Buzz had escaped into the single-wide. We delighted in the thought that they would look everywhere for Buzz, and when they couldn't locate him, they'd have to live with the haunting thought that he was prowling the trailer.

Phase one went off without a hitch We were well hidden, and they went driving by without detecting us. Phase two started off well because they never locked the trailer, but the plan went down the tubes when it came time to catch Buzz. Our snake phobia really kicked into high gear, and none of us had the courage to make the capture. When Buzz saw us, he got all worked up. He just hung out in the corner of his enclosure, coiled and ready to attack. What seemed like a grand idea hadn't really progressed. One person suggested that we just carry the fish tank with Buzz outside and dump it over, but no one would volunteer to carry the old fish tank. Rather than get bitten, we decided to abandon the plan. It was a great idea for a joke, and we laughed quite a lot as we dreamed of all the angst it would have caused if we had pulled it off; however, we needed someone who wasn't scared of snakes, which we did not have.

I mentioned that we would meet and toss around a Frisbee. Aside from horseshoes, tossing the Frisbee consumed quite a bit of our time, and it was a close second to horseshoes in recreational pursuits. We all carried one in the tankers, and we would often take a break from work and play with the Frisbee. Our superiors also frowned upon this activity, and if you were caught playing with a Frisbee while you were on a fire, you could get sent home.

One summer in an attempt to get out of the crew quarters at the ranger station, I managed to get permission from the owner of a place called Moqui Ranch for me and two friends to move in and live there for the summer. Moqui Ranch was an abandoned ranch that consisted of several log houses. I wouldn't call them cabins as the main house had several bedrooms and was quite large. Moqui Ranch was a beautiful place; however, it had seen better days, and it had been vandalized and had suffered from years of abandonment. I always wondered what it was like when people lived there. In its day, it was quite a big deal. I would assume that because of all the abandoned buildings, the barn swallow population was doing well there, and several must have called this place home now that people had quit living there. We would toss a Frisbee around after we got off work each day, and we soon found out that we weren't the only ones enjoying this activity. Every evening as we started tossing around the Frisbee, we would attract a swarm of these swallows. They loved us playing with the Frisbee. They would dart at and dash past the Frisbee in midflight, often several would fly past during one toss. They could literally fly circles around the Frisbee and would play with us until we called it off. There was never a collision as the swallows would swoop within a fraction of an inch from the Frisbee. This was a great pastime for both us and the swallows.

The crew quarters at Blue Ridge housed most of the seasonal workforce, and a young group of guys living together provided a hotbed for jokes and pranks. There were four quarters with four to six guys living in each. There was only one refrigerator and kitchen stove in each quarters, so the kitchen was shared by all. The community refrigerator and kitchen caused some grief because it was not uncommon for someone to eat someone else's food. While some of the guys were good at supplying for their needs, others were not as skilled at shopping or providing for themselves. It seemed like the same guys were always stealing the others' food or always begging for stuff like butter or salt in order to cook their meals.

We all shared a roommate one summer who didn't buy many groceries, and I don't think he took a single bath or washed his cloths all summer long. He was just a little hard to live with. He would have breakfast, lunch, and dinner every day, but they were always the same thing. He would bring back a log of bologna when he went shopping and a bottle of catsup. In the morning he would slice off a slab of bologna and fry it up, smother it with catsup, and choke it down. At lunch he would just have a slab of cold bologna. Then for dinner he would fry up another slab and smother it in catsup again. No vegetables, bread, or anything else, just straight-up bologna and catsup. He didn't wash dishes either, so he had his own gross frying pan along with a knife and a fork. We just wrote these items off and would never use them.

I said he didn't wash his cloths, but that may be an exaggeration. He had two sets of cloths, and he changed them sometimes; however, he would just hang the old dirty ones out on the clothesline while he wore the others for a week or two. He did change clothes once in a while and rotate the ones hanging outside on the clothesline. We always hoped for rain since that might help out with his laundry.

During another summer one of the guys had really worn out his welcome. He was always in need of something and not real worried about just taking something he needed without asking. His behavior kept getting worse and worse, and we thought it needed to come to an end. One evening he started his daily search for food by asking everyone what they were having for dinner. He was always first to finish off leftovers because he rarely had enough food to last him through the week.

Fighting fires is a dirty job, and you get just plain filthy on fires. One of the grossest items of all this dirty work is your feet. A firefighter's socks, for example, can get horribly gross. All the dust and ash finds its way into your boots, and that along with the sweat from mopping up a fire on the hot ground can make your feet pretty gross. Some guys changed their socks daily, and others changed them weekly. Needless to say after a week on stinky feet, socks are very gross and quite stinky.

One evening after work as we all sat around the crew quarters, this guy started his inquiry about what we were planning to have for dinner. One of the guys who was completely fed up with this roommate's inability to take care of himself and who was tired of the daily mooching of food said that he was going to have some burritos and asked if the moocher wanted one. Of course, the guy thought it was a great idea and sat in eager anticipation of a burrito dinner. The guy cooking the dinner had secured just about the grossest sock known to man. He skillfully rolled it up in a tortilla and made a very tasty-looking burrito, and then he offered it to the moocher. His mouth was watering as he looked upon his prize, and he took a great big bite. As he attempted to bite a piece off the burrito, the nasty sock came out. He was just sitting there with that horrible sock hanging out of his mouth. At first, he didn't realize what it was, and he kept chewing on the tortilla. But when he looked down and saw what he had in his mouth, he gagged, which made us crack up laughing. After that, he got the message and started spending more time and money shopping. He didn't trust us with his food anymore.

Most all the employees of that time hunted or at least had a gun or two. I don't know if that has really changed, but guns were a part of our daily existence. One day after work, one of the guys in the crew quarters had just purchased a new .22 pistol and started showing it to all the guys. The group was not following any gun safety rules, but my dad had literally beaten the importance of gun safety into me at an early age. As they looked at the pistol and took turns checking it out, I realized that they were doing just about everything with a gun that you weren't supposed to do. I cautioned them repeatedly, but they ignored my warnings to the point that they were making me mad. We were planning on cooking some steaks out front of the quarters on a barbeque for dinner, and since all my gun safety suggestions were getting thrown back in my face, I decided to go out and start the fire and let these idiots play with the gun.

I went outside and started a fire, fuming about how stupid they were being and thinking about how my dad would have slapped them around a little and taught them proper gun safety. If they screwed up, we surely would not be allowed to have guns anymore, and that would impact everyone. I really didn't understand why they were being such jerks about it.

As I stood outside, a very loud pop came from inside the quarters. Of course, I ducked, and when I realized that I hadn't been shot, I heard one of the guys screaming at the top of his lungs, "I've been shot. I've been shot." Of course, this scared the hell out of me, and I left the fire and ran back inside the crew quarters. When I got inside, I saw the guy who was screaming lying on the floor and holding his leg, saying he had been shot in the leg. The other two guys were holding him down. It looked like he was in a huge amount of pain. I ran over to them and moved the guy's hand off his wound only to find out that he wasn't really shot but just faking it. They had purposefully worked me up by acting unsafe, knowing full well that it would piss me off, and when I went outside to get away from them, they used a firecracker to cause the pop. Of course, this was just about the funniest thing they had ever been a part of, but I felt like kicking their asses because it scared the hell out of me.

I withdrew to my fire and let them laugh like fools about their little prank. Looking back, I see that it was a good trick, but being the butt of their joke still kind of pisses me off.

One night after work, a few of us headed to Mormon Lake Lodge to have dinner and maybe a drink or two. We had dinner with a few drinks and then retired to the lounge to have a few more. We knew quite a few folks there. One drink led to another, and one pool game led to another. One of the guys was the type who didn't take much grief from anyone. He wasn't mean though. He was polite and generally a great guy. He just didn't put up with much. As the evening progressed, he had a few too many libations and ended up just a little on the tipsy side of flat-ass drunk. He was the first to notice, and he decided it was time for him to retire to our truck and go to sleep. So he slipped outside and went over to our truck and lay down in the seat for a rest.

At first, no one knew what had happened to him. We just noticed that he wasn't around. Someone went outside to check there and found him asleep in the seat of our truck. Well, he seemed all right, so we all continued with the evening's festivities. In those days, we all said, "If you snooze, you lose." Our sleeping buddy provided the rest of us with a golden opportunity to mess with him, so we all started thinking of ways to dirty work him.

After several ideas, we decided that we should get some lipstick and go doctor him up. We borrowed a tube of lipstick from one of the ladies at the bar and went out to our truck. When we got there, our buddy was fast asleep. (Really, he was just passed out, but I'm trying to be nice.) We took our time and put some authentic war paint on his face. He didn't even budge as we did. He looked so funny lying there all painted up. We succeeded and went back inside. Of course, we had to tell everyone about our joke. It was pretty funny, but the general consensus was that we needed to go get him and bring him back inside so that everyone could enjoy our handiwork.

We went back out to the truck and woke our buddy up. Admittedly, he was better off asleep because he was truly a mess. His authentic war paint was still on his face as we helped him back in the bar. He was a little tipsy, so we helped him to a barstool so he could hang with the rest of us. People would just look at him and smile, and in his drunken state, he would just bob and weave a little and attempt to smile back. One guy who wasn't clued in on our little prank walked up to him and stared at him. Our buddy started to get somewhat upset and asked him just what the hell he was staring at. The guy said, "What the hell? Are you on the warpath or something?" Then he started laughing at our buddy. We all immediately knew that this had crossed the line with our buddy. We managed to grab him and direct him back to the truck before he focused on the guy long enough to punch him in the nose. It was the end of the evening too. We headed home and thanked God most of the war paint ended up either smeared on his face or his pillow by the next morning. He wondered what the hell it was, but we all acted like we had no clue what had happened and why he looked sunburned.

One activity that occurred quite a bit in the years I started was smuggling drugs. While Blue Ridge is quite a ways from the Mexican border, there was a time when it was the hotbed of smuggling activities. Light aircraft would land on pretty much every straight stretch of road in this area. While the Meteor Crater Road and the road to Chevelon Ranger Station were probably the most popular, people would drop off loads on Highway 87, which seems pretty brazen.

This activity usually took place in the wee hours of the morning and in total darkness. The smugglers would usually line the road with flashlights or a few vehicles in order for the plane to locate the road and then land and drop off the goodies. Sometimes they would refuel the plane and leave. Sometimes the plane was stolen, and they'd just leave it wherever the deal went down.

One afternoon I was driving down Meteor Crater Road, and as I passed through Chavez Pass, I saw two guys in full camouflage carrying M-16 rifles scurry across the road. This was not a common sight, and I found it rather alarming. I thought I had stumbled into a smuggling deal. I left the area and reported my sighting to the ranger station. The district ranger loaded me up in his truck for a little drive, which was usually his way of chewing you out. We drove down the road a few miles, and he told me that I hadn't seen anything and that I shouldn't go down there for a while. This little talk got me wondering just what the hell was going on.

On my next day off, I drove down there to see what the hell was going on despite the weird warning. It was early in the day, and as I passed through Chavez Pass, I noticed a little smoke coming from the thick juniper trees. A thunderstorm had passed through the area the evening before, and I thought that maybe there had been a fire start, so I walked over to it to check it out. As I approached the smoke, I saw it was campfire with two guys who immediately stood up and ran off. It was apparent that they had been there for quite a while as there was litter all over the area. I was spooked again, so I turned around and hauled ass out of the area.

I stayed away until my next day off, but with a week to get my curiosity and courage up, I decided to just do a drive-by and see what was up. As I passed through Chavez Pass, I noticed something white to the north on the road. When I got closer, I saw it was a little Cessna airplane that was upside down in the borrow ditch of the road. There were parachute flare canisters lying around and flashlights all over the side of the road. The light came on, and the two guys I had seen earlier were feds staking out the road and waiting for the load to come in. They were the worse litterbugs too. They'd left all their stuff at their camp and along the road.

Another smuggling attempt in the same place led to a car chase across the flats. Luckily, the culprits were caught, but only after the chase. The local ranch was rounding up the pasture that the cops had chased the culprits through the next day, and one of the cowboys found a little suitcase that contained $10,000 in cash along with some personal stuff. One of the smugglers must have tossed it out during the chase. Ten thousand dollars to a cowboy is quite a sum of money; however, like most cowboys, this guy was as honest as the day was long, and he turned it in to law enforcement.

The money was entered as evidence and held for the trial. However, if they admitted the money was theirs at the trial, they'd have to admit their guilt, so the money went unclaimed. It was eventually returned to its finder after several months, so honesty sure paid off in this instance.

One summer some unknown folks purchased one of the old homesteads about ten miles north of Blue Ridge Ranger Station. These guys were a little weird, and they told everyone that their intent was to develop a dude ranch and build some cabins for their clients to stay in. The first thing they did was construct the main street, which was quite long and went straight through a meadow that ran the length of the property. We were in the area almost daily, burning cabled junipers that had been removed as a range improvement project. Because we passed the area on a daily basis, we did have some contact with the folks staying there and waited for them to start construction of the cabins, though it never seemed to start.

We started thinking that it was all a sham. The main street seemed to be the only thing that they'd constructed. One evening while puzzling over their real intent, we decided that the main street was a runway and that they were smugglers and not dude ranchers. The very next day as we went out to start our daily burning and passed the dude ranch, we saw scads of federal vehicles there, and we found out that they were busted the evening before for flying in drugs from Mexico.

A guy who lived at one of the old timber camps often drove into Winslow to have a few drinks. As this guy headed home, it wasn't uncommon for him to get tired. Or he was just unable to drive because he was a little drunk. So he would sometimes just pull over to the side of the road and take a nap. On one such night, he had done just that. He pulled over and went to sleep in his truck. The stretch of road where he had pulled over was referred to as the runway, as it was often used to land smuggling airplanes. When he woke up in the morning, to his surprise, the back of his truck filled with kilos of marijuana. He returned to Winslow and turned it in to a surprised police force, which caused him some undue teasing from all his workmates. The guy was very much opposed to marijuana, and he never considered getting involved with smuggling at all. After that, though, folks often joked and asked him if he could get them some pot. Those requests never quit pissing him off.

The first several years I worked in the rim country, several separate logging companies were active in all but the dead of winter. This resulted in quite a bit of traffic as all the loggers went to and from their timber sales. The companies kept the roads well bladed, and all of them had a road crew or contracted road maintenance out to a separate contractor. Everywhere I've been in the west, the local folks drive fast as hell on gravel roads in their area. The rim country was no exception, with the roads well maintained, just about everyone who lived or worked there was guilty of driving along too fast.

Logging trucks were common, and with several companies hauling logs, the truck traffic could get pretty busy. The logging trucks were like everyone else. They took advantage of the good roads and hauled ass to and from the sawmills. All this speedy driving around on the gravel roads resulted in just about everyone seeing their lives flash before their eyes. They'd come around a corner and stare at the grill of a Peterbilt logging truck. It was a known safety issue, and people discussed it often at the district safety meetings. I'm sure it was brought up with the loggers too. The first years I worked, the truckers got paid by the load, so they didn't let any grass grow under their feet. Of course, we were equally guilty because we always drove around too fast and completely out of the safety margins if we were headed to a fire.

Looking back, I find it amazing that there weren't more wrecks because of everyone hauling ass around the woods. Everyone just took it for granted that you might have to take the ditch to avoid an accident. One year the district ranger reached a deal with one of the biggest logging companies to paint a number on the logging trucks. This was a twofold issue. The marks provided a means to identify which truck ran you off the road, and because people would be able to identify them, the trucks would hopefully drive in a safer manner.

This was one of those ideas that looked good on paper but didn't really work out. Meeting a logging truck in a bad spot happened often. As these close calls happened, no one was able to get the number off the bumper. The first thing you saw was that huge Peterbilt grill. Then you were looking toward the barrow ditch, looking for a place to get off the road. I don't think anyone actually got a number and turned it in, but it was a good concept. In most of these encounters, both drivers were going a little too fast and therefore shared the guilt.

One morning I was headed out to Battleground Ridge to construct an earthen dam-water catchment as a wildlife-habitat-improvement project. The route I took followed a good but narrow gravel road that cut across the many forks of Miller Canyon. I was pulling a fuel trailer I would use to refuel the dozer that I was supposed to build the tank with. This road was pretty narrow, and there was a quite a thicket of pine regeneration on the shoulders. As I was tooling along as I came around a curve in the road, I was shocked when I met a loaded logging truck that was also tooling along. I took to the ditch with no real idea what evasive actions the logging truck driver took. I was busy trying to not wreck my truck and the trailer. This scared the hell out of me, but as quickly as it happened, it was over. I was all right, and the logging truck kept going. I just chalked it up as one of many narrow misses.

I arrived on the site of the water tank and started working on the catchment with the dozer. Basically, I was digging a big hole in the ground to catch water runoff from the barrow ditch of the road. I had been working for an hour or two when as I turned to look. As I backed up out of the hole, I saw a parked logging truck, and a logging truck driver was standing there and watching me. I immediately thought that this was the guy I ran off the road coming out this morning, and he probably wanted to kick my ass for running him off the road and scaring the shit out of him. I figured he wasn't going to leave, so I parked the dozer and walked over to visit with him. I was a little worried, but I tried not to look scared as I walked up to the guy. As I got there, he right off the bat said he was sorry for our meeting that morning and hoped that everything was all right and that I hadn't wrecked anything. I was relieved and thought it was pretty damn nice that this guy actually stopped to see if everything was good to go. I also apologized since we'd both been tooling along at a pretty good clip. I don't think either of us actually slowed down after that, but it was good to know that the logging truck drivers didn't want to run us into the ditch on purpose.

One day we were headed somewhere in the pumper. I was accompanied by a young Hopi guy who'd been sent out to Buck Springs as a relief crew member because of the high risk of fire danger. I don't recall where we were headed, but during our journey we came upon a Hereford cow that was caught in a cattle guard. The old girl had stepped into the cattle guard, and her back leg was down to her hock. This cattle guard was on an allotment boundary fence, so she could have belonged to either rancher that grazed the two separate areas. She was a hairy old gal, and while you could see where she was branded, you couldn't really read the brand because of her long hair.

It was at a time when Hereford cattle were popular, and each of the two ranchers ran Herefords. We wanted to notify the correct owner to come out and cut her out of the cattle guard, but we were unsure who she belonged to.

I knew if we got the hair around the brand wet it would be easier to see who this cow belonged to, and the pumper had a canvas bucket that folded flat and was easy to store in the pumper. I mentioned that if the brand were wet, we could see what it was, and my helper for the day volunteered to toss a bucket of water on the cow so that we could identify who she belonged to. I might throw in here that my Hopi relief was a small guy, but he could run or walk all day. Like many of his tribe, he was pretty fast on his feet.

We dug out the canvas pail and filled it up with water from the pumper and gave it to the Hopi guy. I got into the pumper to call our find in on the radio as the Hopi guy approached the trapped cow and proceeded to throw the bucket of water on the area of the brand. The old cow was keeping an eye on him as he approached, and when he threw the bucket of water on the old gal, she didn't really like that at all and yanked her foot out of the cattle guard, lowered her horns, and charged the poor little Hopi kid with the bucket. It was a good thing that young Hopi guys could run like the wind as he dodged and jumped, missing her advances like a top-notch rodeo clown. As he ran, he was kind of yelling, not really screaming. I don't think he was speaking the English language, but it was pretty damn funny. As my Hopi crewman reached the pumper, which was a large Dodge power wagon, he leaped onto the hood. Only later did he really see any humor in the ordeal.

The ungrateful Hereford cow just stood there right in front of the pumper, shook her head a few times, and wandered down the road, bawling for her calf. Luckily, the calf was on her side of the fence. I could tell now because the brands matched.

Something else happened at the same cattle guard several years later. We got a report that a bull was trapped in a cattle guard on the rim road. I wanted to see what the deal was, especially since the rim road was popular and heavily traveled. I knew this could be a pain in the ass, so I loaded up and headed out to see what we needed to do to get the bull out.

This cattle guard was on an allotment boundary fence that separated two separate ranches. Not all grazing permittees are created equal, and while one of the ranchers was top-notch, the other didn't have the savvy or the background, which meant he was always a problem. The bull belonged to the lesser of the two permittees, which added to the complexity of the dilemma.

I radioed into the office and had them attempt to contact the rancher and let him know about the situation, and to my surprise, they radioed back and informed me that they had actually contacted him and that he was on his way out. He informed the office that he didn't have the equipment to cut the bull out and repair the damage done to the grid of the cattle guard, which was of no great surprise and meant that I had to return to the office and grab a welder and cutting torch to get the bull out.

I returned to the ranger station and secured everything I needed to get the bull out of the cattle guard, and then I headed back out to the scene of the entrapment. Upon my arrival I was surprised again because the rancher had actually beaten me out there. He was usually slow to react, and his prompt arrival was a surprise. The bull was planted well into the grid with all four feet down in the grid. No bull in his right mind was going to stand there and let you cut his feet out of a cattle guard, and this was a concern of mine. The rancher quickly produced a vial of sedative that some veterinarians had used to sedate animals when needed. This particular sedative was called Rompin. I had used it before actually. It was very strong, but it was a popular one since it was pretty safe to use and animals seemed to recover quickly after getting a dose.

The rancher produced a large livestock vaccination syringe and started filling it with the sedative. I had used this drug before but only on smaller animals, and I was always surprised at the small amount needed to put a dog into la-la land. He kept filling and filling the syringe, and I thought he was going way overboard with the dose. I told him that I felt if he gave the bull a shot like that, he would probably kill him. The guy told me that he might not use it all but just give him some of it and see how that worked, and if he didn't go out, he could just give him a little more until the dose provided the desired effects. After all, what did forest service guys know about animal husbandry? Or so he thought.

With a loaded syringe, the rancher approached the bull from behind and then stuck the syringe in the bull's butt. Upon getting stuck in the butt, the bull started raising hell, which caused the rancher to inject most of the sedative in the struggle. In the fiasco the bull was injected with enough Rompin to sedate a blue whale in one quick prick. The struggling bull slowly turned into a dishrag and went down.

With the bull either sedated or overdosed on the sedative, we quickly cut him out of the grid. We had to hook a logging chain on him to drag his limp body out of the cattle guard and off the road so that folks could get by. I repaired the cattle guard, and we all left with the bull still lying there, barely breathing.

The next day I went back out there to see how the bull was doing, and he was still just lying where we had left him, barely alive. He looked dead, but if you paid close attention, you could see his flanks moving.

Thankfully, he was breathing and hanging on. I took off my tee shirt and laid it over the bull's head as flies were having a field day on him and he didn't show the slightest movement. I put a softball-sized rock on his cheek to hold the T-shirt down and went on my way.

On the second day, I went out to see if the bull had gotten up yet, and he was still in the same place. On the third day, I also drove by, and to my surprise, the bull was gone. He had finally stood up and walked away. My T-shirt along with the rock that I had used to keep it from blowing off was lying on the ground where the bull had been.

I've often wondered what became of that bull. I never saw him again, and I always thought it was a good possibility he woke up and stumbled off the rim. At least he didn't stumble back into the cattle guard.

Relationships can be good or bad, and they can bring up a host of different feelings. They're also hard to come by if you live at a ranger station several miles from any community. While it wasn't my task to bring any of these up in this book, one may provide—at least in my version—a unique take on issues at a ranger station. Early in my career, my roommate and I gained permanent positions, and because we were single guys, we secured a single-wide trailer, which got us out of the crew quarters. My roommate attracted the affections of a lady, and as time passed and they became better acquainted, she started spending the night with my buddy from time to time.

They didn't think I was aware of these evenings as my bedroom was at the opposite end of the single-wide, and these nightlong visits were kept a secret from me. It wasn't really possible to keep a secret like that, but we all played the game that no one knew what was up. This lady had the habit of using quite a bit of lotion each day, and as a result, she smelled of the lotion, which was a rather pleasant smell. When she was visiting, the sweet smell of her was always lofting around the single-wide, which was a good improvement to the normal smells that were associated with our abode. The brand of the lotion never changed, and you could literally smell her before you saw her as she rarely missed her daily applications. I liked the smell because it overwhelmed the smell of smoke, sweat, and dirty socks that were the common smells of our trailer.

As time passed, this relationship started suffering from problems. Before long, she quit coming over, and we were on our own again. She may not have been present, but her scent from her lotion remained around our trailer for much longer. I found it amazing that that smell could last as long as it did. Other than the stench of a skunk, I've never smelled anything that lasted as long. This stuff had a half-life of several weeks. This started bugging my roommate as it reminded him of her.

One evening I was overcome by the thought that I may be missing one of those quality moments in life and a great chance to play a little prank on my roommate. The next trip into town, I purchased the brand of lotion she preferred and started my little trick. I started rubbing a little on his pillow one evening, and when he woke up, he would come into the living room and complain of smelling her in his bed. I started putting the lotion every few days on something he would smell. I doctored up a few T-shirts and a couple pairs of socks, and I made sure the couch and his bedding got a refresher from time to time. He would strip his bed and wash the sheets to get rid of the smell, and then I would sneak in and reapply some more lotion to keep the memory alive.

He became more and more hostile to the smell, and as he tried to erase the smell from our trailer, I would adjust things with the flowery smell. He would complain and ask what the hell was in that lotion that made it keep its smell for so long. It really bugged him. After a few months, I tired of my little trick; however, I never told him what I was up to, and he never figured it out. I don't know what happened to the lady, but I'm sure she still smells great. Every time I smell that particular lotion, it puts a smile on my face.

CHAPTER 4
BEELINING

We were working on a prescribed burn one beautiful fall day up on the Mogollon Rim of Northern Arizona. These were the days of Indian summer. Nighttime temperatures dropped below freezing, but the days were full of sunshine, calm, and warmth.

We burned all morning with great conditions and broke for lunch at about noon. We all got together to eat lunch at a stock tank. A stock tank around here was a water catchment common to the area. I've seen outsiders drive past tanks, looking for a steel tank because the outsiders called tanks ponds or some other thing. So we were all sitting around, eating and bullshitting when one of the guys noticed that there were a lot of honeybees getting water from the tank.

We ended up discussing honey and honeybees, and another guy and I brought up how to find a beehive by following the bees back to the hive. We both had seen this done before, and we were both instructed on the fine art of beelining by friends who had done the practice for years.

With beelining, you wait at a water source that bees are working. Then the bees will fly in a straight line back to their hive. (I'm no expert, but I assume that's where the term beeline comes from.) We have the Beeline Highway in Arizona, but that has nothing to do with this story. It was as easy as just watching which way the bees headed from the water and then following that line until you found the hive.

We all worked in an atmosphere in which joking was quite common. Not many people there were buying into the beelining instructions. One of the guys then said, "I've been watching these bees leave, and they all are headed in the same direction." This planted the seed of doubt in the burn crew, so as we continued to eat lunch, they gave more attention to the bees, which led everyone to believe that they were in fact all leaving the tank and headed up the hill in the same direction.

Everyone figured that the hive would have to be nearby because while the bees were headed in the same direction, you could only see them for a short distance before they disappeared. So the instruction continued. We talked about how we could just walk over to where we saw the last ones and then wait. We could watch as a few of the bees fly by and then continue along that line, always going to where you saw the last bee. As I said, it was calm, so you could hear them fly by too. While it might take you a few bees to actually see the little devils and figure out which direction they were headed, you could hear them buzz over you, headed for home.

The guy who introduced me to beelining had a great trick if you lost the beeline. He would get a cake pan and place it on the ground wherever he lost the line on a slight incline. He'd put sugar water on one end and flour on the uphill side. In theory, the bees would locate the sugar water (one of their favorite things), land, and start fiddling around in it just like the stock tank. Then they'd walk into the flour prior to their departure and coat their sticky little feet. This had a double benefit too. Because of the weight of the flour, they couldn't fly as high, and because they have the white flour stuck all over them, they were easier to see. Both of these benefits helped you continue along the beeline. If he still kept losing the beeline, he would put a piece of window screen over the cake pan, trapping the bees that had been lured to the sugar water. Then he'd take the cake pan along with bees down the line to where he'd lost the trail and start the process again.

One key tidbit of bee knowledge that helps with this process is that bees cannot keep their little mouths shut. All it takes is for one bee to locate the bonanza of sugar water. As soon as it gets back to the hive, it starts blabbing about the discovery. News travels fast, and soon the hive is buzzing around the popular cake pan.

None of these little tricks were needed this day. Every man and certainly everyone on the burn crew had a little boy buried in their soul, and the idea of chasing these bees around brought out the Tom Sawyer in all of us. The day's burning was quickly abandoned for the adventure of following these bees to their hive. By now even the doubters were in the chase and starting to believe in the realities of beelining.

The beeline led us to a huge green oak tree, and sure as hell, there was a hive. About twenty feet up in the tree was a little hole about a half inch in diameter that was busy with bees coming and going. We all felt the thrill of success. Both the doubters and the believers were so proud of themselves. But now that we had located the hive, how were we going to steal the honey?

All the guys looked to us for advice. Now they were convinced that we actually knew what we were talking about, and they eagerly awaited further instructions. While we had proven that we were beeliners, I realized that our knowledge ended when you reached the hive, and how to retrieve the honey from the hive had not been part of our instruction. Not wanting to show our ignorance, we had a little forum while we watched the bees come and go from that little hole in the oak tree.

Looking back, it's hard to believe that the group came up with such a foolproof plan to secure the honey, but this is how it played out. Our real job that day was a prescribed burn, so we had a bulldozer with us. How simple would it be to push the tree over, grab a chain saw, cut open the hive, and get tons of sweet honey. The plan was put into action. We walked the dozer up the hill, and as we all stood around and watched the dozer guy walk the bulldozer up to the tree really slowly and attempt to push the tree over. Gamble oaks have a good root system and are damn near impossible to push over, and the dozer didn't have the guts to get the job done. So the operator then backed up a little and took a run at the tree, hitting it hard. It's hard to believe how many bees are actually in a hive, but that smack with the dozer made most of them buzz out of the tree to see what the hell was going on. We all ran screaming and laughing down the hill as the swarm of bees flew around the area.

A smarter grouping of guys may have abandoned the bee tree and gone back to burning; however, just because one great plan failed, we weren't giving up so easy. We conducted another forum, one that far exceeded the first in intelligence. This time, believe it or not, the plan consisted of just sawing the tree down. Each of us would get three or four pine knots burning really well, and when the tree hit the ground, we would all run up and place them near the little hole to the hive. This pile of burning pine knots right at the door to the hive would burn the wings off the bees as they exited and leave them helpless to defend their honey trove.

We quickly put the plan into action. One guy ran down to get a chain saw while the rest of us gathered up a bunch of good pine knots and started them on fire. One guy volunteered to saw down the tree while the rest of us got the knots burning. The saw seemed to bug the bees a little, but they weren't disturbed too badly. We all had our hands full of burning pine knots, ready to rush the tree when it hit the ground. The tree began to lean, and all of us knew it was time. As it hit the ground, we all headed to the little hole in the tree at a run.

As soon as the tree hit the ground, the bees came out in force. There were many more than all that had come out to see what the dozer was doing to their tree. As we rushed in, they rushed out and attacked us with a vengeance. All of us heading for that little hole made for excellent targets. We immediately abandoned the plan, and without any discussion, we tossed the burning pine knots into the air and ran like hell to get away from our attackers. When they calmed down a little and our stings quit hurting, we went back to the hive and laughed. The ground was littered with burning knots, and not one was anywhere near the little hole.

Now we are wounded and mad but determined to get that honey more than ever. One of the guys brought up that he had learned in the second grade that when a bee stings you, it dies. You don't have to be a skilled beeliner to know that. With so many bees dead or dying after defending the hive, one of the guys decided that we would achieve success. He put on a couple pairs of pants a few coats two pairs of gloves and wrapped his face with a bandana or two. Everything was secured with a roll of duct tape, and then he went in to secure the honey.

While he did discover that not all the bees had died yet, he gutted it out and did open the hive and scoop several shovels of honey, placing it all in plastic bags and our lunchboxes. He got in and out quick, and he left some of the honey for the bees because "winter was coming," as he said. To the group, which was observing from a safe distance, it looked more like he just got tired of having the bees commit suicide and pulled out early. However, none of us voiced our concern that he could have got more of the honey.

We went out in the morning to do a little burning, and all came home after participating in the ancient art of beelining. News of our success spread fast around the ranger station and surrounding community. It seemed there were quite a few ladies who liked to use honey to bake with, and now that they were all aware of our skills, each year they all made a request to secure honey. While the beelining portion of our quest never changed, our honey retrieval methods did improve. We found some beekeeper hoods that fit rather nicely on a full-billed Bullard hard hat. That with a few pairs of cloths, a roll of duct tape, and a bare back bronc riders skill in tape application, made for a far less painful method of retrieving the honey.

One evening we were watching a movie on the television. We were quite a ways from any community, and as a result, we only got one channel. That night we were watching a movie about a giant swarm of bees that was threatening mankind. (I forget the name of the movie.) The film was one of those many movies that addressed different ways the world was going to come to an end by a host of different causes. The movie about the giant swarm of killer bees interested us because of our vast knowledge about the little guys. At the end of the movie, the world was saved when the humans managed to lure the giant swarm of killer bees a huge football stadium where they lowered the temperature to a point where the bees were unable to live, fly, sting, or anything.

This caught our interest. We had learned in second grade that bees died after stinging something. It was their one and only shot at defense. However, cold temperatures rendering them helpless had never made the lesson plan. We soon realized that if the bees were just lying around like pebbles in cold weather, the honey retrieval should take place in those conditions. This would bring a real boon to beelining technology.

As the annual requests started coming in for honey and as we gained more information about bee behavior, we were quick to go out and find a hive. All we had to do was to wait for a nice cold day and then head out to the hive and secure gallons of sweet honey. Then the day came. Temperatures hovered around zero, so it was nice and cold. We went off to the hive, full of confidence and knowledge, eager to secure enough honey to accommodate everyone's needs. When we got to the tree, there was not a bee in sight. They were all paralyzed inside the hive, helpless to a couple of beeliners. So we fired up the chain saw and began the honey retrieval.

I've heard on movie sets that there is a position called the authenticity director. This person's task is to ensure that the movie plot is believable and stays on track in order to make the movie an honest depiction of whatever the movie is about. The movie about the killer bee swarm must not have employed one such individual because the idea that bees were paralyzed by the cold was a bald-faced lie. In reality, all the bees in the hive were just hiding and waiting for some moron to cut into the hive.

Robbing a bee tree in cold weather just ensured that all the bees were home and none were out looking for sugar water. They were all there and united in their efforts to protect their home. The idea that a beesting hurts less if it's cold out is also one of the unfortunate falsehoods experienced by sage beeliners.

So now you know the finer aspects of beelining. If you decide to give it a try, remember that bees like their honey a hell of a lot more that you do. Good luck.

CHAPTER 5
CHANGING TIMES

One of the reasons I have written this book is to note some changes that have occurred during my time fighting forest fires. I will be the first to admit that when I started my career, I was just out there digging line for the most part and not exposed to the higher-level decisions or inner actions required to keep the ship afloat. It was my role to just keep my mouth shut and follow orders. While we lived with the tactics and the decisions that others made, I don't really remember anyone asking me what I thought or if I had any better ideas. I don't feel that I had any better ideas; however, I think that we knew our roles, and quite frankly, it was just generally accepted that this was the way it was. We respected our superiors and their efforts to fight fire because they knew what to do, and besides, all we had to do was accomplish that.

It seems that the whole firefighting process was simpler and more direct in those days. There are definitely more rules and regulations to adhere to today, not to mention increased political pressures. Fires have also become more complex to manage with a host of issues that didn't exist when I started my career. I hope to compare some of the old ways with the new ways to display how things have evolved.

Most folks think that fighting forest fires is hard and dirty work, and they are right. If you're in fire camp and trying to figure things out, it may not be a physically demanding job, but for those out there digging a line, it is just as hard and dirty as it ever was. We were often expected to work extremely long shifts with little downtime to rest up and recharge until you were back at it again. The eight-hour shift was never a part of a firefighter's workday. We would commonly put in shifts of eighteen to twenty hours, and at the extreme, we might work for thirty to forty hours for a shift. I have done several shifts that have exceeded the forty-hour range. This was just the way it was, and while I'm sure managers tried to limit this occurrence, if you were caught up in these long shifts, you were just expected to keep your mouth shut about it and tough it out. After these long shifts, you just got as much sleep as you could and hit it again. After a few shifts like these, we were all like a bunch of dirty zombies walking around. After all, when you are dog-tired and offered a few off hours, cleaning up is last on the list of things you need to do.

When a fire team was assigned to a fire, they were expected to stay on that fire until it was contained. This did offer incentive for success because you knew you were there until the proverbial fat lady sang. While it seemed that fires back then did not gain the tremendous acreage that they do today, the team was there until they succeeded. While the large fires today are attributed to the effects of years of fire suppression and the effects of global warming, I wonder if the fire teams of today were expected to stay on a fire until it was caught if some of the larger fires in current times would have a smaller footprint. My longest stay on a fire was forty-eight days.

Today, the guidelines for rest and work have become the rule. Now it is required that firefighters be off for one hour for every two that they work. It is also a requirement that the incident commander approves any shifts more than sixteen hours prior to working that shift. Another rule now is that a fire assignment can only last fourteen days in duration. While there are means to extend the length of an assignment to twenty-one days, all effected parties must agree prior to that extension. So too, after you return from a fire assignment of fourteen days, you have to take a mandatory two days off. If these two mandated days off fall on your scheduled workdays, then you are paid to take the days off. In times past when you returned home after a fire, you were generally busier than you were on the fire as you tried to catch up with all the stuff you missed while you were gone.

While a fire team would stay on a fire until it was contained in the past, today it is commonplace for a fire to outlast several teams, each doing their fourteen-day stint on the fire and then passing it to another team. Each year there seems to be a fire that goes through several teams, and in the past few years, some of these fires burn for most of the fire season. I really do feel it was a huge incentive in the old days to catch the fire or stay there until you did. Now it is down to working your fourteen days and then passing the fire to another team and hoping they were more successful than you were.

This can and does cause some degree of friction between teams. In getting a fire that has had another team on it, commonly called a "used fire," often the incoming team is critical of the outgoing team's efforts. For example, my team took over a "used fire" from a fire team from Florida. The fire was burning on the Flathead National Forest and threatening to spread into Glacier National Park. When we arrived on the fire and looked at what that team had accomplished during their fourteen days of effort, we were taken aback to see the small amount of line they had controlled. Fire maps showed the controlled fire line in black, and the uncontrolled lines were shown in red. Looking at the fire map, there was only about an inch of controlled line. This was not a good showing for fourteen days on the assignment. We took over command of the fire with high expectations and determined to do a better job that the team we relieved. The fire had different goals and quite frankly kicked our asses and spread well into Glacier National Park. Then our time was up, and we were forced to transition the fire to another team. As luck would have it, the team that we transitioned with was the same team we took the fire over from. As that team showed up and our transition began looking at the fire map, they realized that our fourteen-day efforts had secured just about one more inch of line, and I'm sure they were thinking the same thing we were when we had taken over.

The same holds true for everyone on a fire. They work their

fourteen days and then leave for a few days of rest. While the guidelines about rest and work do serve a purpose, it is a huge change from the way things were when I started. Today it seems like there are more issues stemming from crew behavior in fire camps. However, this issue was limited in my early days. When you got into camp, you ate and lay down because you were spent and had little energy left to get into trouble.

While night shifts are not completely gone, they are fewer than they were in the past. On a large fire nowadays, night shifts are only used for a few shifts if at all. In my early years, there was always both a day and night shift on every fire. It didn't seem to matter if there was anything to do or not, and every firefighter of that era no doubt spent some boring times on night shifts. The night shift on a desert fire was one of the worst you could get. Being from Arizona, most of my contemporaries and I spent many nights on desert fires. Most of the things that would bite and sting didn't venture out during the heat of the day. They would wait until darkness had fallen then make their way out of their hiding places. As a result, you often had to deal with snakes, scorpions, centipedes, and all those wonderful desert dwellers. I have already mentioned my sissy behavior around snakes, and my phobia was even stronger during the darkness because they were not really visible until they scared the hell out of you.

If you worked a desert night shift, you also had to attempt to get some sleep during the heat of the day. Today while the incident command base is usually at a school or near some community, a gymnasium or some other building is used to provide a sleeping area during the day. In the past, however, this was not the case. Fire camps didn't need to be around electricity because there were no computers. Day sleeping areas consisted of wherever you could find the best shade. It proved hard to get any good rest chasing shade around a mesquite tree. After a few days of this, you became dog-tired. I've seen many firefighters fall asleep only to get extreme sunburns because they failed to keep moving into the shady area. I have seen many guys take off their boots and socks only to accidently sunburn their feet so badly that they couldn't work.

One of the reasons that night shifts are not used as much today is the competition for resources. It isn't uncommon to not get all the firefighting resources you need to staff a night shift. Staffing a night shift for a few shifts in order to burn a line or to serve some other purpose is more the common practice currently.

What firefighters wear has also changed quite a bit. When I started, the only thing that was issued to you was a metal hard hat. While eight-inch leather boots with laces were required, it was up to you to purchase your boots, and it still is to this day. We were instructed to wear cotton clothing, which was easy to do in those days as the newer synthetic fabrics were not as prominent as they are today. Levis and a cotton shirt was the norm, while some of the guys who had been on fires in California had managed to steal one of their fire-resistant shirts, which were orange. None were actually issued in this area. Gloves were not a requirement yet, and if you wanted some, you bought your own.

Hearing protection was unheard of. I guess you could have provided your own; however at this time, I don't think we knew that hearing loss could occur by running a chain saw or all the other associated noises of firefighting. Currently, hearing protection is provided, and many safety discussions address this topic too.

Fire shelters, which are a requirement today, were also unheard of. The fire that made them a requirement was the Battlement Creek Fire in Colorado. Four members of the Mormon Lake Hotshot Crew were trapped in that fire, resulting in three fatalities and one suffering severe burns. This occurred in 1976, five years after I started. In this tragic event, the crew was issued fire shelters in an effort to test them and see if they would benefit the safety of the crew. The shelters were new, heavy, and not a requirement to have on the fire line. Because of the expected shift to be primarily a mop-up assignment, with little threat from the fire the shelters were left in camp. This tragedy was instrumental in making the shelters a requirement. Currently, everyone that is on the fire line is required to carry one. On a personal note, these fatalities were friends of mine, and losing them was the first time I truly considered the consequences that fighting fire could have.

As things progressed, the term *personal protective equipment* (PPE) came into the fireground. Fire-resistant clothing was developed, and pants and shirts soon arrived on the scene and became a requirement. These items—commonly referred to as NOMEX because of the first manufacturer—became another item that was issued to all fire-going personnel. This clothing is still the norm, and everyone wear these yellow shirts and green pants as a requirement. Gloves also became a requirement, and they were issued to all line-going personnel.

The metal hard hats were the next to disappear because of the developing threat of electrical accidents. Consequently, they were outlawed and replaced by plastic hard hats. This small rule hit home with everyone. At the time, your *bucket* or hard hat was generally one you had forever. Many folks had theirs painted to their fancy, and they were quite proud of their hard hats. Getting your hands on a single-bill Bullard hard hat was just about the most fashionable thing at the time. Some guys had their single-bills chromed, and they all made sure their hats were polished up bright. I can remember one such guy who had a chrome hard hat. He had been a division boss on the Verde Fire on the desert north of Phoenix, Arizona. After a long and very hot shift, he just left all of us peons out on the desert and headed into camp alone. We felt quite abandoned and somewhat upset that he just went into camp without arranging anything for our transportation. We observed his beautiful chrome single-bill Bullard hard hat lying on the seat of his unlocked truck. It somehow found its way under the dual tires of a hotshot bus and was pancaked into a shiny Frisbee, and then someone put it back into his truck.

In my early days, canteens were the norm. These canteens were one-gallon canvas canteens that were often called "banjos." These canteens had long straps that you could place around your shoulders in order to carry them like a backpack. That was the popular way to carry one too. With this technique, it was out of your way as you dug a line or did other jobs on the fire. While one may still see these canteens, they have for the most part gone away, and most crews would rather be caught dead than carrying one of these cumbersome canteens around. They were a pain in the ass to pack, but they were the only way to take water along at the time. Because of the cumbersome canteens, everyone was always looking for a different means to pack water. Well-dressed firefighters of the era started using military-issue canteens. The military also had duty belts and web gear that canteens hooked onto. These systems also had a shoulder strap to distribute the weight to your shoulders. This was quite a hit, and the setup was commonly referred to as "hips." The firefighters soon began hitting up military surplus stores to outfit themselves with these and to avoid packing around the cumbersome banjos. In the past, a potable water truck generally provided drinking water and hence a means of filling up your banjo prior to each shift.

Eventually, quart plastic water bottles were developed and became the norm. The military web gear was adopted and then provided a means to pack around these new quart-size water bottles. Currently, a quite a few folks are using these, but the new camelback water containers seem to be the popular means of packing water on fires now. The potable water truck has also been replaced. Now pallets of bottled drinking water provide water for the firefighters, and consequently, discarded water bottles litter the fire area and travel routes.

Line packs are another item that no one had when I started. If some well-outfitted firefighters were to see how we went to the fire line, they'd think we were a group of idiots. We didn't take along line gear. All you had was your tool, your banjo, and a sack lunch that you put in your shirt or tucked into your belt. It is a standard deal now for everyone to carry a small backpack on fires. (These are called line packs.)

Before line packs came onto the scene, some of the hotshot crews obtained cruisers vests, which provided a means to carry additional supplies along with you, but they were not issued. While these were uncommon my first few years, they did become a fashion item for a while. Carrying the banjo on your back didn't allow for a pack. Now there are multiple line packs available with a host of attachments to aid the firefighter. These packs provide a means to carry your lunch, jacket, extra batteries, a fire shelter, and whatever you feel you may need during your shift.

Fortunately, you can now stuff Gatorade or some other brand of electrolyte-replacement fluid into your line pack prior to hitting the fire line. This is also a new item that didn't exist in my early years. The hotshot crew that worked for me my final years with the outfit approached me with a request to purchase a couple pallets of Gatorade to put in their fire cache. I balked at the order because I felt it was somewhat in excess, and then I was informed by a hotshot that it was a requirement to fight fires. I told them that people had fought quite a few fires before Gatorade hit the scene. That comment just made them think even more that I was old school and needed to get current with their needs.

Feeding the troops has also changed over time. I have seen many changes to the rules about how everyone gets fed. One thing that was common when I started was military surplus "C rations." These came in individual cardboard boxes, and you didn't have a clue how old they were. They usually had one entre, a can of fruit, a juice, some canned crackers or bread, pound cake or pecan nut roll, a tin of peanut butter, cheddar cheese or jelly, a packet with condiments, a small box of four cigarettes, a book of jungle matches, and a pack of instant coffee. Everyone had their favorite items that came in them, and maybe you preferred the pecan nut roll to the pound cake or the spaghetti to chili beans. When a meal break took place, it was a common practice to trade some of the contents. One of the entre items offered was Spanish rice. I have never seen anyone eat the can of Spanish rice and not puke in less than an hour. They all came with a little government-issue can opener that was call a "P-38" for some unknown reason. Everyone usually carried a P-38 on their key ring in those days. Eating the rations was better than starving to death, but no one desired them. One neat item that they did have was the small tins of jelly, cheddar cheese, or peanut butter. These items were not all that good to eat, but people often put them into warming fires as they provided a great little explosion. This was something that occurred more than once, and they provided some good laughs when they exploded around an unknowing group eating around the fire. That practice came to an end among me and my buddies when a tin of jelly blew up and sprayed us with molten jelly.

Another food item that thankfully went away was the old "boil in a bag" dinners. They were even less desirable than C rations. These consisted of a plastic net bag that looked like a hair net and contained a variety of food items. They were placed in a large caldron of boiling water and fished out and given to us to eat. We called these "gut bags," and the quality of their contents was not far from just plain horrible. I particularly remember the peas and carrot vegetable packet. I don't know how you could even flavor food to that taste they had achieved because it was not at all what peas and carrots tasted like or really anything that you had ever put in your mouth. The gut bags weren't on the scene for long, and if you're a current fire fighter, you should be thankful you missed that tragedy.

The old C rations were replaced by the current military equivalent called meals ready to eat (MREs). While one hopefully uses these are for emergencies, they are mostly used by hand crews that choose to spike out. I really don't know if they are any good to my palette. So far, I have not had to try one out.

Not all the meals in the past were bad. Locally, we had crews of folks who would cook for the firefighters and would prepare top-notch meals. During my first few years, these cook crews were common and provided excellent meals. The state game and fish department staffed one such kitchen and provided excellent food for several fires while they were in that business. Some forests also had a group of folks who would cook for us, and they, too, really put out some great meals. I think this was also common around the nation, and some places you went provided well for the workers. One of the best of these cook crews was from the Shasta-Trinity National Forest in California. I heard that the crew consisted of the wives and relatives of that forest service's employees. At any rate, if you were lucky enough to get on a fire with people who cooked for you, you were always well fed and taken care of. I haven't heard of them for years, but everyone was grateful for their efforts.

Commercial caterers are now used for any large fire. It has become a requirement if the number of people on the fire reaches a threshold. These outfits provide three meals a day for the fire personnel. They provide both vegetarian and regular meals. They also provide tables and chairs so that people can sit down and eat their meals. In cold weather, heated tents are often set up for a dining hall, and you can actually eat your dinner before it freezes. While you still hear quite a bit of complaining about the food they offer, I just always thought back to the day of the gut bag, and then I was very content with their service.

On the Mogollon Baldy Fire, which was in the Gila wilderness, a friend and I took two Southwest firefighter crews to the fire. This fire was far inside the wilderness, and the two crews were flown into the fire. One day we were shorted for lunches. I don't remember why, but we ended up with one crew that had lunches and one that didn't. One was a Navajo crew, and the other a Hopi crew, and when we discovered the mix-up at lunch, we suggested they share the lunches with the other crew. This was not well received to say the least. Then the crew that had lunches asked if we were going to share our lunches too. Of course, we agreed to share our lunches because we were all in the same boat. My buddy opened his paper sack to find out his lunch, which he had been packing around, consisted of only packets of salt, pepper, and sugar. This information did lighten the mood but did little to feed the troops.

In the foreword I mentioned the story of the hotshots not believing the story about paper sleeping bags. I've always wondered who designed those paper sleeping bags and who sold the government on such a questionable concept. There have been a few different kinds put in use, but the ones that we discussed were the first. I have nearly frozen to death attempting to sleep in one of these on too many nights. If the temperature dropped at all, you were a fool not to just climb in with every warm piece of clothing you had with you, boots and all, to fight off hypothermia. You could only get one a day from supply, but if you were there enough days and got another every day and kept putting one inside the other, after a week or so, you could take off your boots. If it happened to rain or snow you can imagine what happened. If you are curious about what these sleeping bags looked like, imagine those large bags of dog food. The dog food sacks have about the same look, although they are a bit shorter. However, the sleeping bags had just about the same amount of insulation. There was a new development in paper sleeping bags after the first ones, and they were a lot warmer. They were insulated with some kind of white synthetic fuzz. This white fuzz would stick to your face after a few days without shaving. I'm sure there are readers who remember them for that reason.

We didn't take a lot of stuff to fires in my early days. I didn't know if that was because I was a grunt and that was just what grunts took to a fire. The folks on the fire teams may have taken along more stuff, but as worker bees, we were limited on what we took. Since bedrolls were always furnished, even if they served little purpose other than keeping bugs off you, we didn't take them. Sleeping pads were not issued though, so it was just your paper sleeping bag and a rock-free area to sleep on. Some relief came if you followed the bag-a-day tactic and started stocking up on them.

Everything we took along with us was crammed into canvas knapsacks. We were each given one for fires. Usually, you would take a coat, a bunch of pairs of socks, one change of clothes, a bathroom kit, and whatever else you could fit in your pack. These packs are currently used as hose packs, that carry fire hose and fittings and not used for much else. If they were issued for the same purpose today, the guys would probably just throw them away. Now a host of new packs are offered. If rain threatened the area, you could usually get some plastic sheets from supply and construct a lean-to for shelter. Tents for individuals were not provided or taken as they are today. One thing that kept most of us from complaining was that when we reached camp, most of us were dog-tired from long shifts, and we really didn't feel like throwing much of a fuss.

Communications have really improved too. That may not be saying much. We didn't have a radio at all on some fires, so any communications would have been an improvement. When I started, we didn't feel that communications were lacking at all. We had a mobile radio in the tanker and a pack set that we could take in the cabin with us or take with us on trips away from the tanker. These pack sets were pretty cumbersome by today's standards, but they were our only option. They were a little bigger than a lunch box, and they needed fifteen D-size batteries. So they were also pretty heavy by today's standards. There were only two channels, and all the radios were set to these channels. Channel one was for fire and emergency traffic, and channel two was for administrative traffic. The frequencies for these radios were set and couldn't be changed, at least not by us.

If you went out of the forest on a fire, these radios just didn't work. When you arrived at a fire, it was common to have no communications. Officials may have already handed out radios, but they were very limited. If someone in your sector had one, that seemed to be enough. I said that they didn't work if you went out of the forest, but while driving to a fire in Utah, we were blabbing away on our channel 2 only to find out that our channel 2 was the Dixie National Forest's channel 1. They didn't think very much of our discussions.

Currently, the norm is programmable digital radios. They are very small and light. They operate on nine double-A batteries, which probably don't weigh as much as two D-size batteries. While the older radios had only two channels, you can program the new ones to carry more than a hundred frequencies. They are easy to program, and therefore, you can take the radios from your home unit and clone or program the fire's frequencies. Then you're good to go. Boxes of these radios can be ordered from the fire caches around the country and are available in fire camps if anyone who didn't bring one from home needs one. In the past, if a hotshot crew had one radio, they were hooked up; however, I'm not sure how many radios are common for a hotshot crew to carry now, but I would bet it is between six and ten for a twenty-person crew.

Before my time there was a telephone line that hooked the ranger station to the guard stations. It was strung from tree to tree and held in place with white insulators usually placed about twenty feet up in the trees. I've heard that you had to be careful using these during thunderstorms, or you could get shocked; however, I never used these. They utilize nine-gauge uninsulated wire to make these connections, and my only exposure to these old phone lines consisted of rolling up miles of the old wire that seemed to be strung all over creation. When I started, we had only one phone at the ranger station—a radio phone that provided sketchy service at best. Now new-age radios cell phones, smartphones, and satellite phones have come onto the scene, and while communications were a little primitive once, those days are long gone.

Computers have changed firefighting in tremendous ways. They have changed all the functions of groups working on fires and really the functions of all federal agencies in general. One of the changes I have noticed is the location of fire camps. In my early days, fire camps were placed as close to the fire as possible without burning the whole place down. While this did happen on occasion—and still does, I may add—fire camp was generally established in more remote locations. Now in order to power the electronic systems, fire camps have moved into towns. Schools that are not in session during fire season are prime locations. Available phone lines and electricity are more of an issue than being close to the fire. It would take volumes to relate how computers have changed the process of fighting forest fires, but they clearly play a role in just about everything.

Computers have many fire prediction programs that are designed to tell you where a fire is headed and when it will get there. Incident meteorologists can watch real-time weather changes and broadcast them if they impact the fire. The finance shop can track fire costs with a greater efficiency and in a timely manner. All equipment and personnel time is recorded on computers. The ordering and tracking of supplies is all completed online. The public information shop can spread information about the fire on websites and maintain hundreds of contacts.

I remember when the forest service got the first computers. They were called the "data generals," and they showed up without any instructions. It was up to us to figure them out, and through trial and error, we slipped slowly into the computer age.

The compass was a key piece of firefighting equipment. While most of us knew our way around our home turf, if we went to a fire in a foreign place, we needed compass skills to find our way around. You generally received a topographical map, but without any compass skills, you could end up in the wrong place. With the global positioning system (GPS) in place, the compass has taken a back seat. If you're unaware, the global positioning system is composed of several satellites in orbit around our planet that can pinpoint your location. There is no question which is more accurate, and GPS offers a host of benefits. People have forgotten the old system of counting dots from a dot grid to determine acreage. Currently a GPS perimeter of the fire is established with just a push of a button, which immediately determined the acreage with more accurate. GPS systems are in all aircraft, and just about every unit on a fire has one. This is a tremendous advance in firefighting, and while it has caused many to abandon the compass, it far exceeds its capabilities. Instead of leaning on the hood of your truck with a topo and a compass, now topographic maps can be loaded upon your tablet, and GPS will tell you exactly where you are.

The tool selection to go out and dig line has changed as well. In my early years, the choices were limited to a fire shovel, Pulaski, double-bit ax, McCloud, and maybe a brush hook. Council rakes and swatters were also around, but we had little to no use for them. Chain saws were not new, but they were very large and heavy. All the saws were gear-driven, and they predated modern clutch-driven saws, which are quite a bit lighter and improved. Tools were expendable. And after you worked a shift with your tool, you would eventually head to supply and turn yours in for a sharpened one. The tools firefighters now carry are much better. The standard tools we used have been bent, welded, chopped up, and customized in just about every way imaginable. Because of the modifications to these tools, you can't just go to a supply and get another one, so crews tend to keep their tools, and sharpen them theselves.

Hand crews have also evolved from my first days of firefighting. During my first few years, we didn't have any hotshot crews on the Coconino National Forest. When I started, hand crews were gathered in any way possible. They might meet at a bus parked at a local unemployment office, and the first twenty guys who showed up were loaded into the bus and driven to the fire. Southwest firefighter crews (SWFF crews) were staffed by most of the reservations and small towns in northern New Mexico. These crews were always sent with a crew liaison officer (CLO) who had a lot of knowledge about fires and could ensure they followed safety procedures as well as keep their time. While there are still a few of these crews today, they have diminished in number.

Currently, there are several hotshot crews around the nation. These hotshot crews, which are officially referred to as interagency hotshot crews (IHC), are a national resource and are positioned at several locations around the nation. They are type 1 crews, and they, too, have evolved from modest beginnings into the groups they are today. The first IHC that worked on the Coconino National Forest was the Coconino Hotshots, and they were quickly joined by three additional crews, giving the forest four crews. The first IHCs didn't have all the bells and whistles as they do these days. The first crews were transported in flatbed trucks. The old knapsacks were issued for fire packs, and all the older fire equipment I mentioned earlier was all they had. The first IHC at Blue Ridge lived in wall tents for the summer. They also had a few ladies who cooked their meals for them while they were home. This was the practice for several years before new crew quarters were constructed.

IHCs now have nice crew carriers that look better than they run, as it is common for them to not make it home, breaking down often. These crew carriers have a full host of supplies, food, water, fire packs, a traveling saw shop, burning fuel, and just about everything you could ever want on a fire. The superintendent's vehicle was generally equipped with a water pumper unit, computer, and everything that didn't fit into the crew carriers. Most crews have all-terrain vehicles pulled on a trailer behind the superintendents truck. IHCs are very well equipped these days and provide a significant punch in fire suppression.

It seemed for years that the National Guard deuce and a halves were used to transport folks around a fire. It has been several years since I've seen these used. I remember how cold you could get if you were headed out to the fire in the morning on one of these vehicles. They did have canvas covers not unlike like a Conestoga wagon of the old west. While these covers did cut down the windchill, they were seldom used. Most roads utilized in fire suppression would get horribly dusty. It's not uncommon for the dust to be several inches deep. If people put the covers on the deuces, the back was open and sucked unbearable amounts of dust into the vehicle. We all chose to freeze rather than be suffocated by dust, so we generally left the covers off. The suspension for the deuces was very stiff and provided a very rough ride. The seats were made of wood and went along each side of the back of the vehicle, so you had to pay attention, or you would get whacked by the limbs of low-hanging trees.

Another big change is the current participation in wildfire suppression by municipal fire departments. This did not hold true in California because they involved fire departments earlier than most of the country. In the rest of the nation, you never saw fire department resources on forest fires. With urban sprawl, which has affected most of the areas around the country, forest fires started burning into subdivisions and communities around the west. Fire departments were thereby involved whether they wanted to be or not. Most fire departments had no wildland engines, and the staff had little training or qualifications in wildland fire suppression. The risk grew as the communities around the nation did, and this additional risk got several fire departments involved in the wildland fire arena. Fire departments started training in wildland practices and developing qualifications. As departments could, they started getting wildland engines, and with the equipment and qualifications, they have currently become one of the key participants in the fray. Now it is uncommon to get to a fire and not have fire department resources engaged in the battle. I think it's safe to say that all incident management teams have members from municipal fire departments, and most may not be able to fill the teams without their participation.

Contract firefighters were not yet on the scene. Currently, multiple hand crews, engines, water tenders, and those who offer just about every option of equipment work as contractors for fires. In the past every engine on a fire was from one of the federal or state agencies. I have been on many fires today where there is not an agency engine but mostly contract resources. If there was a need for any extra equipment, they could sign up, but this was uncommon.

The aircraft used in suppression has also changed quite a bit. In my first few years, helicopters were used, but for the most part, they were used for reconnaissance flights and initial attacks. Helicopters in that era didn't have the power and capabilities that the current ones have. Their payload was limited, and they lacked the power to overcome high elevations in hot temperatures. Nowadays helicopters play a huge role in fire suppression as newer ships have quite a bit more power and significant payloads. "Bucket work," which is a common use of helicopters on today's fires, was yet to begin, as the buckets, or "bambi buckets," were yet to be thought of. While crew shuttles were done, they required several flights.

I think the best and most effective tool with helicopters that came into being during my career is the interior tanked type 1 helicopters. The most effective of these today is the Sikorsky Sky Crane, which can deliver large drops of water or retardant with spot-on accuracy. Generally, turnaround times are quicker than heavy air tankers, and they can fly in stronger winds than most feel comfortable flying in with heavy air tankers. Plus they are assigned to your fire and are not diverted as frequently as air tankers.

Today helicopters are utilized for a host of missions. They are vital in reaching inaccessible country, and they help with shuttling crews, supply transport, reconnaissance flights, backfiring, mapping, and medical evacuations. Most of today's firefighters haven't worked without helicopter support. Just know they save you a lot of walking.

Air tankers, which were referred to as "slurry bombers" or "borate bombers," consisted of mostly military bombers that had been converted to drop fire retardants. They were all prop-type aircraft, while some did have jet engines that the pilots would turn on after drops to make their exit. Some converted commercial aircraft were outfitted as well. I never got tired of watching them work on a fire, and I still find it to be one of the neatest things to observe. The old planes, which dropped retardants from alarmingly low elevations, would fly over so low that you could see the pilot and the rivets on the plane. You could feel the power of the engines as they flew past. While watching a retardant drop is neat, it is also very dangerous. At times the retardant would break off several trees, knock over snags, or send rocks rolling down a slope. A retardant drop could also send you flying if you were in the way, and I have seen many injuries from folks who didn't get out of the way.

Single-engine air tankers (SEATs) were not yet on the scene. These aircraft are the type commonly used as crop dusters for agricultural fields. Many now have been converted and can apply fire retardant. The older military bombers are not used any longer, and currently, many are developing a new fleet of air tankers. There were a few tragic accidents involving some of the older tankers, and for safety reasons, most of the older military air tankers were grounded. The newest addition to the fleet of air tankers is the very large air tanker (VLAT). These are commercial jets that are currently being used in fire suppression activities.

One of the changes that I have noticed in my career is knowledge about wildland fires. When I started my career in wildland fire suppression, there was one way to gain this knowledge, and that was by fighting fires. The mentors that taught me about fire suppression were veterans on multiple fires, and they gained their knowledge by their involvement over many years of actually fighting fires. As I have stated, firefighting was not an option but rather a duty, and most everyone was required to either work in a support role or out on the fire line.

I doubt that many universities offered classes in wildfire management or fire ecology in my early years on the job. While most of the folks in the professional series did have degrees in some sort of forest management, I doubt that there was much discussion of wildfires. People gained this knowledge on the ground by fighting fires. Most of the actual firefighters fell into the forestry technician series rather than the professional series as defined by the forest service. This has changed throughout my career because of the change in participation in fires by people in the professional series. In the era when everyone was expected to take a role in fire suppression, there were more folks in the professional series who were involved in the fray, and therefore, more educated folks had a better working knowledge of fire suppression.

Since fire suppression duties are more of an option rather than a duty in today's world, many of the folks in the professional series opt out of fire duties, and therefore, they don't have as good a working knowledge of the process. The days when forest employees wore many different hats and engaged in a host of work and responsibilities in differing fields are fading, if they aren't already gone. While there will always be exceptions, I feel most of the professional series now are specialists and choose not to fight fire.

I strongly feel that to gain a working knowledge of wildfire suppression, you need to start at the basic level, which is humping line, and through working multiple fires and encountering different fuel types, you can build a firm knowledge base of the process. I have read many books and reports that discuss and document wildland fires, and I have come to a conclusion that I find peculiar. I feel there are two techniques to gain this knowledge. One is through on-the-job training, and the other is by attending a university. I feel there are two distinct groupings of wildland fire knowledge. In my experience, I find that there are few documents published by the worker bees, and a host of them are published by the academics. I have digested much information, cautions, practices, and guidance in wildland fires written by folks who may have master's degrees in fire ecology but have little or no actual experience in fire suppression.

One key change that occurred in my tenure of firefighting is the pay one received for fighting fires. When I started and well into my career, you were limited to how much money you could make while on fires. If you exceeded the limit, you "maxed out," which resulted in you working for free. I am unaware of the amount of money you were limited to at this time, but it was an issue that impacted many firefighters in the past. This may be an issue that most of everyday folks are unaware of, but it does show the commitment that people once shared in the firefighting business. This issue didn't impact the employees with lower levels of pay; however, as you moved up to higher pay grades, the impact followed you, and with the higher pay grade you attained, the fewer hours you could work before the threshold was met and you started working for free.

Pay on fires worked like this: If you were actually on the line with an uncontrolled fire, you received hazard pay, which was a 25 percent increase of your base pay. As you worked your forty-hour workweek and overtime started, you got 50 percent more than your base pay. If you were working on one of the federal holidays, you got double time or twice your base pay for all hours worked. If you worked overtime while on the line of an uncontrolled fire, you were supposed to receive the 25 percent for hazard pay and the 50 percent for overtime, and in actuality, you were supposed to receive your base pay plus the 75 percent increase. Holiday pay was double your base pay, and that was all you could get because hazard pay and overtime were trumped by the holiday

While this issue was limited to some degree with the required work/rest guidelines discussed earlier in this chapter, it did impact some of the folks in a higher pay grades. As I progress up the pay scale, I was impacted by the cap placed on all firefighters, and I grew accustomed to the "max out" check amount come payday. This pay structure was eventually changed, and with exception to the highest pay grades, firefighters started getting paid for the actual time they spent on fires. I remember the first check that I received after the rule was changed. I was scared as hell because I was sure that I had been overpaid. Overpayment can become a big issue as you are required to pay the overpayment back with interest, which is usually an unwanted surprise for family finances. I always wondered why the payments had to have interest attached. Not only were you working for free, but you also had to pay back more money than you actually got. You never knew about most of the overpayments, or they weren't your fault at all; however, they always came as quite a surprise.

Currently, you do get paid for the actual hours you work unless you are among the highest of pay grades. I have a close friend who's an active firefighter and has been promoted to a high-paying job with the forest service. One season that was moderately busy resulted in him going to several fires. As the season came to an end, he found out that he had exceed the new cap and owed the government a huge amount of money. While he just took it on the chin, his wife had a completely different take on the dilemma and pretty much grounded him. As with pretty much everyone, paying back the excess didn't bode well with their family finances.

Another big change in the wildfire business can be attributed to the current condition that the years of fire suppression have put our nation's forests in. I think it is common knowledge that the size and intensity of fires has increased tremendously. The forest environments have been choked with vegetation because we have taken fire out of the ecosystems. Add the global warming issue and urban sprawl to the overstocked forests, and it becomes obvious that forest fires are a growing issue.

Logging, which was the most common way of treating forests,

has fallen on tough times. The fight to halt logging is just one of the issues that has led to the current hazardous state of our forests. On a national level, overstocked forests have become a prime target for insect damage, and most states in the west have seen vast stands of trees impacted by disease and insect attacks. All the above reasons have resulted in huge and intense fires. Most of our forests are in desperate need of thinning, and without logging, this thinning is a costly and time-consuming problem. While fuel treatment projects can reduce the threat of catastrophic wildfires the vast number of acres that need to be treated far exceed the agency's ability to fund and accomplish these treatments.

The new thought is that we need to allow fire to resume its natural role in the forests around the nation. This is a startling conclusion in fire suppression. Rather that put fires out, many believe we should manage them and allow them to burn, which will reduce the unwanted intensity and size of fires in the future. This is fueled by the tremendous amount of unhealthy forests caused by decades of fire suppression. The end product is that hundreds of thousands of acres can be treated quickly and without the huge costs of fuel treatment projects.

This is not to say that all fires are managed and not suppressed. One requirement to managing a fire is that it has to be started by natural means and not a man. Historically, all fires were suppressed regardless of the ignition source. Today common objectives include suppressing a percentage of a fire, protecting private inholdings, and allowing the fire to burn on the landscape on another area. If treating multiple acres with fire is the objective of this idea, it is surely working. Fires that could be suppressed at little cost or exposure to the safety of firefighters are becoming huge, and this burning can last for weeks on our national forests.

I'm still on the fence for this fire management strategy. While I see the need to allow fire to resume its natural benefits, I feel that the size of the treatments are somewhat overboard. If allowing these fires to burn creates a healthy end product, that's great, but the intensity and impacts to watersheds and citizens are sometimes not of great concern. If there were not such huge populations of people, the natural role of fire would be much easier see and predict. I guess there is still enough of my upbringing in fire suppression to think that some of these fires are just wrong and bad management. The idea of natural fire cleaning up the forest and reducing the risk of catastrophic fires in most of our forests has been given the green light. Some of these management fires produce the same catastrophic impacts they are designed to prevent. I was attending a public meeting at one such fire, and a rancher stated, "The idea of burning the forest up to prevent fires is like setting your house on fire to eliminate the threat of it burning down."

Don't get me wrong. Many of these changes have created a better environment for the firefighter. Hopefully, with the noted changes, the current firefighter will appreciate how it is now and agree that while things were different in the past, their job is much safer and more comfortable today.

CHAPTER 6
INCIDENT MANAGEMENT TEAMS

I have already mentioned that the highlight of my years working for the forest service would have to be the years that I was part of incident management teams. At the time of this writing, I have participated on teams for more than thirty years. I have worked with the finest groupings of people anyone could wish for.

There is no doubt several folks who have never heard of incident management teams or who don't have any knowledge of how they are structured or what they do. I thought I should provide a brief outline to give some insight into these teams.

When I first started with the forest service, these teams were called fire teams. The management term "large fire organization" (LFO) was the command structure, and these teams were organized in order to battle large forest fires, which were called project fires at the time.

Early in my career, the LFO structure was replaced by the incident command system (ICS), which basically changed the names of the positions of the team structure, and I suppose this new system made it more reflective of things to come. Most of us who were used to the LFO system thought it was just a change of terminology, and we were a little reluctant to go along with the change. Most folks now are unaware of the change even happened.

Incident management teams (IMTs) make up the command structure of the incident command system (ICS). If you're not aware of IMTs and how they function, I have included some discussion of the parts and functions of an IMT. The team consists of several separate groups that work collectively in order to manage a large forest fire or any other emergency. The ICS has the organization to handle a host of different situations. I've often heard that the training and skills should bring order to chaos.

While large forest fires were the reason that ICS was developed, teams are currently used for a wide variety of emergencies. If a national emergency is declared, it has become common to activate an IMT to assist in the management of the emergency. For years forest fires were their only focus, but currently, teams have been utilized for a host of differing situations. Teams have managed earthquakes, floods, hurricanes, and just about any national emergency.

Notable assignments that show the diversity of incidents to which IMTs have responded include the following: Two responded to the attack upon the World Trade Center in New York City. Another team responded to the attack on the Pentagon. A team managed the Exxon Valdez oil spill along the Alaskan coast. The recovery of the space shuttle *Columbia* was also assigned to an IMT after that tragedy occurred.

While these assignments were all over the national news, some assignments were not so well covered. One such assignment with several teams in various parts of the country was the Exotic Newcastle Disease. This disease, which was extremely contagious and impacted poultry, was a threat to many different nations. If a chicken had the disease, a team was tasked with setting up a one-mile perimeter around the infected chicken, and the team then disposed of all chickens within that perimeter to prevent the spread of the disease. If an infected chicken was found outside the perimeter, a new perimeter was established, and the entire process started again. It is no secret that IMTs weren't happy about these assignments, but teams did respond until the threat was diminished. These assignments were commonly referred to as "chicken-choking assignments." While many looked down at this term, it wasn't far from the truth.

IMTs are organized into a command and general staff, and several unit leaders work directly for the general staff positions. The command staff is made up of the incident commander (IC), which is the lead figure, the public information officer (PIO), the safety officer (SOF), and the liaison officer (LOF). The general staff is compromised of the operations section chief (OSC), the finance section chief (FSC), the planning section chief (PSC), and the logistics section chief (LSC). Any of these positions can have assistants, which are called deputies. For example, an assistant to the IC is a deputy incident commander (DIC).

Each of the general staff positions has a host of people who perform separate tasks that all make the team function as a whole. I will briefly describe each of these functions as well as the command staff.

The incident commander is the lead for the team and the contact with whatever agency or agencies placed the order for the team. On each assignment the ordering agency will designate an agency administrator. The agency administrator provides marching orders for the team and represents the host agency in all matters concerning the incident. The agency administrator develops documents that outline what the host agency expects from the team and assists the incident commander in development of the incident objectives. Incident objectives set goals that the team will work toward accomplishing. The incident commander supervises all the command and general staff, and he or she also keeps the hosts agency updated on the strategy and tactics the team will take and reports on the accomplishment of the incident objectives.

The safety officer, which works with the command staff, is responsible for the safety of all the incident personnel as well as the public associated with the incident. This position often has subordinates who are referred to as line safety officers, which actually work in the field on the fire line and out with whatever operations the assignment requires. This position observes all operations and conditions at the incident command base (fire camp) to ensure the safety and welfare of all personnel associated with the incident. On most if not all incidents, the primary objective is firefighter and public safety.

The public information officer is also on the command staff and is responsible for preparing any news releases or updates concerning the incident. This position is the main contact for any television, newspaper, or radio updates for the incident. All public meetings are coordinated by this position, and subordinates often establish trap lines in order to get the information out to the local points of interest. It is common for politicians to visit incidents, especially on election years. I have been on multiple fires where governors, senators, representatives, and even the president of the United States have visited incidents on a few occasions. PIOs generally works with their staffs to coordinate the visits to ensure they see whatever it is they want to see and get the proper news coverage to get the word out that they participated. This shop answers the phone assigned to the incident and also keeps the social media sites current and with incident information.

The liaison officer is the final member of the command staff. This position coordinates with any and all agencies that are impacted or needed to meet the incident objectives. Generally, these contacts include county and state governments, public service providers such as electric and natural gas companies, and local and state law enforcement agencies. This position is a contact point for any assistance required from their agencies. This assistance can involve road closures, evacuations, road blocks, or interruption of services. Through this position, all these participants are kept appraised of current and future needs, and everyone is briefed on accomplishments and shortfalls.

The following are general staff positions:

The finance section chief manages the financial accountability for the incident. Each incident has a financial cap that the team is supposed to work within. The finance section chief manages the cost unit leader, the time unit leader, equipment time recorders, personnel time recorders, and the compensation and claims unit leader. The total incident cost is compiled daily to ensure the cost still falls within the financial cap established. Any claims or compensation issues and land use agreements also fall within this function. Time and the cost for all personnel and equipment are recorded by this unit.

The logistics section chief manages the needs for all assigned personnel such as camp, feeding, ordering, and equipment needs. The logistic section chief manages a host of unit leaders, such as the medical unit leader, communications unit leader, supply unit leader, food unit leader, ordering manager, base camp manager, facilities unit leader, ground support unit leader, equipment manager, and receiving and distribution unit leader. The branch also takes care of the personnel—caterers, shower units, mechanics, transportation needs, medical necessities, equipment inspections, ordering of supplies and equipment, communication network, and the camp layout.

The planning section chief manages a host of unit leaders that supply all the planning and documentation needs of the incident. One critical product of the planning section is the incident action plan (IAP). The IAP is required for each shift. It is a packet of information that captures a huge amount of information that includes the incident objectives, overhead listing, safety message, division assignments and staffing, communications plan, air operations plan, medical plan, weather forecast, fire behavior forecast, human resource message, and maps. The IAP covers each shift, and it ensures that everyone is informed of each team's actions, safety issues, and all that pertains to that shift of activity. Accuracy and availability are paramount. The collection of all this information from the different functions, and printing the document are a big part of each shift for the planning section. Positions that fall into the planning group include the situation unit leader, resource unit leader, demobilization unit leader, documentation unit leader, training specialist, fire behavior analyst, IT specialist, GIS specialist, human resource specialist, and an incident meteorologist.

The final member of the general staff is the operations section chief. It is common for a team to have two to three operation section chiefs. For years teams only carried two operation section chiefs because of the potential need to staff both day and night shifts. Most teams carry a third operation dude who is called "the planning ops." The third person free up the day or night operations section chief so that one can get more involved in actual operations as the planning operations person handles most of the camp activities. The operations section develops the tactics needed to meet the incident objectives and assign the resources needed to accomplish those objectives. All actual firefighting personnel and equipment, including all aircraft, are assigned to the operations group. The rest of the group consists of the air operations branch director, which manages aircraft usage, the air support group supervisor, and hopefully, two air tactical group supervisors. The incident is typically divided into divisions, and each team carries four division/group supervisors who directly manage all resources in their divisions. A structure protection specialist is sometimes required, and this person is tasked with the protection and coordination with local fire districts or fire departments when structures are threatened.

There are actually three types of IMTs, and they are each given a number rating. The highest level for IMTs is type one. These teams are called national teams. Type 1 teams have a higher level of training and experience, and they are in place to manage the most complex situations. Type 2 IMTs are more numerous than type 1 teams, and they are generally assigned to their geographic area. Both types of teams are dispatched across the country as needed, and they are expected to manage whatever kind of incidents they are thrown into. In past years, type 3 IMTs generally managed fires at the initial phase or remained on the forest or home unit. People on these teams don't require as many qualifications, and they have quite a few less participants. However, in the last few years, type 3 teams have been thrown into some incidents that pushed type 1 complexity. A complexity analysis should be completed to determine which IMTs are necessary. In busy times when IMTs are at a premium, the need for an IMT to aid in management can trump the complexity.

Nationally, there are several IMTs that are available for yearlong stints if the need arises. There are government teams, and some states and fire departments have created their own teams that can manage a crisis if needed. Teams can get a multitude of assignments as noted earlier, and they may be assigned anywhere. For example, my teams and I have gone out to incidents in California, Oregon, Washington, Idaho, Montana, Nevada, Utah, Wyoming, New Mexico, Florida, Louisiana, Georgia, Tennessee, Kentucky, West Virginia, Virginia, and my home of Arizona. I have had multiple assignments in most of these states throughout my years of participation.

I've stated that my participation on IMTs has been one of the highlights of my career. It's hard to explain the comradery within teams. The bond is perhaps similar to the one I created with people during my time in the military. I've had assignments that were great, and the team kicked ass and had a blast; however, I've been on other assignments when nothing seemed to work out and tough things happened. Good or bad, the teams power through and get things done, and you have as good a time as you can in the process. I am proud of all the different IMTs I have been a part of, and each team was also proud of their fellow members. If you were on an IMT and you didn't think it was the best team there was, something was wrong. Teams will work through the haze when things go completely to hell, and they will get back on track by helping one another and overcoming the issue.

Early in my career, these IMTs were touted as being "the best of the best," and participation on the teams was a desirable pursuit. There was stiff competition for getting on a team, and many people who wanted a team position had a hard time securing one. Currently, it is difficult to fill teams as there are actually more people working for the forest service but fewer folks who want to participate in fire suppression. The number of teams has gone down because of this problem. I think this problem is the same all over our nation. The Coconino National Forest actually fielded two IMTs when I started. Now there is just a handful of employees who participate.

I think that most of the people who want to be on an IMT are not lazy or do-nothing types of people. I would bet that in their real jobs, they exhibited the same work ethic and are the go-to folks at the home unit. This may be one of the reasons that those at the home don't want them to join IMTs and get swept away in the middle of the night to work at some faraway place.

The command and general staff on IMTs is separated by two different classes. Type 2 command and general staff positions must pass a class called S-420 or "command and general staff." Type 1 command and general staff members must pass S-520 or "advanced incident management."

Both of these classes in past days were hard to get into, and they made for quite an intense session. Passing the class was not guaranteed. I will discuss S-520 as it was probably one if not the hardest of all government fire training to get through in its time. I believe this class was once called "fire generalship," and I've heard and firmly believe it was established to phase out people who didn't cut the mustard.

Now this behavior is not allowed in government agencies. This class was held once every two years on a national level, and the session was conducted at the National Advanced Resource Training Center (NARTC), which was located at Pinal Air Park near Marana, Arizona.

Every two years, twelve teams that consisted of the command and general positions went through the course. It was difficult to get a spot in this training, but it was a requirement to serve on a type 1 IMT. Each region or geographic area of the nation could fill a few seats in the session, so when you went through this training, you were placed with people you didn't know prior to the session. Each team had a coach that was assigned for the full two-week class to assist everyone and steer them toward success.

When I took the class, the liaison officer was not a common position on IMTs, so my team consisted of the incident commander, safety officer, public information officer, logistic section chief, finance section chief, planning section chief, and the operations section chief. In later years two operations section chiefs were placed on each team. My team members came from Washington, Montana, Florida, California, Wyoming, and Arizona, and we were complete strangers as we started the session. Our coach was the director of fire and aviation from the Northern Rockies.

Life at NARTC was limited as it was quite a ways into town (Tucson), and barracks were there along with a cafeteria and a bar called the Roadrunner. All the faculty and attendees were expected to stay on site, and for the entire fourteen days of the class, we were allowed one day off. Classes would start at 0800, and almost every day they would extend well into the evenings as the teams would meet after the day's sessions to compare notes and prepare for success. Often our team would work until 2200 and then head to the Roadrunner to have a drink before turning in.

The session consisted of daily presentations about incident management, and attendance was required. Two written exams were required to complete the course. Simulations of forest fires were also a huge part of the session, and they were also necessary to complete the course. The simulations consisted of scripted fire scenarios that a simulation, team would run you through. Each simulation had its own sim team. These sim teams had generally the same people from session to session, and they were adept at providing an active and busy simulation. They could really turn up the heat and give the teams a genuine run for their money. The simulations had several inputs too. The team going through the simulation was kept in a room with just a phone, radio, and fax machine for the entire time. All the inputs from the sim team were received by these instruments or some actor coming into your room. Evaluators viewed the teams from inside this room, and they determined who should pass or fail.

All the sessions actually led up to the final simulation. Some of the mentors I had looked up to in my career flunked this class. Everyone had been there for several long days, and we were stressed about the final sim and passing the course. It was pretty common for stress and fatigue to figure into the course just as it would in a real-fire situation. The final sim was the very last session, and that was when everyone found out if they passed or not. I was one of the fortunate 47 percent of my class that passed. I had never been to a training session that anyone had flunked. I was relieved that I had squeaked through but appalled at the amount who hadn't. It goes without saying that the old Roadrunner was full of two separate kinds of drinkers that night. Those who had passed were incredibly relieved and happy as hell, and those who had been there for two weeks and felt they had wasted their time were pissed off. I remember thinking that I was so glad I had passed and that I would never have to go back to S-520.

A year or so later on one afternoon, one of my old ICs who had moved into fire and aviation at the regional office in Albuquerque called me. He asked if I was interested in instructing the Southwest's portion of the classes at S-520, and I agreed to help. At the next session, I was on the cadre and started helping with the session. My involvement lasted until my retirement. I eventually became a team coach. Then I became an operations section subject matter expert and while I tried to fight it off, I was an evaluator during my last year. This introduced me not only to the up-and-coming members of the nation's type 1 IMTs but also to some of our nation's leaders in wildland fire management. I really feel I stumbled into this; however, it was one of the highlights of my career and something that I looked forward to as I met some of the best people in the business.

As I stated earlier, there was a rumor that one of the objectives of this class was to cull people who had difficulties passing the ordeal. It sure felt that way when I went through the training, and I'm sure the folks who didn't pass felt the same way. Year by year, the class slowly started changing. NARTC was replaced as a new training center was built in Tucson—the National Advanced Fire and Resource Institute (NAFRI). IMTs started facing trouble in filling positions, as the desire to join an IMT started to decline. The course was eventually shortened to a week, and the written exams were done away with. The sim teams that were there for years were replaced, and new simulations and sim teams were put into the session. Because of their knowledge, the original sim teams could really turn up the heat and make you sweat. Now the class is a pass-only deal, and everyone who takes the class gets their ticket punched. This was another change that I always felt bad about, probably because I took the class when it was pure hell for two weeks. I think anyone that took S-520 in those days would agree with me.

CHAPTER 7
ENVIRONMENTALISTS

When I started my career, there weren't any environmentalists, and if there were some, they pretty much kept to themselves. If someone claimed to be an environmentalist, it would probably have a different impact than it does today. I'm an environmentalist in that I don't want to see our environment ruined for me or future generations. However, I have had to deal with current environmentalists and what the term means to some today. I have yet to meet one who in his or her own mind didn't feel I had barely the intelligence of a German shepherd. As I mentioned earlier, my education never reached the level to achieve professional status with the forest service. This provides a great way to dismiss these writings as those of a mere technician, and therefore, one may think this book has no credibility. Therefore, if you are a modern-day environmentalist, there is no need to spend a lot of time disputing this portion of my writings. Just blame it on my lack of education, and move on to saving the planet.

I realize that my views on this subject may seem biased or offensive to some members of the environmental community. However, I really don't care as I have been ridiculed, cast as a liar, and taken to court on many occasions for just trying to do the job I was paid to do.

I started fighting fires before the rush of environmentalists, but I did see the seeds of the movement planted and flourishing into the huge deal it is today. While congress passed several acts prior to the start of my career, they really didn't hit the home front until a few years after I started. Some of these acts include the Endangered Species Act (ESA) and the National Environmental Protection Act (NEPA). While I do think the basic thought for these acts was admirable and needed to some degree, I doubt the writers of these acts knew what the long-term impacts were. I feel the novelty of being an environmentalist was spawned from these and many more acts passed by congress. These acts changed the complexion of the forest service and the lives of many people who worked on federal lands.

The Endangered Species Act (ESA) was written in order to reestablish species whose population was falling and could possibly become extinct. A survey was started decades ago and continues to this day to determine species of animals and plants that are threatened with extinction or have limited numbers. This act mandates that a recovery plan is developed and adhered to until each species has recovered to the point that it has reached historic numbers (whatever that is). Upon reaching historic numbers, it is then removed from the list. A species of plant or animal can be classed as sensitive, threatened, or endangered, and through the individual recovery plans, the species is protected from harmful impacts. Habitats, both current and potential, are also afforded protection under this act.

The other act that I mentioned is the National Environmental Protection Act (NEPA), which says that prior to an undertaking on federal lands, an environmental analysis is needed so that people can review the impacts of whatever the project activities are and determine if there would be any unfavorable environmental consequences. If researchers found that there would be no irreversible environmental issues, an environmental analysis (EA) was prepared and submitted.

If it was determined that there could be some serious environmental consequences, an environmental impact statement (EIS) was required.

For example, your run-of-the-mill grazing allotment management plan would require an EA instead of an EIS since an EIS would generally only be necessary for larger projects such as Glen Canyon Dam which forms Lake Powell. The appeal process varied between the two documents. As for an EA, anyone could appeal. All a person needed was a stamp to mail in the appeal. Under the appeal process of the EA, the burden of proof was upon the agency, so after an appeal, the agency was required to prove that the EA was complete and unbiased and that there were truly no indications of long-term impacts. If you wanted to appeal an EIS, the process was more difficult. The appellant had to prove that the EIS was faulted, and this was quite a bit more difficult and expensive, especially since a lawyer or a team of them was usually required. If the appeals are not mitigated, they end up in court, and the judicial branch of the government would make the decision concerning the proposed project.

Another factor that compounds these issues is the Freedom of Information Act (FOIA). This gives environmentalist groups or individuals the ability to request and receive all documentation gathered during all these studies so that they can review them for inaccuracies. While it may seem like a trivial thing, it could take a week to copy and mail all the information from one request. I have received FOIA requests, and they've been granted for every single document in our office. While working in range management, we were literally forced to copy every document from the past several decades. It took several weeks of work to copy everything, and the paper would have literally filled up several pickup trucks with boxes. These documents were reviewed by the antigrazing factions that wanted to bring an end to livestock grazing on forest lands. All their efforts and the costs we incurred did not halt grazing on forest lands, as every avenue they pursued proved to be invalid. However, the fight to halt grazing is still ongoing. The antilogging faction lost groves of trees just to provide the paper for this process.

The list of threatened plants and animals is constantly growing as additional species and management practices are added through their recovery plans. The US Fish and Wildlife Service (USFWS) has the task to compile and manage these species as well as develop the individual recovery plans. This interaction resulted in the hiring of a host of biologists, botanists, environmentalists, attorneys, and scientists of various fields in order to meet the requirements of the acts.

With these acts, environmentalists and environmental groups came onto the scene. The battle cry to halt timber harvesting on federal lands, and soon livestock grazing on federal lands was a hot topic as well. Most supporters of these new fads had little ties to the land or factual knowledge of either of these practices. The acts previously discussed fueled these discussions, and the appeal process often forced these matters into court. Hence, this process has provided a boon for environmental law, and now it's a huge employment opportunity for many. Most environmental lawyers prior to these acts probably needed to secure a second job to buy their kids a new pair of shoes, but now the field has grown into a huge business.

One of the first species that fell under the protection of the Endangered Species Act—and initiated all of us who predated the act—is the Mexican spotted owl. This should not be mistaken with the northern spotted owl, which did not live around here…ever. Prior to the time when it was determined that the Mexican spotted owl's numbers were in trouble, life was easier.

With listing the Mexican spotted owl, which few of us had even heard of at the time, researchers determined that the reason they were fading from the landscape was their dependence on old-growth forests. If we lose our old-growth forests, these animals would fall into extinction along with the many species we have already lost.

Timber harvesting was probably the biggest function of the forest service, and several logging companies actively logged forest lands. Maintaining multiple use and sustained yield was the mission of the forests. Timber sale receipts were returned to the US Treasury, while some were allocated back to the forests for reforesting harvested areas, road maintenance, wildlife-habitat improvement, and the administration of the program.

The logging industry consisted of a large portion of the economics of all the neighboring communities. As compliance with the new acts progressed, the logging industry went out of business. Mills were closed throughout the Southwest. The loss of this industry was considered quite a victory for the environmental community. The long-term impacts were thought to be a step in the right direction, but eventually, that would change.

Not long after the logging industry was shut down and the Mexican spotted owl became protected, another issue developed. Forest fires started burning into communities and destroying hundreds of homes. Because of decades of fire suppression and increased tree density, the forests were extremely overstocked, causing increased intensity of fires and a major threat to communities. As new subdivisions were developed and the urban sprawl spread across the nation, a new term, the *wildland urban interface*, came onto the scene. Forests were in dire need of thinning in order to reduce the fire intensity and to keep wildfires out of the growing communities springing up throughout the nation's forests. Hundreds of thousands of acres were in need of thinning to reduce this threat. The problem was that there were no loggers left to accomplish this process.

As the logging industry was shut down, so were the markets for wood products. Not only were there no loggers, but there was no market to sell any wood products. This was a huge issue. Instead of gaining any revenue from the forest products, the forest service was forced to spend millions of dollars, in efforts to thin the overstocked stands of trees. Road maintenance, which was a part of all timber sale contracts, was also pretty much abandoned as the forest road crew could not provide the level of maintenance the logging companies provided contractually.

Some of the local environmental groups that were instrumental in shutting down logging blamed this dilemma on the forest service's inability to run a logging show, and they banded together to show us how it should be done. They would show us how to redevelop the market, how to lay out timber sales, and how to get off our asses and do it right. I felt this was a pipe dream when they became involved, and I still do as after a few decades. They have yet to prove their claims.

It's required that we comply with the ESA in regard to environmental documents, so prior to submitting an EA or EIS for approval, one must gain the approval of the USFWS. This review by the USFWS is there to ensure the listed species or any current or potential habitat will not be impacted. The reference to potential habitats also opens up an entire bucket of worms. The review process is time-consuming, and with each year, this became more and more complex as additional species were added to the listings and court rulings defined new boundaries.

All these requirements changed the makeup of the forest service. In previous years there were a few specialists who were usually working in the supervisor's offices of forests. Now every district has a host of specialists, all of whom were needed so that the agency could comply with this new way of doing business. The era when a forest employee wore many different hats started fading away, and a new group of specialists started emerging. Fire suppression became an option rather than an expected duty. While the number of employees increased, the participation of employees in fire suppression declined.

I have been involved with several environmentalists for decades across our nation. Because of my involvement in fire management, I have literally worked with folks from Canada to Mexico and the Pacific to the Atlantic Oceans. I've protected species ranging from grizzly bears to the Florida panther, from twin spotted rattlesnakes to the Pacific salmon. In my travels and experience, I have yet to meet one of these politically active environmentalists who did not live in a city. I have never met one who worked on the land as a logger, rancher, and/or farmer. I have never met one who fell into the technician educational level either. Most sport advanced degrees from one if not many of our nation's universities.

Not only did the environmental movement change the way the forest service did business, but it also changed the lives of many people who had ties to federal lands. Many of these people became the target and victims of the maze of environmental law. I have had the pleasure of knowing many such victims that were dyed in the wool environmentalist because their families and entire existence was dependent upon their environment. As with the forest service, they, too, have been caught up sorting through the fog of environmental issues and court rulings. I have no doubt that these political environmentalists and their followings feel they are saving the world. I suppose it's a credit to our society that they have the time and finances to pursue their efforts.

I have spent many years monitoring vegetative condition while working as a Range Technician. On several situations when the monitoring data did not suit the environmental community, these studies were determined to not be statistically sound. This gave the environmental groups a valid reason to ignore what actual monitoring displayed. However, the fact that these recovery plans mandate we manage for the protection of a species until such time that historic numbers are achieved seems to violate the soundness of the plan. For instance, who has or will determine what the number of Mexican spotted owls was historically? I'm sure that there is a table or matrix of spreadsheets we can use to make this determination, but it seems to me to be nothing more than a scientific wild-ass guess (SWAG) and not even statistically sound.

Environmentalist everywhere are looking for species that they can list for ESA protection, and in so doing, potentially establish new regulations in order to fuel whatever fad they are supporting. These acts gave the teeth to those who felt that global warming was being caused by cattle farting and belching methane gas into the atmosphere (one of my favorites). This was supposedly another reason to stop livestock grazing on federal lands. From my technician view, I look at the throng of traffic that every city endures day and night, and I don't lose any sleep because of livestock flatulence.

Groups of these city-dweller environmentalists started banding together to voice their particular fads, and in so doing, they developed quite a following of individuals. These groups would appeal just about every action that went through the NEPA process. If these appeals were not mitigated to the environmental group's satisfaction, they progress to the judicial branch of the government to make the final decision. This is a long, expensive, and frustrating process.

As the environmental community evolved into groups, these organizations solicited political support. This political pressure added yet another level of complexity to an already complex situation. On many occasions when members of the environmental community didn't get their way, they would seek a congressional inquiry, which is also undesirable and time-consuming. Some elected officials became active in the environmental fray, especially on election years. Of course, they often took the path that contained more votes rather than investigating what was good or bad for the environment. This political pressure added to the quagmire of sorting through the increasing maze of environmental laws—a process which was already lengthy, expensive, and frustrating.

Here's a quick example of how the process works. The Mexican spotted owl, which I must admit is a pretty neat creature, was listed, which required the development of a recovery plan. When the recovery plan was developed, a draft was submitted for our review. This document was a fairly large one, maybe not as thick as the King James Bible but close. I was concerned because when this document was approved, we would all have to live by what it said. In attempts to moderate this, I reviewed the lengthy document. One portion discussed hiding cover for prey species for the owl. In order to protect the food base for owls, a sufficient growth of plants was needed so that we could protect the rodents the owls fed on. It went on to say that this hiding cover was only forage species and that these forage species couldn't be grazed below a certain percentage in order to provide substantial hiding cover for prey species.

Fearing that this was somewhat bias and fueled by the antigrazing crowd, I offered my input. I didn't understand how it was determined that "forage species", or plants that animals ate, were needed to provide hiding cover for the prey species of the owl. If you're a mouse slipping around in the woods, does it matter if you're hidden and protected by tumbleweeds or a clump of orchard grass? By limiting the hiding cover requirement to forage species, the plan fanned the flames for all the folks who wanted to halt grazing on public lands. People listened to my suggestions, but they dispelled. When the final recovery plan was approved, the language was actually worse than it had been in the draft. I must have pointed out a soft spot.

As we all embarked on this era of the forest service, another item also moved things away from the old way of doing business. Computers were introduced, and all business is done on them now.

Another change I've seen is the level of education. When I started, it seemed that everyone who attended a university obtained a bachelor's degree and hit the workforce. More and more you see people earning their master's degrees. Because of this phenomenon, people are publishing theses on just about anything you can imagine. These are available online, and you can find them as you sit in your office. These drive many of the arguments and discussions on how to best manage our resources. While some are valid and offer useful information, some are pretty biased or just plain wrong. However, right or wrong, if they are published, they fuel the fire for those who want public lands managed to their liking.

One such document that came to light in Flagstaff, Arizona, was a paper that said the prescribed burning of mature ponderosa pine would kill all the old-growth ponderosa pines. This paper went on the state that it was required to rake the pine needles from under every mature ponderosa pine prior to prescribed burning. It was written that because of the lengthy and unnatural breaking of the cycle of natural fire, pine needle cast had built up to the point that enough heat would be produced during burning to damage the roots and/or cambium of the tree and cause it to die. At that time, we were funded to burn more than ten thousand acres a year, and raking around that many pine trees would have brought our program to a halt. I had been on the forest for decades, and I knew of the hundreds of thousands of acres burned with prescribed fire didn't bring about the mortality that this paper warned of; however, that brought little solace to those who believed the document. The nonbelievers set up monitoring plots in our burn blocks in order to prove we were wrong for a few years. We didn't kill any mature ponderosas, but I'm sure there are still those who think we cheated somehow.

One of the most frustrating deals I got involved in concerned the antelope population in an area on the forest called the Anderson Mesa. We were going through the NEPA process to issue a new allotment management plan. A group felt that livestock grazing would eliminate the antelope population on the mesa. We had set up a public meeting to discuss what we were planning, and this meeting was attended by the ring leaders of the group that wanted to stop livestock grazing. In their view, livestock removed the grass crop, which was critical to providing cover for hiding antelope fawns. This lack of standing forage supposedly allowed coyotes to find and eat the fawns. The meeting was also attended by a wildlife biologist from the forest service's regional office in Albuquerque. After listening to their concerns, he stood up and said that the lack of cover for antelope fawning was due to the livestock overgrazing a species of grass called Arizona fescue to the point it didn't occur upon the mesa any longer.

Arizona fescue is a species of grass that grows at higher elevations and typically under stands of Ponderosa pines. It's a coarse grass that isn't eaten to a high degree by livestock. It often is not grazed at all and therefore provides a deep old-grass bed (i.e., hiding cover). The issue I had is that Arizona fescue doesn't occur on Anderson Mesa at all and hasn't since monitoring started decades ago. I would be surprised if the biologist from the regional office had ever set foot on Anderson Mesa. Somewhere back in geological time, maybe palm trees grew on Anderson Mesa. Who can say for sure? This statement was not only totally wrong, but it also set the stage for an expensive and long-term debate over the antelope issue. The expert went back to the regional office in Albuquerque after he had made his alarming and long-lasting statement, and he never got his Tevas dusty.

To further fuel the antelope debate, the state game and fish department's expert declared that if this issue with antelope hiding cover wasn't resolved, that antelope would disappear from the mesa in a few years. Obviously, this person was a member of the antigrazing group. Another game and fish researcher who had actually studied antelope on Anderson Mesa for years offered an unbiased study that didn't fit with the information from the antigrazing fad. The group searched far and wide to find an expert to justify their claim. They found a guy from Wyoming who supported their group, and actual research lasting years was shot down. The state game and fish— even with their thoughts that the antelope population was doomed if grazing wasn't stopped—still allocated tags for antelope hunting, which seemed counterproductive to me.

The game and fish researcher that had his studies discounted was a top-notch guy. I had worked with him on other projects and was always impressed by his hard and truthful work. One of my biggest issues with the Anderson Mesa deal was how this guy was kicked to the curb. A fine thank-you for a job well done.

Another example of this whirlwind of activity is a grazing allotment that needed to have an updated allotment management plan. This allotment is a pretty big piece of land. In fact, it encompasses an area starting at the Verde River, which is a low-elevation desert-type habitat, and runs north up to the top of the Mogollon Rim into the ponderosa pine habitat. Because of the varied elevation differences and vegetative types that occur within the allotment, it is home to a large number of ESA species. An EA was initiated, and all the processes I've been complaining about were started. An EA was completed and subjected to the approval of the USFWS and the environmental community's appeals. This process of approvals, appeals, and mitigations continued nonstop for years. The regional office decided at one point to prepare an EIS to stiffen the appeal process, as the allotment was without an approved NEPA document. Further mitigation determined that this presented an unfair appeal process, and the EIS was shot down. Then another EA was started. As I stated, this process dragged on for years, and during the years of preparation, additional species were found and determined to meet the protection guidelines of the ESA, which in turn required additional evaluation and restrictions. With each new species, new requirements would be brought forth, and additional appeals and studies would be filed. I participated in this process for more than ten years, and I never got an approved NEPA document for the management plan for the grazing permit. I can't say if it was ever finished, but I know it went on for at least an additional five years at a tremendous cost to the government agencies. Who knows how much this process cost or the frustrations it has caused? However, it's parallel is a puppy chasing his own tail.

Compliance with the acts impacted firefighting as well. I want to focus on fire stories, so I will offer a few issues that occurred when we tried to do the right thing, though that didn't always work out as planned. While I worked as a division supervisor on a fire team, we were assigned to the Thunderbolt Fire, which was burning upon the Boise National Forest in Idaho. This fire was adjacent to the south fork of the Salmon River, which fell under protection because the critical Pacific salmon spawning beds that were present. The fire consisted of just a few thousand acres, and upon arrival, the team thought that we could catch it quick and keep it small if we were allowed to utilize bulldozers to construct a fire line around the fire. However, it was mandated that we could not use dozers because they could add silt and debris into the river, making the spawning beds unusable. We were directed to utilize hand line meaning one constructed with hand crews to contain the fire.

Construction of the hand line in heavy timber is tremendously slower and less safe than a dozer line. This resulted in the footprint of the fire growing from a few thousand acres to tens of thousands of acres. The slopes of the Salmon River are pretty steep and while the dozer line may have added some silt and debris into the spawning beds, the result of the fire burning for miles down the river chasm no doubt added tons more silt and debris. The requirement of the hand line also placed firefighters in a more hazardous situation by prolonging their exposure.

The Coffeepot Fire was one of the fires in the Ryan Complex that burned on the Cibola National Forest in New Mexico. The fire was within the Apache Kid Wilderness west of Socorro, New Mexico. As the team took over management of the fire, we were informed that there were several MSO nests in the area that the fire was burning. We were instructed that fire suppression activities were to avoid impacting these nest sites at all cost. The district assigned a biologist to assist the team in order to meet this objective.

The environmental community was concerned that if people found out the location of a MSO nest site, they would just kill them and thereby eliminate all the management fuss from that area. This resulted in most of the biologist maintaining lots of secrecy about MSO nesting locations. This was the mind-set on this fire, and the assigned biologist would flat-out refuse to disclose the location of any of the nests. In order to avoid impacts from the firefighting efforts, each day we would review where line construction was to occur, and he would approve or deny our direction and intent. Each shift we would report our progress, and each shift we'd gain his approval for our intended direction the following shift.

One day as we were plugging away and digging a line down the bottom of a canyon, I got a call from one of the hotshot crews. They informed me that they had just cut down a tree that contained a MSO nest, and they took a crew vote and agreed that they needed to report it. I immediately asked if they were sure that it was in fact a spotted owl nest. I was hoping it was some other kind of owl. They then informed me that it was indeed a MSO and was indeed a nest tree. Hoping to find some solace, I called them up and asked if it was in use or vacant, hoping for the latter. Then they informed me that there were three eggs that had been destroyed, so there was no avoiding the issue.

When the news got to the biologist, he went ballistic. Of course, it was our fault, and he claimed that we just had just thrown out his inputs and had completely disregarded his direction. We felt just the opposite though. Each day he reviewed where we planned on constructing lines, and because we were following the bottom of the canyon, we had not strayed in our projections. We were chastised for this error, and the blame was pinned on us; however, the secrecy of the locations proved to be the demise for one MSO family. Secrets suck when you're working fires.

The Willow Fire burned in the Mazatzal wilderness on the Tonto National Forest. During that time, I was asked by a district ranger on the Coconino National Forest to fill up a stock tank that was drying up on that forest. He asked that I send one of the type 1 helicopters on a mission to this location, which was several miles away. He requested we attend to the stock tank because it was a critical habitat for the Chiricahua leopard frog. This stock tank was in an area that historically had no water, and consequently, it was an unlikely frog habitat. This stock tank, which was built as a range improvement for livestock, was purposely placed in an area that had no water before. I find it somewhat of a miracle that frogs actually found this tank as they would have to cross miles of arid land to Its location. They had fenced it off now, and livestock were excluded from its use. All this was done to protect the habitat for the frog, which no doubt was put there by somebody not by hopping across miles of country.

I bring this up as this is another issue. Creating artificial habitat for endangered species is a growing peril. I didn't approve of the helicopter missions, as I felt it was beyond our authority and just plain wrong. However, the creation of artificial habitats and then the forcible management of them for species should be against the law.

The elusive willow flycatcher provides another a great example. Along with the ESA listings, there are plants that are classed as noxious in federal terms. These plants were not native to our continent but bought here for one reason or another. Some were introduced as erosion-reduction plants, some because they had nice flowers. Some just found their way here because they were stuck to something or someone. Some of these plants have done quite remarkable here and spread across North America.

The tumbleweed is one such plant that was introduced and has since taken over quite a bit of land. The salt cedar has also taken over many waterways, especially in the Southwest. The salt cedar has become one of the dominant noxious plants in the Southwest. It seems that the willow flycatcher doesn't feel the ill effects of this plant. Researchers have found that it is now a critical nesting site for the endangered bird. While the noxious weed program would like to irradiate certain exotic species, these would impact the recovery of the willow flycatcher.

This might not sound like a big deal, but the consequences can become far-reaching. Roosevelt Lake is a large reservoir in central Arizona. It was constructed several years ago, and it provides both water and power. A huge project to make the lake larger was undertaken. The dam was raised several feet in total. The new construction would require they build a bridge for the highway as it used to pass over the old dam. Along with the new bridge, the existing highway and campgrounds would be submerged under the new pool level of the lake. So along with the bridge, several miles of state highway would need to be elevated. New campgrounds and new boat ramps would also need to be constructed—all above the new lake levels. I have no clue how much all this cost, but several million dollars may be too low of an estimate.

You can imagine how long this all took. After several years of construction, it was completed. The salt cedar that I mentioned earlier loves water, and the pool level of the old lake was riddled with these noxious plants on the shoreline. Within these noxious plants, there were a few willow flycatcher nests. Another issue with salt cedar is that it produces a seed that floats, which explains why it historically occurs all around the pool level of the lake. Environmental groups that didn't really like the new construction of the reservoir brought the nesting birds to the forefront.

When it came time to fill the lake to its new level, it was halted by the judicial branch of the government because of appeals about the willow flycatcher. It was determined that if the lake was filled, it would inundate nesting birds, which was a violation of the ESA. The filling of the lake was put on hold. It was later determined that the lake could be filled but only after the nesting period had been determined. But the nesting period was the same time as a snowmelt in the higher country that produced the bulk of the runoff to fill the lake each year. Because of the invasive nature of salt cedar, as the new pool level of the lake rose, the increase in shoreline was tremendous, and that increase would have increased the areas of salt cedar which would become available for the willow flycatcher. This was eventually resolved, but it is an example of the teeth that the ESA has.

The Arizona Department of Transportation approached one of my friends and asked him for permission to remove some of the hazard snags along State Highway 87. This project was requested as a safety measure for public travel along the highway. It was my friend's job to accommodate such requests. They made this request in the middle of the winter, and the actual work was scheduled to be done during the winter months. When the district biologist became aware of the project, it was shot down because of ESA reasons. It seems that the threat of killing a Chiricahua leopard frog was just too great to allow this project to go on. I'm surprised that the little spuds are listed as they have to be pretty tough to be out hopping around in the middle of winter miles from any water source. It does show the level of stupidity we have to deal with.

Political pressure can have impacts on ESA management. A prime example is the Salt River wild horse herd on the Tonto National Forest. Riparian areas in the Southwest are few and far between. There are a host of endangered species that are dependent on theses limited areas with riparian values. As a result, most of these areas with any remote riparian value—large and small—have had to be excluded from livestock grazing. This riparian protection was required in order to comply with the NEPA and ESA requirements. Livestock grazing in riparian areas is one of the major reasons that environmentalists have used for years in their attempts to halt grazing on federal lands.

Because of the increased population of the wild horses, the Tonto National Forest decided they needed to remove them from the Salt River, which by Southwest standards is a major riparian area. The wild horses actually are trespassing as unauthorized livestock, and they never should have been allowed there in the first place. The proposed action to remove the horses caused a huge political battle, and many people formed a group to save the wild horses and prevent their removal. The local TV stations carried stories every night covering this issue. Groupies of the "save the horses" faction were filmed feeding the wild horses apples and treats as they and all the wild horses stood around among the tables of a campground. Tears were shed, and threats were issued. It turned into quite a big deal. The huge amount of press and media coverage stalled the proposed removal of the horses, and the wild horses are still hanging out in one of the best riparian areas, awaiting their next apple from the defenders of trespassing livestock.

To cut to the chase, horses are livestock just like cattle. It is unfortunate that the issue of these trespassing horses was not dealt with in a timely manner in the past. While horses were present in our continent's last ice age, these are an exotic species that the Spanish introduced to this country just as cattle were. The wild horses are just about as native to the Salt River as Bengal tigers would be. If these wild horses had been wild cattle, I can't help but think how the proverbial shit would have hit the fan.

I wonder where the mass of environmentalists are in this dispute. The issue of livestock grazing in riparian area is one of the primary issues that involves both the environmental movement and the US Fish and Wildlife Service, which plays a role in ensuring ESA species are protected. Livestock grazing in a riparian area is accepted in this instance because it is more of a political hotbed. It's upsetting that while the battle to absolutely halt grazing in riparian areas by cattle and sheep is such a sharp knife, while the trespass horses are given a free pass. If you're a riparian plant does it matter if your eaten by a cow or a horse? I also wonder how the Tonto National Forest feels about the lack of support from both the environmental community and the USFWS, in dealing with this issue.

Unfortunately, I could go on and on with these examples. Little change will come as a result of my writings, and it is a heated issue with me. Rather than have a stroke capturing some examples, I'll leave it at that. As I stated, I feel I am an environmentalist at heart. I also feel that most of the environmentalist I've been railing on would starve to death if it weren't for the corner grocery store and live-in houses that are constructed out of old-growth forests. They should be happy that there is ranching, farming, and logging because if there weren't, they would be busy trying to feed themselves and wouldn't have so much time to bitch about the environment.

In closing this portion, I offer an old quote that predates the current environmental frenzy by an ecologist named Frank Egler, who said, "Ecosystems are not only more complex than we think but more complex than we can think."

CHAPTER 8
SHIT HAPPENS

This portion about shit stories is somewhat weird. On a recent golf trip, the gang was talking about the aches and pains that come with the years, and we collectively agreed that when it came to talking about problems shitting, we were too old to golf and should quit hanging out together. While it isn't a great topic at the dinner table, most parents, dog owners, and cowboys have been forced to deal with their own shitty deals. Few things are absolute; however, while we may not get to Bora Bora or sail around the world, we will all die, and we will all shit.

The team was activated and given an assignment at the Los Conchas Fire in New Mexico. People from our sister team from the Southwest were on the fire; however, they were getting their butts kicked, and the region had decided to zone the fire and have our team join up to help manage the fire. As usual, after the initial callout, the phone calls started coming from all the operations guys who wanted to make sure they got the word about what intel we had about the assignment. It was standard to communicate via cell phones while en route, and through this correspondence, we all decided to meet in Albuquerque at a Blake's Lotaburger for lunch and get together prior to the briefing, which was scheduled for later that day.

One of my favorite things about New Mexico is green chili. I don't know where else you get the quality of green chili that comes from New Mexico. Surely, it doesn't come from the canned varieties available around the country. If you have eaten at a Blake's Lotaburger, you know you can order real New Mexico green chili on your burger. That was the main reason we chose the Lotaburger for our lunch gathering. The operations gang gathered and had lunch. We stretched our legs from the drive and then headed up to the briefing.

After the briefing we scattered to see what we had just bitten off. The division guys went out to the fire, the air guys went to the airport in Santa Fe, and the operations guys jumped in a helicopter to do a recon and see what our options were. The fire was pretty big, and because of the lay of the land, our portion was going to make it a lot bigger. This recon flight had me, one other ops guy, and our trainee. The recon was going along well, and about thirty minutes into the flight, my stomach started to growl. I was not too concerned. As I said, the area we were looking at was pretty big in broken country, and the flight was starting to drag on as we looked for a place to start our efforts. We flew over roads to see where they went and whether we could use them. We flew over ridges to see how they connected. All the while, my stomach continued to growl and started churning around, bubbling, and stewing. I didn't think there was any real emergency, as we had pretty much covered all the country. Plus I thought we would be getting low on fuel soon and return to the helibase. My operations buddies did not have the same idea or the same churning gut, and they kept wanting to fly over another ridge, look for another water source, and see just about everything there was to see.

At about that time, the churning in my gut got out of hand, and I calmly declared an inflight emergency by saying, "If we don't get back to the helibase, I'm going to shit my pants." Rather than expressing the smallest amount of sympathy for my condition, my cherished teammates thought that it was the funniest thing they had ever heard. Their initial reaction was to try to make me laugh, but I was focusing all my energy on trying to prevent an inflight catastrophic failure. They wanted to look at one more ridge. In my defense, I was in the front seat of the helicopter, and the pilot noticed how serious a problem it was. I was balled up in the fetal positon, sweating and in obvious turmoil. Unlike the idiots in the back seat, he didn't want me pollute his aircraft any more than I wanted to.

Finally we turned toward the helibase. You could see where it was as we turned, and I didn't think there was any chance I would make it so many miles away. The back seat crowd was having the time of their lives, really laughing it up like two little boys in Disneyland. My eyes were fixed on the faraway location, hoping for the best. I think that was the slowest I've ever seen a helicopter fly. I started using the Lamaze breathing technique to keep from turning inside out. The pilot was getting worried, and he asked if I wanted him to shut down before I got out of the helicopter. But I didn't even need to answer. we finally made it, and with the rotors turning, I bailed out. It was obvious I was not in peril of getting struck by a rotor, as I was doubled over with pain and heading to the Porta Potty. I did make it there, but much to my teammates' remorse. They still think it was funny, and I'm still waiting for a chance to get even. One of my favorite things about New Mexico is still that great green chili.

The team was activated for an assignment because of Hurricane Francis on the west coast of Florida. Florida had just been nailed by Hurricane Charlie, and a national emergency had been declared. The team was flown to Atlanta, Georgia, and staged there as the hurricane was yet to make landfall. The Federal Emergency Management Agency (FEMA) wanted us at the ready to head to Florida after landfall occurred. It was early in the morning when we got the call to mobilize because the storm had made landfall. We quickly loaded up in our rental vehicles and headed to Ocala, Florida, which would become our incident command base. While the hurricane had already made landfall in Florida, it was just getting to Georgia, and our path took us into the teeth of the storm. Through the wind, rain, and debris on the interstate, we drove to Ocala.

Our assignment was to feed a National Guard unit from Kentucky that had been activated, and we were supposed to provide any assistance we could to lessen the impact of the storm. A caterer from Wyoming was en route to feed the troops, and the team would manage that endeavor. The National Guard from Kentucky had their own kitchen and didn't want or need the caterer. With our one job taken from us, the team was left with nothing to do but go to two meetings each day. They told us to stand by and said that they would get back with us at the next meeting and give us an assignment. After the caterer from Wyoming arrived and was sent home, which made for quite a drive, we had no tasks. Occasionally, a small task would come up; however, those few didn't take very long, or they needed but a few of us to accomplish.

The team would have dinner at one of the local restaurants as power was restored. This was the highlight of the day. We would sit around all day, and then it was off to dinner, which may have included a beer or two. We soon found out that one of the hot spots in town was a place called the Wing House. After another boring day, all the ops guys headed to the Wing House to check it out.

The Wing House was jumping. A Florida State football game was on, and the place was packed. As we arrived, we asked for a table and were put on the waiting list. One beer led to another, and after waiting four hours for a table, we were informed that they had a table ready. Though not all our gang had been drinking, a few had, and it was entirely possible that they had had too much to drink during the four-hour wait. At any rate, we ate and returned to the ICP.

The next morning at our briefing, we were informed that yet another hurricane was approaching Florida. Our mission now was to retreat to Atlanta and wait for Hurricane Ivan to come ashore and then return to resume our mission of assisting in whatever way we could. The team loaded up and headed north to Atlanta. About halfway there one of the division guys who may have drank too much the night before awoke in the back seat from his hangover and informed us we needed to stop quick, as he needed to "blow mud."

At the next exit, we pulled over, and there was a Stuckey's Pecan store, the only place that offered facilities. We all went into the store to browse around while our buddy headed to the bathroom. If you've ever been in a Stuckey's, you know it's usually one big room filled with goodies made from pecans. We started to notice the horrible smell of mud creeping throughout the store. It was both amazing and gross that the stench was penetrating the entire store. The customers were headed out the door with sour looks on their faces. One little boy said to his mother, "Phew, Mom. What stinks?" Our buddy emerged from the bathroom, and we hauled ass before the hazmat team arrived. I don't think any of us have been to a Stuckey's since. We currently use that term "blow mud" as needed.

Our team was activated and went to a complex in Northern California. It consisted of several fires in the Six Rivers, Mendocino, and Shasta Trinity National Forests. A few of the fires were within the Yola Bolla Wilderness. We met in Redding, California, for the team briefing. Another team from Alaska was currently managing the fires but were timing out soon, and we were to take over the mess. At the briefing one of the forest supervisors informed us that she'd allow us to use retardant in the wilderness if lives were threatened. She informed us that approval for the usage of retardant could only come from her and if retardant was used without her approval, she would press criminal charges against whoever had authorized it.

After the briefing the division supervisors scattered to the different fires to gain whatever information they could prior to our takeover. There was a super scooper aircraft from Canada assigned to the fire. These aircraft actually fly low over a lake and scoop up water, which they then drop on the fire just like a heavy air tanker. This aircraft was being utilized in the wilderness in lieu of retardant.

One of the divisions went to the fire in the wilderness, and upon his return, he quietly informed me that the Alaska team was using retardant in the wilderness. This concerned us because we obviously didn't want criminal charges filed against us. I asked the operations guys from Alaska whether they were in fact using retardant in the wilderness, and they denied the charge immediately. They said they were using the super scooper with the water they were dipping out of Ruth Lake and that was all. Shit, I would have lied too!

I tied back in with the division that had made the report that they were not using retardant in the wilderness, and this really pissed him off. He informed me that he was hunkered down and taking a dump, and without any warning, he was nailed by a salvo drop of retardant. He went on to inform me that if I doubted it was retardant, he would drop his drawers and let me see his red ass as evidence. I didn't want to check, and we escaped without any criminal charges.

In regard to the same incident, one of the division supervisors called and wanted to have a face-to-face with me and requested that I come out to his division for that meeting. As I arrived, I saw his truck there, but he wasn't around, so I asked one of the guys on an engine crew if he knew where the he was. They informed me that he had gone to the bushes to take a dump and that he would be right back. In short order, the division guy returned to have his face-to-face with me. A few minutes into our meeting, one of the guys on the engine crew started yelling at the top of his lungs, "Spot! Spot!" which was the common way of informing everyone of a spot fire that was over the fire line. Sure as hell, there was a spot fire over the line, and it was building fast. A heavy helicopter was diverted to drop water on the spot fire. Quick response suppressed the spot fire, and all was well. Spot fires are common on a fire, and the division seemed rather overly concerned about this one. I was prodding him about his concern, and he informed me that the spot fire was the result of him burning his toilet paper at the dump site.

While assigned to the Cerro Grande Fire, which impacted Los Alamos, New Mexico, I was at the ICP one fine morning when the urge to take a dump struck me. I really don't know if everyone had the same phobia about Porta Potties that I do, but they can be pretty gross. I attempt to avoid them at all costs if possible. At any rate, things were calm on the fire at the moment, so I decided I would take a drive away from the ICP and find me a nice place to relieve myself out in the woods.

I drove a few miles from camp to a deserted road and decided that this was the place. I pulled over, got out of my truck, secured a shovel and a roll of toilet paper, and headed for the security of the woods. I walked about fifty yards from the road and found a tree where I'd have a nice, secure place to take care of business.

As I started to drop my pants and get on with the issue, I noticed a forest service's green truck driving really slow down the road. What the hell! I had driven away for a few miles from camp and found a secluded road, and now someone was following me. What kind of pervert wanted to witness me taking a dump? I peered through the trees to try to make out who the hell it was. As the vehicle crept through a spacing in the trees, to my horror I saw that it was my truck rolling away. I had left it in neutral. The urge to take a dump was immediately replaced with the fear of my truck rolling away to its death. I tossed the shovel and toilet paper in the air and ran as fast as I could to get in my truck and avoid a wreck. As I approached to road, I started to get in front of the truck, but then I thought that if I slipped, I would get run over. So I cut around the back and managed to get in and slam on the brakes just as it rolled off the road. Needless to say, I was worked up about my near miss. As I looked up, I saw that there was one of the line safety officers about three hundred yards down the road. He was laughing his ass off at my near miss. He assured me that the story would not get out. Here's a little hint. Don't ever believe anyone who says this because he told everyone. I would have too.

The Rodeo-Chediski Fire for Arizona was a pretty complex fire. There were evacuations, highway closures, structure losses, and governor and presidential visits, and multiple city governments were involved in this huge and active fire. Throw all this into a strategy meeting, and it makes for a lengthy one.

While enduring one of these meetings, my guts started to growl, and that feeling that I had better head to the toilet started to build. My initial thoughts were that I could last the meeting as I wanted to ensure I had heard everyone's input. The meeting just kept going on and on, and the issue with my gut kept getting worse and worse. I finally told my ops buddy that I had to leave, and then I got up and left the meeting.

The incident base was at a high school, and leaving the meeting, I had to walk across a courtyard and into another wing of the school to find the bathroom. As I hurried across the courtyard, my situation got really bad, but walking as fast as I could, I finally made it. When I got into the bathroom, there were two stalls, both of which were occupied. I made a plea for the occupants to hurry up, and then I heard a familiar laugh from one of the stalls. It was a Phoenix fire department guy who worked in our medical unit. He realized who I was and what my problem was, and he thought that it was just funny as hell. The more I urged him to hurry up, the louder and harder he laughed.

Finally, he finished up and slowly left the stall, just giggling a little by now. I wasted no time and sprang into action. I jumped in the stall, dropped my pants, and let go. He was still out washing his hands and laughing at me. Then I looked down and noticed that he had stolen the toilet paper. I cussed at the little shit, and he almost had a stroke laughing as he left the bathroom, no doubt to go and tell all his buddies about his little joke.

Well, there I sat soaking up my little dilemma, weighing my options. Then I noticed a hand full of toilet paper reaching under the divider from the next stall. For all bad things, there is a little ray of sunshine. What a cool thing to do. I didn't know who this unseen person was, but you could tell his heart was in the right place.

The next morning at the day shift briefing, which was attended by a herd of folks, a guy approached me and said I needed to thank him. I was trying to place this guy, but I couldn't remember him or any reason I needed to thank him. I didn't want to slight him if he did something great that deserved thanks, but I just could not place him. This guy then acted like he was handing someone some toilet paper under the divider of a bathroom stall, and I knew immediately that he was one of my true heroes. I gave him some sincere thanks and left him giggling about the whole deal.

One fire season I had tenured off one of the Southwest fire teams, as my five year commitment was completed. The type 1 team from Colorado or the Rocky Mountain region had difficulties filling their team, and I was asked to fill in as operations for the summer. This was the first season I hadn't been on an incident management team in several years, so I accepted the offer. I only knew a few folks on that team, and I thought it would be a fun challenge to go out with a new team.

Unfortunately, the winter prior to this fire season, the team had been subject to some internal strife. This strife resulted in several long-term team members not returning to the team, and they had actually asked me to participate so that the team could meet staffing requirements. I had no knowledge of what had occurred when I agreed to fill their vacancy.

The team was assigned to fires in the Stanley, Idaho, area on the Boise National Forest. There were two separate factions of personnel on the team—those who liked the ones who had left the team, and those who didn't like the ones who hung it up. Both factions attempted to recruit me into their schools of thought, and their friendship circle. This made the assignment quite weird for me because I didn't know who was who or what had happened, and I just wanted to remain neutral and do my job. I would be accused of talking to one faction or the other, and it always seemed to piss someone off because I was violating their trust and talking to someone from the other side. This is difficult when you don't know who's who, and I felt it would be a lot easier for me as a newcomer if they wore different color shirts of something to distinguish the two sides.

I soon became frustrated, and this frustration ended with me pitching my tent and camping away from everyone. I had a really neat little place for my tent, and at least I could go hide after the daily stuff was done and sleep away from the fray. We inherited another fire called the Red Mountain Fire. The afternoon we got this fire, it hauled ass. This resulted in us placing a large order for additional people needed to manage the new fire. Within a few days scores of new people were showing up in camp. Soon many of these new folks found my little getaway area, and new resources started moving in and crowding my secret and stable camping space.

I had a great thought, and then I grabbed a shovel and a roll of toilet paper. I dug several small holes all around my tent and stuck just a little toilet paper out of the holes when I covered them back up. It made the area look like whoever was living in this tent had been taking shits all around the little clearing. This worked like a charm, and folks didn't encroach on my little space. When the team pulled out and we were all tearing down camp and packing up, I was over at my tent and packing all my stuff up, and one of the division supervisors on the team came over to visit. With all my stuff packed up and a huge plastic bag of all my trash from two weeks in my tent, all I had to do was pick up all the toilet paper props around my little area. With the plastic bag in hand I started walking around and pulling the toilet paper out of the ground and putting it in the trash bag. This freaked the division guy out, and he yelled at me, What the hell are you doing?" I then told him what I had done, and we both got a good laugh. This trick still works very well, but people look at you kind of weird in camp.

As I previously discussed, New Mexico produces the best green chili. The same goes for the area around central Washington. Rather than green chili, their tribute is fruit. While New Mexico can say they own the quality green chili, Washington may rule the roost when it comes to fruit. I was assigned as an interagency resource representative (IARR) along with one of my mentors and good friends. We headed to the Thirty-Mile Fire, but we were also supposed to work on the multiple fires that were burning in the area.

As we approached Wenatchee, Washington, after the long drive from Arizona, we saw there were acres and acres of fruit trees. Roadside stands selling their fruit were everywhere. Being from Arizona, where fruit is pretty scarce and good fruit damn scarce, we decided to pull over, stretch our legs, and see what they had for sale. There were cherries that were the size of plums, peaches the size of a softball, and apples of every size and description. It was a fruit mecca. What really caught our eyes were the peaches. My traveling buddy bought one, and I remember him saying, "A peach just ain't ripe if you don't have juice dripping off your elbow after the first bite." The peaches were the best I ever had. We checked out the cherries. There were two different kinds—Bing and Rainier. My buddy liked the traditional Bing cherries. I liked the Rainier cherries. They were golden with a hint of red, and as I said, they were the size of small plums. We both bought a basket of cherries and hit the road to Winthrop, Washington, as we had made room reservations for our stay.

My Rainier cherries were the absolute sweetest cherries I had ever eaten. They were huge, and each one was just as sweet as the last. I was in heaven eating these sweet cherries, enjoying each one, and I was just amazed at how sweet and fresh they were. When you're from Arizona, you seldom have the opportunity to enjoy such fabulous fruit. My buddy quietly ate his Bing cherries, also amazed by their quality. We exchanged handfuls of our cherries so we could both enjoy their sweetness. We were driving along and enjoying our cherries, just happy as hell.

I don't recall how far it is from Wenatchee to Winthrop, Washington but we managed to eat almost all our cherries. I don't think either of us had ever eaten so many sweet cherries. If you're from Arizona and haven't been exposed to such quality fruit, it may be easier to overdose on cherries. I've never eaten so many, and my system told me that most if not all those cherries wanted out ... now. My buddy was in the same shape, and we both knew that the cherries didn't like their new environment.

I have always heard that old people eat prunes to stay regular and healthy. I'm here to tell you that if you've eaten a few prunes and haven't had any success, eat a few handfuls of cherries and watch out. I think the fruit stands should have warning signs that tell you that the laxative effects of these sweet cherries may catch you in between rest areas. By the time we reached Winthrop, there was no doubt that they had all worked collectively to cause some great stomachaches in us, and there was only one obvious solution to the dilemma. As we checked into the motel, the lady was very slow and deliberate in the process. I just hoped she got me checked in before I *blew mud* in the lobby.

CHAPTER 9
DOGS

I've always been partial to dogs, and have been the owner/partner to many Australian shepherds. Aussies make great partners and family members. I don't think they have any connection to Australia, but it's hard not to like these dogs. When I was a little boy, my father found one that had escaped from one of the sheepherders that in those days used the sheep drivetrails that crossed the Mogollon Rim. One day while my dad was driving around, he found a little red Aussie puppy that seemed to be lost and alone. The puppy had strayed from the sheep herd and their herder and seemed lost. My dad knew the herder and the owner of the band of sheep, and when he returned the puppy, they asked if he wanted it. Since we didn't have a dog, he kept it. He named the puppy Lucky as he felt that the pup was lucky that he had found the little guy. Lucky was a great partner for me as a kid, and he got into lots of trouble with me throughout my childhood. We both got whipped many times for playing in the irrigation ditches, shooting frogs and snakes with my BB gun, or chasing the huge carp that sometimes found themselves down the ditch to our place. I don't remember getting spanked for something I didn't do, but I do remember getting quite a few spankings. After each one, Lucky would come by and comfort me and show his friendship. He lived for twenty-one years, which is quite a while for any dog, but he was the first of many Aussies that I've had the pleasure of living with. Currently, I'm on number seven.

On a fire at the Custer National Forest, the team was set up near a little place called Fishtail, Montana. Fire Camp was set up in a cut hay field on one of the local rancher's private land. Like so many areas in Montana, Fishtail is a grass-covered valley with mountain ranges encompassing it in all directions.

Fire camp always attracts local pets, mainly dogs, if any are in the area that have the freedom to run wherever they choose. There are lots of goodies in the fire camp, and a dog can get a pat on the head or friendly scratches from the folks on the fire team. I've been in fire camps on reservations when packs of dogs quickly catch on about the handouts, both food items and affection.

On this particular fire, one of these dogs that liked hanging out at fire camp was a Queensland heeler pup that was probably around six months old. She was indeed a cute pup. She was a true hound for affection, and she just loved all the attention she was getting in camp.

Ladies just love puppies. Guys like them well enough, but ladies coo and baby-talk as they give dogs treats and pats on the head. Any dog would it soak up. This all resulted in the puppy hanging out in the finance, and plans shop as there were so many ladies who were there to love on the cute little thing.

Dog attitudes inevitably come into play, especially since this heeler was a ranch dog. She wasn't one that knew the rules of the big city. She wasn't used to walking around the neighborhood and having a human pick up her leavings in a plastic bag. All she had known is the life of a Montana ranch, which builds a different kind of critter.

The ladies just threw out the red carpet for this cute little thing, and I don't think it ever went home. One of the ladies really drank the Kool-Aid for this little girl and started talking about taking her home to Arizona when the fire was over. We said that it wouldn't be cool to just dognap her as she no doubt belonged to someone in the area, and so we made efforts to find out just who the little girl belonged to.

As it turned out, the puppy belonged to a rancher that was unfortunately killed in a car accident not long before our arrival. The ladies found this out while trying to find the owner, and it made them feel horrible to bring up the whole deal once they learned about the tragedy. However, the rancher's widow said that the puppy brought back sad memories of her late husband and that she was willing to let the lady have the puppy.

To say this was a hit back in fire camp would be an understatement. All those pats on the head, meat from sack lunches, and just a general state of giddiness with the change of ownership of the little heeler pup swamped it with goodness. She got a new name, a collar, a bed, a water dish, and just about everything any heeler ever wanted.

The fire finally went out, or we timed out. I forget which happened first, but it was time to head back to Arizona. We had a closing party in Red Lodge, Montana, and the puppy was exposed to life in the big city. She was just in hog heaven as all the team members had some sort of relationship with the new team member. After a night out on the town, we headed home. The route from Red Lodge to Arizona led us through Yellowstone National Park.

While traveling to and from a fire, team members monitor the crew frequency or common user frequency. This is done just in case someone has trouble, and we can just to keep in contact with everyone on the trip home. As we were traveling though Yellowstone, several folks started talking on the radio about never seeing Yellowstone Falls. Hell, we were driving right past it, so we decided that we would all pull in and take a quick trip to see the falls. Of course, the puppy had never seen the falls either, and she was part of our group.

As we pulled into the parking lot at the falls, you couldn't help but notice all the signs that mandated all pets be kept on a leash. The only thing that we had not purchased for the puppy was a leash; however, in true firefighter fashion, we dug out a piece of parachute cord and tied it onto her new collar just so she wouldn't miss the trip.

The parking lot was full of cars, SUVs, and tour buses. Yellowstone Falls is a very popular place, and there were quite a few folks headed down the short trail to a scenic overlook of the falls. We all found a place to park. All of us were in either forest service or BLM vehicles, so we got some attention. We parked, got the cute little puppy on her makeshift leash, and headed down the trail to see the falls.

There are two ways to view what happened next. As tourists are walking down the trail to the falls, they notice cute little chipmunks that are used to begging for treats from the tourists. They just come up and take a treat right out of people's hands. It's so cute. What an experience not only to see the wonders of Yellowstone but getting a chance to actually feed some of the cute little critters. It's no wonder they made movies of the chipmunks. They are just so cute.

The other view comes from the ranch-raised Queensland heeler. If you're a heeler and headed down the trail to see the falls with all your new friends and one of these stupid chipmunks that has absolutely no fear of anything wanders out into the trail, it's time to show everyone some of your talents. An unwary chipmunk in the trail to a heeler pup is like finding a hundred-dollar bill for the rest of us.

If you are one of the many people who have been bitten by a heeler, you truly know how fast they can be when they want to. With that quickness, the heeler pup grabbed the cute little chipmunk in her mouth and shook the shit out of it, and then she dropped it in the middle of the trail. This only took a fraction of a second.

Unfortunately, this horrible and unwarranted attack appalled many of the tourists. Their only exposure to such things must have been limited to the Discovery Channel as they were frozen with awe that such an obscene act of murder had occurred right in front of their eyes. Some were shielding the faces of their kids so they didn't have to view the carnage. "We just fed that cute little chipmunk some peanuts," one of them shouted while looking at the cute little heeler pup like she was a devil dog. Parents were pulling their kids away from the puppy like she was a wolf. They also looked at us like it was our fault that the poor little chipmunk had slept through the lesson about heelers.

Of course, the puppy was proud of her catch, and she awaited the praise for her quick actions from all her new friends. However, we just hurried down the trail to see the falls, take a quick picture, and haul ass before all the tourists got a better look at us or took out their revenge on the puppy.

After a quick glance at the falls, we hurried back along the trail to get on the road and avoid the growing discontent with the tourist crowd. As we approached the site of the massacre, quite a grouping of folks had a quick service for the fallen chipmunk. They had buried it, constructed a small cross made of sticks, and were paying their last respects for the poor little thing. They made up such a solemn group. Of course, they gave us an ugly stare as we walked by. There was also a busload of Japanese tourists who were caught up in the service, no doubt unaware of the heeler's ways, wondering what the hell was going on. None of them thought the heeler puppy was too damn cute.

Because of the mass evacuations and the lack of time to evacuate everyone during the Rodeo-Chediski Fire, several pets missed the bus. The fire impacted not only people's pets but livestock too, and wildlife was also displaced or put in harm's way. News coverage spread nationwide, and people all over the country witnessed the fire's progress and the damage that it was causing.

The news coverage brought this issue to the attention of a national pet rescue group that then went to the fire and set up shop. Their task was to provide shelter and assistance to the rising number of animals that were abandoned or hurt because of the fire. They saw quite a host of animals, including dogs, cats, horses, and even a calf elk, which was rescued and caged at fire camp for its own protection. This was free of charge and quite an undertaking for the residents of the area and their animals.

Because of the number of animals rescued, the crew soon exceeded their on-site ability to house all the animals, so the humane shelter was enlisted in Holbrook, Arizona, which was an hour's drive from the fire. They, too, provided this service without compensation, and both groups should be commended.

As word that rescued dogs were being transported to Holbrook, the operations folks gave the shelter the name Puppy Prison. While a great undertaking, we viewed it as less than desirable, especially for the dogs. Instead of reporting the pets' locations to the authorities, some of the guys began caring for the animals by giving them water and feeding them on a daily basis.

One afternoon the fire made a pretty impressive run toward a small subdivision, a ranch, and a resort. Resources were very limited, and they were committed to other areas of the fire. I was there alone, and I requested some immediate help to try to burn out the area around the structures. A strike team of engines was rounded up and sent my way. My partner and a safety officer from Florida also heard my plea and headed my way.

As my operations partner and the safety officer arrived on the scene, the fire was threatening a ranch house, and we all drove over there to see what we could do to prevent it from burning down. When we arrived in the front yard of the house, we were greeted by two dogs, a Queensland heeler and a pit bull. They were left during the evacuation for some unknown reason. They'd probably been out chasing elk or something when their owners were evacuated. Left alone, they assumed that their job was to protect the old homestead, which they were doing a great job of. All three of us were in separate vehicles, and as we drove up to the house, the dogs ran out and barked madly.

My ops buddy called me on the radio and asked me to get out of my truck first to see if the dogs would bite. Both of us knew the rumors about pit bulls, and both of us knew that heelers just lived to bite intruders, especially ones driving forest service trucks. So both of us sat in our trucks, wondering what to do next when he called me on the radio again and told me to hold tight. He said, "Hold on. The safety guy from Florida is getting out as bait." The safety guy just pulled up and got out of his truck like he lived there and dispelled any of our fears. The dogs were all bark, no bite. They seemed quite happy to have some company.

We successfully burned out around the place. The two dogs greatly appreciated our actions, and they stayed with us as we burned and held the area around the house. As our task was completed and our new friends were sitting in the truck with me, I took a drink of water. Both the dogs looked at me with those big eyes, insulted that I didn't offer them a drink. I found their bone-dry water bowl and filled it up. They both drank it all several times over. We wondered if they were hungry, so we offered them some food. We only had one of the sack lunches from fire camp. I tossed them a few sandwiches, but they both turned their noses up at them.

These two dogs became my charges, and in efforts to keep them from the dreaded puppy prison in Holbrook, I made them a part of my daily routine. I would go over and water them and offer them food on a daily basis. My food offerings consisted of the sack lunches provided for the firefighters. Each day they were waiting for me to show up, love them up a little, and provide water and food. They were all about the water, but they didn't really eat anything. It took them three days before they would eat a sandwich from the sack lunches.

I worked for several years in range management, and for the most part, I worked alone. Some of the cowboys joked about me being the lone ranger as I was alone in my pursuits on most days. My boss at the time was one for fieldwork, and he told me a desk was just something to hide behind. As a result, I spent most of my time in the field, doing a host of range or wildlife projects. We donated quite a bit of time and effort in our attempts to make things better. It was commonplace for me to take my dog with me every day. This was accepted for the most part, and no issues resulted from me taking along my dog. If for any reason I couldn't take along my pup, she would lay a guilt trip on me for abandoning her, upset that I was leaving her home.

When I left Blue Ridge and moved to Flagstaff, I had a dog named Loretta. She started life at the ranger station, and she was used to having her run of the place. I was able to take her along with me to work on many occasions. Moving into a town's ranger district was different, and while taking her along with me was limited, I always took her if I had the chance. I had taken my dogs with me many times prior to my move, and they felt left out when they didn't get to come along. Loretta was no exception, and whenever possible, I would bring her along for the ride. It wasn't as accepted as it was out in the far end of the forest, and I knew that I would eventually get caught and told to leave her at home. I just couldn't bear to break the news to her, so she went along when she could.

I was a para-archaeologist by training. This allowed me to do some archaeological surveys for projects. We were required to do these so that various projects could avoid any cultural sites, and also to record sites found in the surveys. Wupatki National Monument personnel wanted to fence the right-of-way of the highway to the monument that passed through a slice of the forest. For one reason or another, I was asked if I could to this survey so that they could construct the fence. I accepted the job. It was a great way to get some field time, and I knew that Loretta would just jump at the chance to go along.

I surveyed the entirety of the fence on both sides of the highway, and I needed to record the sites that I had found in that survey. One of these sites was a small field house right next to the highway. Upon recording the site, I had to give it a site tag to mark it and record its number. The site tag consists of a small piece of aluminum with the site number on it, and we were instructed to nail it to a tree as close to the middle of the site as possible. I was in the process of nailing the site tag on a tree, standing there with a hammer in one hand and the site tag in the other.

Again, I was right on the edge of the highway, but I was pretty much out in the middle of nowhere. I looked up, and I saw a guy riding a bicycle down the highway. Though we were out in the middle of nowhere, the bicycler caught Loretta's attention. Everything was going along all right, but as this guy passed within five feet or so of me, I noticed Loretta slipping up behind him. She clearly wanted to go in for a quick taste of a bicycler. The guy rode right past me and didn't even speak, nod, spit, or anything. That may be why Loretta was sneaking up behind him, though I'm not sure.

Not wanting my dog to bite this bicycler, I threw what I had in my hand at Loretta, namely the hammer. I didn't aim at her head but rather threw it in front of her to pull her attention away from the foot of the bicycler. When I threw the hammer, the bicycler stopped on a dime and turned around and came up to me and called me a nasty name. He then asked if I threw the hammer at him. I didn't appreciate his approach, and I calmly told him that if I wanted to hit him with the hammer, I would have just clocked him as he rode by. He didn't take that well.

He continued to cuss me out while keeping an eye on Loretta. He was very abusive and expressed his disfavor for both me and Loretta. He told me that I hadn't heard the last of this and that he was going to report me for my assault. He got a pen out of his little fanny pack along with a piece of paper and wrote down the door number and license plate number of the truck I was driving. After that, he got back on his bike and rode off down the road.

Loretta and I just stood there and watched him ride off. Then I nailed the site tag on a tree, and that finished our tasks for the day. We got into the truck and headed back into town. A short distance down the road, we overtook the bicycler as he continued his journey. As we passed him, he flipped me the finger. Loretta barked a few times at him and looked over at me to make sure I wasn't going to throw the hammer at her again.

The next day I was called into the ranger's office only to find out that the guy did stop in and report the incident. He told the ranger that he had survived a dog attack and a horrible cussing assault by me while I held back my vicious dog as she attempted to bite him. He made up quite the story about my abusive language and the aggressive dog that was with me. After listening to the ranger and the story the guy had made up, I had two thoughts. One was that a bike ride into town offered quite an opportunity to embellish a good story, and second, that maybe I should have run the dude over on my way back into town. I was instructed in no uncertain terms that taking Loretta along with me to work was not going to happen again. Loretta was never given a chance to defend herself, and she maintained a lifelong distrust for bicycle riders.

One morning there was a group of guys sitting around and waiting to be briefed for a fire we would soon be assigned to. A young Queensland heeler joined our group and stopped in for a few scratches and pats on the head, and he wanted to see what we were doing in his town. This dog was very friendly and full of energy like many heelers. One of the guys changed his sitting position, and the morning sun caught the crystal of his wristwatch and cast a bright reflection on the wall of a building next to us. This reflection quickly caught the attention of the heeler, and he immediately went after it.

Dogs and even cats find chasing a bright light around to be quite a fun game. I have driven cats to the brink of insanity as they chase around the light produced by a laser pointer. If you have ever done this, it provides quite a bit of entertainment for both the human and the cat. If you haven't done it, give it a try. It will provide some cheap thrills for both participants.

The guy producing the reflection was having just about as much fun as the heeler was chasing it around. We were all amused at how fast the dog moved and how enthralled both the dog and our guy were. Around and around, up and down, over and over again—the dog worked himself into a tither chasing that elusive spot of bright light, and he just couldn't quite catch it. This went on for a long time, and the dog was getting tired but refused to give up. We suggested to the guy that maybe he should give the poor dog a rest; however, he ignored what we said, and the chase continued. We made the same suggestion a few times, and the guy kept it up until the dog was truly worn out. We told the guy that the dog was going to get frustrated and bite the shit out of him if he kept it up, but he refused to quit.

Eventually, our pleadings to let the dog have a rest sunk in, and the guy quit shining the reflection of his wristwatch on the side of the building. Finally, he and the dog settled down for a rest. We were still just hanging out and waiting the briefing to start. The dog was lying in the middle of our little circle, panting and keeping an eye out for the bright spot that had just disappeared into thin air. While the dog was tired and frustrated, he hadn't given up, and he continually scanned the building for the elusive bright light that moved around like a UFO, ready to go after it again if it reappeared.

The guy who cast the reflection on the wall was just full of joy for providing such a fun activity for the dog. I noticed one of the other guys remained very still and seemed caught in thought. I was sitting there, watching this guy, wondering what he was thinking about when I noticed that he had captured the sun's reflection on his watch and was directing the reflection right on the crotch of the guy who had been playing with the dog. The dog was lying there, panting and looking around for that weird light when he noticed the reflection on this guy's crotch. The dog immediately froze, but only the guy pointing the reflection and I caught this reaction from the dog. The dog quit panting and froze, his eye on that damn elusive light. The guy who had been casting the reflection for the dog was oblivious to his dilemma, just visiting with friends and enjoying the morning. His legs were spread wide open with the reflection hovering around his privates.

The dog was as still as a statue, staring in disbelief that the bright light was right there and not moving around as fast as it had been during the chase. The guy shining the reflection made it quiver slightly, and the dog licked it lips a little but remained motionless. Then with the quickness of a bolt of lightning, he pounced on the reflection with a loud growl.

The guy who had been playing with the dog was just enjoying the morning when the dog pounced with a growl. He freaked out and let out a scream, which was understandable. He didn't know the dog was just playing the game as he was unaware he had been the backdrop for the reflection. He thought the dog had just done it out of spite, and he was somewhat upset by the dogs behavior, not to mention our hysterical laughing. He just kept saying, "Why did the dog do that?" and we just recited the story that we had told him before, namely that he should have given the dog a break earlier.

There's another story that I would like to tell that involves an Australian shepherd, a breed of dog I've always been partial to. Both the boy and the dog lived on one of the ranches that I have had the pleasure of working with. This boy's father worked on the ranch as a cowboy, and his mom was a stay-at-home mom who lived on the ranch in one of the houses for married cowboys. This ranch was a large one and had extensive winter pastures, as well as a large grazing permit on the national forest. The cattle wintered off the forest on private land, however each spring the cattle were gathered and driven on foot for several miles to the forest permit for the summer.

The ranch had two headquarters—one for the winter months and one for the summer months. This required all the ranch folks to pack up their homes and move twice a year up to the summer headquarters in the spring and back to the winter headquarters in the fall. This coincided with moving all the livestock up to the forest. As a result, the families may not get to see their cowboy dad for several days at a time.

The boy in this story was a youngster somewhere around seven or eight years old. He was an only child, and at this time, he was the only kid on the ranch. Most of the other kids associated with the ranch were probably ten years his senior and helping with the trail drives. He and his mom had moved up to the summer ranch, and so this young lad and his mom were pretty much alone each day along with his dog. His dad was gone for days on end with the spring works, and his only partner was Spud, his dog. Spud and this young boy were always together. Their days were spent chasing lizards and chipmunks around the corrals, or chasing sticks or balls that the boy tossed.

All the cowboys liked this young lad, and he liked all the cowboys too. When they were together, he liked to hang out at the corrals with the cowboys and his dad. During one afternoon one of the herds of cows and calves arrived at the summer headquarters. They were to be branded there and then taken out to their assigned pasture, so all the cowboys were to remain at the headquarters, which meant the boy could see his dad and also hang out with all the cowboys who worked there. He was elated and he and Spud were at the corrals when everyone rode in.

He stayed up at the corrals as everyone unsaddled their horses and put morals on them. A moral is a bag usually made out of a gunny sack that held rolled oats as a treat for the horses. A rope is attached to the bag and hung over the horses ears so with their noses in the bag eating their ration of oats. All the cowboys, the boy, and Spud were sitting on the corrals, waiting for the horses to finish their oats in their morals when the boy's mom came out on the back porch of their house and hollered for the boy to come home and wash up as dinner was ready. All the cowboys always stayed at the corrals until the horses were done with their oats. The boy wanted to stay more than he wanted go to dinner, so he just ignored his mom.

In a few minutes, she reappeared on the porch, this time a little upset, and she yelled to the boy and his dad that dinner was ready and that they needed to come down and eat. The boy was still more interested in hanging out with the men than he was in dinner, so he ignored her again. His behavior didn't go over too well with his mom, and the next time she came outside, she marched up to the corral and grabbed the boy by the arm and yanked him off the top rail of the corral and started dragging him home. The mom was spanking the young lad on the bottom for ignoring her. The boy was screaming because he didn't want to go and he didn't want a whipping either.

All the guys at the corral thought that grabbing him and dragging him home was just a little bit too much, but we all knew that it was really none of our business. Most of the guys there had probably been yanked off a corral fence and dragged home by their moms. The cowboys all felt that it was somewhat mean and didn't approve, but we all kept our mouths shut. There was one exception, and that was Spud.

Spud was also at the corral as always, and he was a step behind the boy, who was his hero and partner. While we all felt that it was not our business to get involved, Spud had a different take on it. He couldn't ignore his buddy screaming like he was hurt, so he dashed out from under the bottom rail of the corral, ran up, and grabbed the boy's mom's ribs with a determined bite. He didn't let go either. This sent the boy's mom over the moon. She screamed, dropped the boy, and started hitting Spud in an attempt to make him let go. Seeing his mom beat Spud only made the boy cry worse, and the entire deal escalated really fast. The boy finally grabbed Spud by his bobtail and pulled him off his mom. She was just about as mad as anyone I'd ever seen, and she demanded that Spud be shot on the spot. The idea of someone shooting Spud sent the young lad into a fit, and he started hugging Spud and crying. Spud was keeping his eyes on the boy's mom, getting ready for another attack if needed.

The mom stormed back to their house, rubbing her ribs and cursing Spud. The boy sat in the dirt, crying and hugging Spud. We were still sitting on the corral, thinking to ourselves, *Good dog*. The boy's dad went to comfort his son and tell him that no one was going to shoot Spud. This ended the afternoon's excitement; however, Spud was forced to live in exile for a few days until the dust settled. He was readily accepted into the bunkhouse during this exile as we all felt that he did what a dog with a little buddy should do. During Spud's exile he was the hero of the bunkhouse.

CHAPTER 10
BEARS

Most Americans know about Smokey Bear. Some even know the song. However, people don't always know how bears can complicate the firefighting process. Most folks have a few bear stories of their own, but I want to offer a few of mine here.

We were sent to a fire near Lincoln, Montana, within the Helena National Forest. The Sucker Creek Fire was located north of town and just outside the Scape Goat Wilderness Area. For those who haven't been there—the Scape Goat, Bob Marshall, Great Bear Wilderness', Glacier National Park, and Waterton Lakes National Park, which is in Canada, are adjacent. This huge mass of wilderness falls upon the continental divide, and it had afforded the grizzly bear quite a good comeback, an animal that is currently listed and protected as an endangered species.

The fire started outside the Scape Goat Wilderness, but wind and topography both pushed the burn in that direction. Bear safety precautions are discussed and practiced daily in fire suppression activities. We all take this training seriously in this neck of the woods, as we all know that we can be mauled, killed, and eaten by one of these dudes. The district office has a fully mounted grizzly bear on display so that people get an idea of what kind of chance they will have if they don't follow all the rules.

Being from Arizona, which lost their grizzly population long ago, all my grizzly knowledge came from reading articles about them. I don't know if you have noticed, but most of the writing about grizzly bears is about someone being mauled, killed, or eaten in some remote place. Even Lewis and Clark documented that these bears would maul, kill, or eat you. So this is not some new behavior that global warming is causing.

This fire was headed into the Scape Goat Wilderness and into an old fire scar from the Eagle Talon Fire, one that was quite large and probably six or seven years old. As the fire burned into the old burn, the rate of spread slowed to a crawl, so we poured our efforts into pinching the fire into the old burn. As the fire ran, or spotted, into the old burn, it skunked around in the snags and deadfall from the old fire. The fuel in the old burn was heavy, and while the spread of the fire slowed to a crawl, it was still eating its way through the old burn.

There were multiple fires burning throughout the west, and resources were spread thin. Our direction was to stop the fire's spread in the old burn scar as the lack of available firefighters was a concern. We made plans to look at a foot trail that went up a creek and out past the head of the fire as it provided the best location to start a control line around the mess and stop the fires movement through the fire scar. This trail connected with the line we had on the western flank of the fire, and it also provided the quickest and most likely place where we could be successful in getting around the fire.

But resources were at a premium, so our plan fell onto a single division supervisor. He was all alone and miles away from anyone else, stuck in grizzly country. Oh, and he was an Arizona boy too. After he became aware of his assignment that day, he wanted to have a little chat about what we were thinking. So we gave him a good briefing and got him set up with some bear safety stuff, including pepper spray.

While many suggested we give him bells, we couldn't find any in the fire camp.

Hikers in this area are instructed to wear bells so that bears can hear them coming down the trail and avoid them. People are also instructed to carry pepper spray to protect themselves. Locals like to tell guys from Arizona that the way to tell black bear shit from grizzly bear shit is that grizzly bear shit has bells in it and it smells like pepper spray.

Pepper spray is another issue altogether. I think more firefighters have been sprayed than bears in this neck of the woods, boys will be boys. I've seen guys spraying it on their sandwiches to get that pepper flavor. Personally, I really doubt that I would have the guts to stand my ground and squirt pepper spray at a charging grizzly. Obviously, the bear wants to maul, kill, and then eat you, so why would you just spray pepper juice at it and really piss it off? You're probably not going to limp away from this one.

So back to our guy we're asking to go deep into grizzly country alone. He just hung around camp quite a long time, he said he was looking for some bells but I think he was kind of scared of the assignment. I really don't blame him, but someone had to do it. It was discovered that we did have access to a pistol, which is not really allowed on fires however one guy did have a .45 that was offered to the division dude if he wanted. He asked if it was alright, and I thought it was the only way we were going to get him up there to see what was what so I said it was alright.

Then he headed out, armed with pepper spray and a .45. He was driving very slowly as he left fire camp, paying close attention to safety. Having solved the problem at hand, the day went on. However, after getting out of a meeting that afternoon, I saw a deputy sheriff from the local county drive up and motion for me to come over. He told me that there was a report of gunfire in the area of the fire and that he had an officer en route to check it out. We had the area of the fire closed to the public, so the sheriff thought it was someone who had sneaked into the region. My concerns immediately went to our pistol-packing division guy, of course. A guilty conscience can produce quite a few scenarios. All those articles and Discovery Channel documentaries about grizzly violence came back to me.

I jumped in my truck and started in that direction, all the way thinking of all the bullshit I was in and hoping I could find and hide the pistol before the sheriff got there. I didn't have any bells, pepper spray, or bear safety items. My only hope was that the bear had eaten enough of the division guy that he wouldn't want to eat me when I arrived. Shortly after I reached the edge of the fire, I saw a group of folks talking to a deputy, so I pulled up and stopped. They had determined that the reported shooting was just a crew burning out the road by using flare guns. That was the only gunfire in the area. I acted like I knew it all along and tried not to show my relief that I didn't have to explain where a pistol came from when we recovered the division supervisor's remains.

Everyone made it out. The division guy heard the radio traffic about the shooting and knew we had dreamed up the worse. He was amused and figured he was just getting even with us for sending him out there alone, so he let us sweat. The .45 was returned to its keeper, and we decided there was a reason pistols weren't allowed on fires.

On the Moose Fire, which started in the Flathead National Forest and spread into Glacier National Park, another part of grizzly country, a few things happened. We were briefed on bear safety as was the practice in this area. Fire camp was set up at an old aluminum smelter near Columbia Falls. We soon got in a helicopter for a recon flight to see what options we had in suppressing the fire. All the guys in operations usually camped away from everyone else in our own little place. On this fire we camped by the helibase in a little stand of willows at the base of a ridge.

The recon flight went well and as we were returning back to the helibase, our flight path followed a long ridge that was covered with huckleberry bushes, their leaves turning red in the late summer. It was the same ridge we were camping at the base of. As we approached the helibase, I saw at first one and then three bears eating the huckleberries. As we landed, I talked to one of the guys at the helibase and told him that we had seen three bears on the ridge. Then we went to have dinner prior to our next meeting. At dinner we saw the helibase guy we had told about the bears, and he informed us that he had counted a total of five bears working the ridge. That was quite a few bears so close to our camping spot, but we acted like there wasn't issue because we didn't want to seem scared.

On our trip up to the fire from Arizona, the first day's travel took us to a motel in Idaho Falls. As I woke up in the morning, I jumped into the shower, and rather than unpack all my stuff, I used the soap and shampoo the motel offered. The shampoo the motel offered was apple-scented, and it seemed fine that morning; however, as I lay down to sleep in my little tent, all I could smell was apples. So there I was, trying to get some shut-eye, and all I could smell was apples. Bear precautions tell you to never take anything in your tent that smells like food, and now I smelled like apples with five hungry bears feeding just above us on the ridge. It's kind of hard to get to sleep when you think you may be a midnight snack for a bear. You eventually fall asleep as you think about how local motels should include some bear safety training.

On the same fire, which burned with a vengeance for several days, one of the wildlife biologists informed us one day that the fire had burned over a little creek called Mud Creek with such intensity that it killed all the fish. He said the banks of this little creek were lined with dead fish now. I had never seen such a thing, and the next afternoon I thought I would drive out and see this for myself. I drove out to where a road crossed the little creek, parked my truck, and started walking up the creek. I didn't see any dead fish, and I was beginning to think that the biologist had made up the story. I was probably five hundred yards up the creek from my truck when I saw a giant bear track in the mud of the creek. The bear had been working up the creek and eating all the dead fish, and I knew it was a grizzly because of the like five-inch claws in the imprint. As I looked at my truck in the distance, I decided that I should just return before the bear found me and chased me back there ... or worse.

On another assignment in Montana—this time on the Ahorn Fire in the Lewis and Clark National Forest—all the operations guys made our little exclusive camp at a little campground called Double Falls Campground. The incident command post was in Augusta, Montana, which was several miles from our camping spot. This little campground provided us with the seclusion we wanted and was located at the foot of the front range in that area.

For the most part, the Ahorn Fire was within the Bob Marshall Wilderness, which provided excellent habitat for the growing grizzly population. In fact, there was a good population of both black and grizzly bears in the area. The morning briefings, which were held at a nearby Girl Scout camp, had black bears wander through on several mornings. We were briefed and cautioned each day about the bears.

We were not at our camp spot during the daylight hours as we left before sunup to get to the briefing, and in the evenings we had meetings in Augusta, which meant we didn't get home until well after dark. One evening one of the division supervisors saw a grizzly bear run across the road just a few hundred yards away on his way back to our campsite. He shared this information with us, which made it a little harder to get to sleep that night, but other than that, we dismissed it as just a sighting.

The next day while we were visiting with the rancher in that area, we learned that one of his cows had died just below our campground on the creek and that the bears had been feeding on it. This got our attention as the bear sighting the evening before was more than just a one-time occurrence. The bear would probably return each night to feast on the cow until it was gone. That night we all climbed into our little tents and lay there, hoping we would not replace the dead cow in the grizzly's diet.

The area of the campground was open to grazing, and the next night as we crawled into our tents for the evening, a group of cows decided to graze in the area. Lying there and waiting to go to sleep while thinking of being a snack for a grizzly bear was hard, but when you are lying in your bedroll inside a tent with no windows and you hear something walking around outside, you start wondering if it is a cow or a mean and hungry grizzly bear. I'm sure I wasn't the only one pondering the same thing. You lay there and wonder if you should yell and try to scare away whatever is outside or just be quiet and hope it grabs one of the other guys first so that you can escape to the safety of your truck. I knew I was following the bear safety protocols by not keep any food in my tent, but after several days on the fire, I smelled plenty bad all on my own. If the bear was eating a stinky dead cow, he was obviously not bothered by awful smells. I didn't want to be the first to unzip my tent and make a break for safety because the other guys would never let me live it down if it was just cows. There was little I could do but lie there and remember all the horrible bear stories I'd read as a kid in *Outdoor Life* and review all the bear precautions I'd been taught and hope I wasn't mauled, killed, and eaten.

Playing with bears is not limited to Montana. While on the

Rattlesnake Fire, which burned in the Chiricahua Mountains and the Coronado National Forest in Southern Arizona, I served as a division supervisor on a team there. Most of the firefighters who were assigned were camping at a spike camp in a church camp that had been provided It's use for the fire. Another division and I drove up to the church camp to see what was happening and tie in with the crews that were on scene. As we pulled into the church camp, we saw probably about forty or so folks there and the packs and bedrolls of many more who had slept there. There were boxes of stuff and trash where everyone had eaten. It looked just like a common scene of a rushed spike camp on a developing fire. As we pulled in, we noticed a bear standing there and holding someone's two-week pack.

A two-week pack basically has pretty much everything you take to a fire—clothes, socks, and any other personal items. This bear was standing there and just holding the pack when we noticed this rather small lady standing about thirty feet away, staring at the bear. The pack was no doubt hers, and she was yelling at the bear to drop it. The bear was just standing there, holding the pack, and looking at the lady like he didn't understand a word she was saying. Then the bear just set the pack on the ground and went down on his haunches and sat there, looking at the yelling lady.

The lady must have figured that the bear had realized that he had done something wrong and was giving her back her pack. She ran over and grabbed her pack. The lady stood up, and just then the bear stood up and swung his right paw, clocking the lady in the side of the face. This blow put the little lady down hard, and the pack went flying.

This all happened in very short order as we were still sitting in our truck, dumbfounded by what we had just seen. The bear looked at the lady lying on the ground and then looked at the pack. He darted over, scooped the pack up in his mouth, ran about seventy-five yards up a little hill, and started just tearing the hell out of it. We ran over to the lady to see if she was all right. She was doing all right, but the blow from the bear damn sure left a mark. She was more angry than hurt, and as she was rubbing her chin, she was cussing that the bear was still up on the hill, tearing all her cloths out of her pack, and just destroying it in true bear fashion.

I don't know if this little lady ever read all those horrible bear stories in *Outdoor Life* when she was a little girl, but it didn't seem she had. It was a little humbling afterward as we realized that us two grown men had sat in the truck and watched all this unfold and that the little lady was the only one not scared of a bear. We both thought of the old saying "Hell hath no fury like a woman's scorn." While scores of men have learned that lesson firsthand, it was obvious that bears just didn't care.

That afternoon the Rattlesnake Fire hauled ass. The Chiricahua Mountains are unique like many of the mountain ranges on the Coronado National Forest. They range from high desert to mixed conifer in short order. Because of the rough country, coyote tactics were the best way to work the fire.

For those not in the know, coyote tactics consist of line construction until the end of the shift. Then all the crews camp at that remote location and get up in the morning and continue throughout the day. They spend the night there again and so on until they finish. Camping wherever you end up isn't like a fun family camping trip with a tent, lawn chairs, and a cooler of beer. It can mean just eating a ration, putting on your jacket, and lying down in the dirt like a dog and gutting it out. Hence, the name *coyote tactics*.

When I was a division supervisor on the team, I preferred using coyote tactics. Often by not traveling to and from camp, you got more rest, and that was one of the key benefits of this mode of operation. If the logistics group on the team has their shit together, it can be quite a bit better, and on this fire, they were doing a good job. As we neared the end of each shift, a squad of one of the crews would bump up to a place that I chose to spend the night, and we'd cut any trees needed to get a long line from a helicopter so that they could deliver food and supplies to us.

A helicopter can suspend a sling net of supplies on a line and lower the sling of supplies down through the canopy of trees. The line has a hook at the bottom, and the pilot can release the load and drop off supplies. So too, they can remove trash or backhaul in the same manner by putting everything in a sling net and hooking the load up after the pilot lowers the long line down.

In this manner, the logistic group was keeping us well supplied. The evening supplies consisted of the normal things we needed, such as batteries, bar oil, saw gas, maps, and of course, meals and water. Meals delivered this way come to you in containers called hot cans on fires. A hot can is the size of a ten-gallon bucket, and it contains a hot meal prepared by the caterer in the fire camp. Along with dinner for that night, breakfast and sack lunches were also delivered at the same time, so in the morning you didn't need another delivery. You could just eat and get to work.

This was working out well, and each afternoon I would bump up with a squad from one of the hotshot crews and prepare a place to fly in our stuff. If there were any trees that needed to be removed, we did that, and as the helicopter delivered the supplies, we would dig everything out of the sling nets and set the hot cans in a chow line so the crews could eat as they arrived. We'd set aside the breakfast and sack lunches for the next morning. As everyone ate, they would discard their dirty paper plates in plastic bags, and we would pile up all the trash. The next morning we would place it all in the sling nets our stuff was delivered in, and one of us would wait around until the helicopters were up and running. Then they would come out and extract all our back haul.

This meant that every night we were all sleeping around all our garbage as well the next day's supply of food. While this is a great way to fight a fire, it does not follow great bear protocols, and there was a sizeable bear population in the area. Another issue that compounded the upcoming problem was that many of the local bears were used to taking advantage of campers. They knew that if they desired a change from bugs, roots, and their natural diet, they could just visit some unsuspecting camper and eat their Twinkies or soap or whatever they wanted.

On the first night, we had no problems. Everything went off like clockwork. On the second night, we were raided by one bear. And while the bear had not bothered all our breakfasts and sack lunches, he had dragged off and ripped to shreds all the plastic bags of trash. It took about an hour to locate and pick up the mess and get it into the nets for the back haul. Bears just love to tear stuff up, and if PetSmart catered to bears, they would sell plastic bags of garbage as bear toys.

On the third night, the news of the food delivery on the mountain had gotten around, and we had at least two bears, maybe more, digging around through our stuff in the middle of the night, which didn't help the crews get any quality sleep. We thought it was the same bear because he had dragged off our trash bags into the timber and tore them to shreds. On the fourth night, it got completely out of hand. Now there were several bears digging through all our stuff, and to make things worse, the bears started fighting one another for our goodies, which caused quite the disturbance in the quiet spike camp environment. Some of the guys got up and tried to chase off the bears, but it didn't accomplish anything but waking up folks who were actually sleeping through the bear fights.

When the sun came up, we discovered that not only our garbage but our breakfasts and sack lunches had been torn to shreds or dragged off into the trees. Some of the crews scattered and were able to locate some of the food that had been left. Luckily, we were able to scavenge some food items for the day, but now we decided things had to change both for our safety and hunger. The next night we put all our breakfasts and sack lunches in the helicopter nets and tied them up in a tree out of harm's way. We didn't have enough nets to tie up the garbage, so we packed them away from the place where all the crews were sleeping and piled them up. In the middle of the night, we were all awakened by a hotshot yelling that there was a bear in the back haul. One of the guys shined a light over to the pile of back haul and yelled out, "Shit! It's not a bear. It's a skunk." That got everyone up as it seemed that a skunk was worse than a bear. It's funny how things work.

Everyone has heard of Smokey Bear. He was found burned and abandon, and he eventually became the trademark for forest fire prevention. As this fire was winding down, we all got the tragic news that the old boy had cashed in his chips and gone on to the great beyond. That afternoon I got a call from one of the hotshot crews saying they had found a bear cub all alone. In true hotshot spirit, they thought that it would be a great idea to capture the little tyke and keep the Smokey story going like the sequel to *Star Wars* or something. My knee-jerk reaction was to just say hell no, but I had second thoughts as I didn't think that the bear's capture would be a simple as picking the little fella up and cuddling him. That was something that I wanted to witness.

When I was a young boy I always wanted to capture a baby bobcat and raise him to be my partner and pet. The opportunity never presented itself until I was in my early twenties. That was when I found a bobcat den with three of the little cuties in it. My childhood dream of a pet bobcat came back to me, so I went in for the capture. There is a reason some folks call these critters wildcats. They are just mean as hell, and I dare anyone to pick one of these little devils up. It took only one attempt to realize that if I did grab one, I would probably bleed to death before I made it back to my truck, so I abandoned one of my childhood dreams in an instant.

My bobcat experience coupled with my knowledge of how sharp puppy teeth and claws were made me want to witness the bear cub's capture, so I told them I was headed their way and to hold on. By the time I got there, the mama bear had come back and retrieved her cub and ran off, so I didn't get to see the attempted capture. This was probably the best outcome, but it could have made for a good anecdote for my bear stories.

Before I was ever on a fire team, I was sent to the Divide Fire, which was burning in the Gila National Forest in New Mexico. The fire was burning in the Gila Wilderness, and while I wasn't on the team, I did know some of the team members. I was assigned to be a gofer for a team division supervisor. I was friends with him and his buddy, who was also a division supervisor on the team. He was balding, and he had taken to shaving his head. Always looking for a better way of doing things, he had decided to apply a hair removal product to his head and see how that worked for him. But he had an allergic reaction that caused quite a bit of irritation and made an ugly mess on the top of his head. It was one of those things that was hard to look at. He was definitely not someone you would sit next to at dinner or trade hats with. Of course, everyone was sympathetic of his problem, and we didn't talk about his condition in front of him anyway.

I was assigned to his division, and one day as we were digging a line on a ridge that was a very narrow portion of the continental divide. The lead crew bumped a mama bear with three cubs. Mama ran all three of her little squirts up in a fir tree and hauled ass. This was a very narrow ridge, and there was no alternative way around, so the three cubs halted their progress. The initial thoughts were to just scare the hell out of the cubs and run them off so that we could continue building the fire line. This was easy enough to put into action, and the hotshot crew all started yelling and running toward the tree the three cubs had climbed up. It did scare the hell out of the cubs. They all started screaming at the top of their lungs for their mom to return, and they just climbed higher in the tree.

I had never heard a bear cub's distress cries before, and it was something that I would always remember, especially since there were three of them giving it their best shot. We started worrying that the noise from the cubs would bring back their mom with an attitude, so we backed off a little and waited, but nothing changed. Their mom had just left them in the tree. We thought that maybe if we had a helicopter fly by the tree, they get down and run off. A helicopter was ordered and flew by the tree, which did scare the cubs, but that only made them cling tighter to the tree. We thought that if the helicopter hovered above the tree, maybe that would do the trick. We called the helicopter back and asked him to hover over the tree. That did make the cubs have to really hang on because of the rotor wash and scared them worse putting additional urgency in their calls out to their mom.

All this caused quite a bit of radio chatter as better minds offered advice or wanted an update as to how our efforts were working. Everyone knew about our dilemma and our failure to get the cubs out of our way. Then the division boss's buddy on the other side of the fire called him up and told him to just take his hard hat off as that would scare the shit out of anything. By the time we all quit laughing, the cubs had disappeared from the fir tree, and we could continue with the line.

Our line going down the continental divide met up with some other guys who were coming at us from the other direction. We were pretty much done, and so we were getting ready to walk out of the wilderness. The summer monsoon season was starting, and that night as we sat out there in the middle of nowhere, we watched a huge thunderstorm approaching from the distance. It eventually came over us and just pounded us with rain and lightning. As mentioned, I was once struck by lightning, so I can get very nervous in a storm. Consequently, this was a long night for me as lightning popped everywhere, and we were on the highest ridge around. It was a long night, but I did entertain everyone as I flinched at every flash.

The next day we were all walking out of the wilderness, and it was quite a hike. The weather forecast for that day was heavy thunderstorms, and after the night filled with lightning, I thought I should get an early start to at least get off this ridge before a storm moved in. The early start didn't happen as the helicopter that we were waiting for to hook up our back haul was late. As soon as we had taken care of that, one other guy and I started heading out, which consisted of following the line back down the continental divide. The clouds were building fast and right on top of us, so we walked faster.

We had only traveled a few miles when a rumbling started coming out of the clouds above us. There was no lightning hitting the ground yet, but you could hear rumbling up in the dark clouds. We knew we were in for it, and we were going as fast as we could when out of the blue, a hailstone hit my hard hat, which was about a half inch thick. Then the cloud just turned loose and pelted us with hail. There was the head of a draw off on the Pacific side of our ridge that was full of Douglas fir regeneration, so we ran down to it, just getting pelted with hail.

We were protected by the tight canopy under the smallest trees we could find, and we grabbed our rain stuff from our line packs. I always carried two large trash bags. They were light and didn't take up a lot of room in your pack, and they worked well as rain gear. I put my line pack in one bag, poked a head hole in the other, put it on, and hunkered down with the other guy. We had just got tucked in and were freaking out due to the intensity of the storm when we heard the cries of a bear cub right next to us. These were soon joined by some of their fellow cubs. We thought we were in good shape, but now we wondered if we should stick it out or move. I was bundled up in a garbage bag, and I knew bears just loved tearing the hell out of garbage bags.

We decided to stick it out as we were more scared of the storm than of the bears' cries. We knew that their mom was good at ignoring them from our previous contact. They were probably just as scared of the storm as I was, and I would have been crying too if that other guy hadn't been with me. I wouldn't have known what the cubs crying sounded like if we hadn't heard them a few days before.

A serious bear story happened on the Freeze 2 Fire, which occurred on the San Carlos Apache Reservation in Arizona. Fire camp was set up at a place called Point of Pines. One evening in the middle of the night, a couple camping at a nearby lake were the subjects of a black bear attack. A bear grabbed a lady out of her lawn chair and mauled her horribly. This location is about ninety miles from the nearest community, so it is pretty isolated. The bear seriously hurt this lady, and she suffered life-threatening injuries from the mauling. Her husband loaded her up and headed out to try to get her to a hospital.

About two miles from the lake, they saw the lights of our fire camp, which they rightly pulled into.

Every fire has a medical unit there to provide first aid to the fire personnel. When the couple pulled into camp, they woke up some folks who ran and got the medical people to treat the lady. They provided lifesaving first aid, got her in a helicopter, and flew her to a hospital in Tucson. The general consensus was that the lady may have died in transit if they hadn't seen the lights of our fire camp. We were all very proud that they were there and did such a great job of treating this lady's injuries.

The tribal game and fish department was helping us with security on the fire, and they were informed immediately about the issue. Two officers went to the lake to try to find the bear that morning. As they were searching in the darkness, one of the officers saw the bear sneaking up behind his partner and shot it. That added to the weirdness of this entire event. We were informed that the lady would be all right, but she required multiple surgeries and time to heal up.

The summer prior to my employment with the forest service, I was employed by one of the ranches up on the rim. This was a great place to work, and during the summer I stayed up on the mountain. They had just constructed a new bunkhouse that was quite nice. The bunkhouse had a large living room that we would all gather and visit in after dinner. One evening we were all discussing an article in a *Western Horseman* magazine. The article was about California in the old days when it was still a part of Mexico.

This article was about the *vaqueros* roping grizzly bears. The ropes that the vaqueros used were *riatas*. Unlike ropes currently used by American cowboys that are made of nylon or hemp, a riata is made from braided rawhide. A riata is usually quite a bit longer than a modern rope and not as strong. As we all visited in the bunkhouse, everyone thought it was crazy to rope a grizzly. That's saying something in a group of cowboys who are half rope crazy at best. By this I mean that most wouldn't pass up the chance to rope anything. In fact, many of the wild animals that shared the ranch had been roped in the past. The longtime foreman of this ranch had actually roped several mule deer bucks and just about everything else.

In one of the small holding pastures close to the ranch headquarters, a cow had been held up because she was sick, and she was placed in the small pasture so we could easily find her and doctor her back to health. After our bear-roping research, one of the cowboys found her the next day dead under a mature ponderosa pine that had been struck by lightning. A bear had found the dead cow and was now actively eating her. The cowboy hurried back to the ranch to share the news because while bears were always around, they were seldom seen.

This was news at the ranch, and we all stopped whatever we were doing and headed down to see if the bear was still there. The cowboy that had found the bear was still on horseback, and while most of us just jumped into a truck and drove over there, he headed back on horseback. As we all approached, we saw that the bear was still there, and as we all invaded his space, he ran up into the pine tree and stood on one of the lower branches, not real happy that we had disturbed his breakfast.

This was not a giant bear, and we all felt that it was a yearling or a two-year-old at most. He just maintained his perch on one of the lower limbs. One of the observing cowboys dared the cowboy that was on horseback to rope the bear. He immediately acted upon the dare. As I alluded to earlier, most cowboys are aching to rope anything. The mounted cowboy rode up to the tree and quickly and skillfully dropped a loop around the bear's neck, and took his dallies. If the bear was slightly freaked out before, it went completely nuts as it was roped. It swatted at the rope and fell off the other side of the limb, and the bear hung just like a horse thief in an old western movie. To all us onlookers, it was a shock to see the bear hanging by its neck, squirming around like a horse thief would have in the past.

We immediately started yelling at the man to cut the rope, to let it go, or to not kill it. We all showed concern for the hanging bear. The cowboy immediately let go of his dallies and freed the bear, and the animal hit the ground. In a flash, he jumped back up on the tree and hauled ass, climbing even higher, dragging the rope behind him. We were all grateful the bear was all right, and we were all pretty well amused by the whole ordeal; however, then we started worrying that the rope was still around the bears neck and had gotten all tangled in the limbs of the tree as he ran up the tree to make his escape. We thought that he could still easily hang himself again as the rope was tangled on several limbs and the loop was still firmly anchored around his neck. We all felt that we needed to remove the rope. The cowboy wanted his rope back too, but this was the least of everyone else's worries.

One of the cowboys was a huge man of Swedish blood, and he was always up for any challenge. He decided that getting the rope back was no problem. He could just climb into the tree with a pigging string and tie the bear's feet with it and remove the rope. This guy was easily bigger than the bear and arguably as strong. As I said, he was a big guy. A pigging string is a short piece of rope that is used to tie the feet of anything that needs to be roped. If you have seen a calf-roping, the pigging string is used to tie the calf's feet after it's caught. While no one else thought they could accomplish this task, no one objected to this guy's willingness to attempt it.

With a pigging string tucked into his belt, the guy climbed into the tree with the bear. The bear didn't really seem to like that as it tried to get away, and in so doing, it got the rope tangled in a bunch of limbs, making the deal worse. The bear had gotten the rope so tangled that it was literally at the end of his rope again; however, this time it was not hanging by its neck. It could not move any farther away from the tree-climbing cowboy, who was approaching with his pigging string. The cowboy climbed into the tree until he was just on the opposite side of the tree from the bear. The bear was scared, the cowboy determined, and the onlookers stared in disbelief.

With bear and the cowboy sitting on limbs on their respective sides of the tree, the cowboy decided it was time to tie up the bear. That's when the bear got mean and started growling and snapping his teeth at the cowboy. The cowboy was only a few feet away from the bear, and the crowd stared in shock. He decided that he may not have thought out his idea, and so he gave up and came back down, much to the approval of all us spectators.

We then decided that we could shoot the rope near the bear's neck and break it. Then the bear could make its escape for good and do whatever bears did. A few folks drove back to the ranch to get some guns and shells and returned to the tree to solve the problem. The tree the bear was in was within sight of the main road, and the group of folks standing around the tree drew the attention of anyone driving by. My mom and dad just happened along and came over to see what the deal was. Upon seeing the scene, my mom said that they had their movie camera with them and that they wanted to take a movie of the bear when we released it. This camera was one of those old Kodak 8 mm deals, the first movie cameras that families had in those days. With guns galore and the movie camera rolling, the shooting started.

The bear was quite freaked out when the shooting started, and it was slow to understand that we weren't trying to shoot it but rather shooting at the rope in order to free him. It managed to get even more tangled up trying to get away from all the shooting. Finally, after the first fifty or so shots, it calmed down, or maybe it was so tangled it couldn't move anymore. That provided all us deadeye shooters with a good shot at the rope that didn't have the bear in the line of fire. The rope was a nylon rope, and eventually enough of us hit it that it showed a fraying spot, one that we all aimed at. This went on for a few hours, the movie camera ran out of film, and we ran out of shells.

A runner was sent back to the ranch to go through all the glove boxes in the ranch trucks, dresser drawers, and wherever a .22 shell may be as we had almost shot though the rope, but because it was a nylon rope, the last little bit was proving difficult. The bear had long since quit moving, growling, snapping his teeth, or in any way objecting to our shots. The runner came back, and we shot all the remaining shells at the rope, which left it frayed but not broken. We were done and felt we had done all we could do. One of the smarter guys among of us said that we should just leave it alone and see if it could get away if we all left. With all our options spent, we headed back to the ranch, leaving the bear in the tree.

We did go back just before dark. To our amazement, the bear was gone, and so was the rope. It had managed to get down and leave on its own. We all hoped it managed to free itself of the rope, and we kidded with the bear roper quite a bit after the dust settled. I'm sure that bear thinks that cowboys are the absolute worse shots in the world.

In between Yellowstone National Park and Teton National Park, there's an area called the John D. Rockefeller Jr. Memorial Parkway. This portion of Wyoming is one of our nation's natural wonders and such a beautiful place. I was sent there to a fire as a division supervisor many years ago. Prior to heading out for our first shift, we all attended the briefing for the day shift, and we were informed of the potential for running into bears. While the number of grizzly bears was low, the many black bears and the possibility of confrontations with grizzlies were not out of the picture. Bear safety is a huge concern on fires, and we discussed it then for safety reasons.

After the briefing I headed out to the fire to check out the area that I had been assigned to. We had a couple of hand crews, and we were supposed to start lining the northern portions of the fire. There were no roads in the area, so we would cut the line away from our vehicles and head deep into the surrounding forest. I got with one of the crew bosses and a field observer who had been assigned to my division. We were scouting the best location for the fire line and flagging it so the crews could start cutting the hand line.

As we continued with this process, we found ourselves quite a distance from the crews cutting the line behind us. We ran into a large pond in a meadow that was a result of a huge beaver dam that had been constructed across a small creek. The opening was pretty large. It either had standing water or was very boggy. We thought that it could be a safety zone for our division as there was little other breaks in the dense timber on our flagged line. We all took a break and explored the beaver's dam, and then we were ready to continue with our line location. We grouped up again and headed upstream to find the quickest way around the beaver pond to continue with our line. As we were walking around the end of the pond in knee-deep grass, I noticed that a baby moose was lying there curled up in the deep grass. Wow, he was a cute little guy. I called the other two guys over so that they could check it out. The three of us were standing there, looking at this cute little moose calf when his mom noticed us and came trotting out of the woods near us.

We don't have any moose in Arizona, and I have never really been around any. We do have deer and elk, and if you find one of their babies curled up in the grass, they really don't care if you look them over. This is not to say that they like it. The mother's instinct is still there, but looking isn't a foolish or unsafe thing to do. Moose mothers have a completely different take on the safety of their young. To my eyes, moose are a weird-looking animal. Their legs look too long for their body, their hind quarters seem way too small for an animal their size, and their round snout and big ears make them look rather stupid.

The three of us were standing there, watching the approaching moose mom. We were standing flat-footed when we realized that she wasn't just running over to her baby but running at us and very pissed.

Like horses, moose pin their ears when they are mad. As this mama moose approached us, two things were very apparent. She had her ears pinned back against her neck in anger, and she was absolutely huge. I stand six feet six inches, and her shoulder was quite a ways over my head. Our knee-jerk reaction was to run, and run we did. We all took off in different directions as fast as we could. The moose singled out the field observer and started chasing him. I ran over to a nearby tree, and just as I thought I was safe, the mama moose stopped in her tracks and wheeled around and stared at me. I guess she thought I was closer to her baby than the field observer was, so she turned around and ran toward me, again with her ears pinned to her neck. I had no choice but to scramble up into the tree I was standing by. As a result, I was now in the tree with the moose standing her ground below me.

She must have known she had the upper hand because she just stayed there and looked up at me. She must have been amused that she had treed a firefighter. After making successful escapes, my two partners got back together and watched me in my tree from a distance, a mad mama moose standing guard. I was out of her reach, and they were quite amused by my dilemma. I think they were just relieved that it wasn't them in the tree, and they were not the least bit grateful that by letting the moose tree me, I had allowed them to make their escapes. This moose did not want to leave and had been there for a long time when one of the guys called me on my radio and suggested that I turn the volume all the way up and then turn the squelch knob all the way over. The static noise on my radio might scare her away.

As I was hanging on up in my tree, this didn't sound like such a bad idea. While this moose didn't seem like the kind to be afraid of anything, it was worth a try. I turned the volume knob all the way up and then cranked the squelch knob all the way over to create that horrible noise. This really pissed off the moose. I don't know why, but she got her second wind and stood up on her back legs with her ears pinned and started pawing at my tree. While I had thought I was high enough up in the tree, I didn't realize how far up the moose could actually reach, and I had to scramble up higher. She kept pawing at me until I gained some height, and then I turned down my radio. As I turned down the noise from my radio, I could hear the two guys laughing their ass off from their safe distance.

Eventually, she got tired of not being able to stomp me and listening to the sound of the chainsaws from the crews working on the fire line. She soon left the tree and gathered up her calf and wander into the dense timber. When she left, she did cast one last glance at me to ensure that I was still scared and still in my tree. I climbed down and went over to the two guys who had been watching, and then I had to listen to them laugh it up. I was all scratched up from my rapid ascent into a fir tree, and I really didn't see the humor in the situation; however, I was glad to be safe.

The next day at the morning briefing, we were again instructed on the ins and outs of bear safety. Then the safety officer asked if anyone had any questions. I raised my hand and said that maybe we should discuss moose safety. He said with great concern, "Oh, yeah. Watch out for moose. They will kill ya."

The fire team was assigned to the Toadlena Fire, which was burning in the Chuska Mountains in northeastern Arizona upon the Navajo Reservation. A few things happened on this fire that merit discussion. One afternoon my operations buddy and I were taking a recon flight in a helicopter to see how the fire had progressed and to check things out in general. As we circled the fire, we would talk to the different division supervisors to see how things were going. The division which had the east side of the fire wanted us to look at something, but we were having a hard time seeing what he wanted from the air. He told us that he would walk out on a cliff that had some bare rock and that we should be able to locate him then.

While he walked out to the cliff we were hovering above in the helicopter, the pilot said that he saw a mountain lion. Mountain lions are a very reclusive animal, and it is very uncommon to see one. At first, neither of us saw it, so the pilot asked if we wanted him to swing around to show us the lion. Of course, we were all in and said, "Sure, let's see if we can locate it again." We eventually saw the lion. We were at a pretty low elevation, and as the lion ran up the side of the mountain, we were right on it. As we chased the lion up the side of the mountain, the division supervisor came out on the bare rock cliff. The lion dashed up that same cliff and ran about twenty feet from the division supervisor. It scared the hell out of him later because he didn't know that we had seen it and that we were following it up the side of the mountain. He thought it was after him. We had a good laugh at his expense.

When the fire was under control, we all headed into Gallup, New Mexico, for the closeout meeting with the tribe. Our planning section chief on the team was running late, and as he headed into Gallup, it got dark. As he was headed down the highway, he ran over a sheep that was in the road. When he got to the meeting, he informed us that he had hit a sheep on the way to Gallup. We immediately started giving him hell for his hit-and-run accident. We tried with some success to make him feel as guilty as possible for his ruthless crime. We brought up the incident at all possible times to raze him and hopefully protect any sheep that grazed in the area.

Several years later after many sheep jokes and sheep presents, we were assigned to a fire in Montana. One of the locals we had the pleasure of meeting had a daughter who was raising a lamb for a 4-H project. We explained about the ruthless slaughter of a sheep several years ago when the planning section chief did the hit and run. We asked if they could bring the sheep over to a planning meeting to play another prank on our section chief. They thought this would be a grand idea, so that evening during the planning meeting, they turned the lamb loose in the yurt where that meeting was being held. The lamb wondered up to the front of the meeting, looked up at our plans chief, squatted, and peed all over the place. It was quite a good prank. A few days later, this 4-H lamb was killed by a grizzly bear just about four hundred yards from where we were all sleeping.

CHAPTER 11
RUBBER BOOTERS

When I started my career fighting wildfires, there was little to no municipal fire departments involved in the fray—unless, of course, you were on a fire in Southern California, where it was common to see municipal fire departments fighting wildfires. If you saw a red truck on a fire around here, it was broken down, stolen, or lost. However, this has changed tremendously. City, county, and state resources are common on the fireground today, and they're firmly involved in all aspects of wildfire suppression. I have to give all these departments some kudos as they have pretty much started training their employees in wildland fire suppression and the incident management system on a nationwide scale, while the federal agencies remain as stupid as we ever were in structural fire suppression. In a charming way, I refer to these fire department folks as "rubber booters" because they wear those whenever you see them all dressed up in their fire gear. At least in the movies they do.

Another thing that has changed in the course of my career is the threat of structure loss in a wildfire. During my first years, if a structure was threatened, it was usually a ranger station, ranch house, or some other isolated structure. While there are always exceptions, this was generally the rule. Now it is uncommon to be on a fire that doesn't threaten multiple structures. This threat is one of the reasons communities have become active in wildfire suppression. Multiple fires have burned hundreds of homes, and thankfully, the teams now enlist structural firefighters in their ranks.

Another bonus is rubber booters have medical credentials. This is a major part of all their normal jobs as they respond to medical calls frequently. My team had several of these guys on staff, which was great for the troops. They provided medical aid on the host of issues ranging from blisters to heart attacks, and they also managed the transport of any victims as needed. I cannot think of any incident management team that doesn't currently employ many of these people on the teams, and the teams are stronger for having them.

But rubber booters also seem to have an unquenchable need to screw around with those who don't have that title. The bulk of downtime in fire stations must be spent researching practical jokes and practicing them on one another. They all seem so well informed of such things. Being cast into the world of wildland firefighters provides a virgin pool of victims who haven't evolved with the constant threat of firehouse pranks. Even old traditional pranks were unknown in the wildland ranks, providing huge opportunities. Our medical unit delighted in playing little reindeer games in fire camp and keeping up their unwritten obligation as rubber booters to screw around with as many folks as possible.

For example, they would sneak around at the morning and evening briefings and squirt foot powder on everyone's butt while they were paying attention. I know it is a little deal, and they never denied it. They just kept doing it, and we treated it like it was just a minor infraction. At first, we raised a little hell, but then we kind of got used to it and just let them have their fun. This didn't go over well with the medical guys. As we ignored them, they escalated their butt-powdering. They started targeting some more influential people like district rangers and forest supervisors. One forest supervisor who was being a pain in the team's ass took the stage one morning to give us all a pep talk, and we all shit as she turned around to walk off the stage and we saw that she had been powdered. They were cautioned after this incident; however, that warning fell on deaf ears, and the powdering continued. I never saw them get a congressman or governor, but those people are harder to sneak up on and usually have some folks watching their backs.

In the recent past, I worked on one fire near a small Arizona town that prided itself on being a great place for rednecks. The medical unit guys informed us that they had a great new sunblock product, and they passed it around to us all to give it a try. So we all lathered up with the stuff. Shortly after most of those present had applied the new sunblock salve, I walked outside into the full sunlight. To my horror, I had colored sparkles all over me. The sunblock had sparkles in it, and we were all sparkled up like little girls. It was great fun at the medical unit, but dealing with the locals when you have sparkles all over your exposed skin is quite humbling. One of the victims was accosted by some of the locals while he was getting gas at a local gas station. They thought he was a sissy and an easy target. They accused him of being from Hollywood and made fun of his sparkles. The sparkles really glued onto your skin and didn't just wash off. Several months later if the sun hit me just right, I would pick up one that had been stuck there and remember the medical guys' good humor.

They always told me that I looked dehydrated, and they wanted me to stop in for a quick IV to pick me up. I always felt that if I went in, there was no telling what they would do. I sure as hell wasn't into the idea of an IV, and I always thought they would give me an IV filled with estrogen just for the hell of it.

One thing about playing tricks on people is it plants the seed for revenge. Those who know that others are seeking revenge are always waiting for the other shoe to drop. The medical guys knew not to let their guard down, but we were not in a hurry to get even. Watching their paranoia was some justice, but not enough.

An opportunity for revenge came a few years later as the team was assigned to a fire in Montana. The assignment was on the Custer National Forest and was a complex of two fires deep within the Absaroka-Bear Tooth Wilderness.

The medical unit leader usually worked as a law enforcement

agent, and because of this, he needed to return home to serve a warrant and make an arrest. Or maybe it was his turn to buy doughnuts. Who knows? But he was ordered home either way. We drove him to Billings, Montana, to catch a flight home, and he was scheduled to return in two or three days. This left all his staff running the medical unit in his absence.

This gave those of us seeking revenge a couple days to plot out a scheme to even the score. Very discreetly, we found out when his return flight was scheduled to get into Billings. We also found out that one of his guys was going to the airport to pick him up and bring him back to fire camp. We also determined that at one of the trailheads into the wilderness had absolutely no cell service. One of the ladies was all too willing to be an accomplice.

Plans were laid out with quite a cast of characters. Here's how it went down. I ordered a mandatory meeting with the entire medical staff, and because of the issues and fire activity, I needed to have the meeting at the secluded trailhead. We intended to get everyone from the medical unit out of cell phone coverage, and because their boss was absent, they reluctantly agreed to the meeting. They did have one issue. Someone was supposed to pick up their leader at the airport. I stressed the importance of the meeting and said that I would make arrangements with someone else to pick him up in Billings. I told them that I knew of a lady who was going to be in Billings anyway and that she had agreed to pick him up. Problem solved.

There were two basic ways to get from Billings to fire camp. You could go through Red Lodge, Montana, or take Interstate 90 west and get off at Columbus, Montana, and then head south through Absarokee. The westerly route along the interstate had a rest area located between Billings and Columbus worked well into our plan. At any rate, that was the route we decided on. We had two guys hiding in the vegetation with a video camera to record the impending sting at the rest area.

As the medical unit leader landed in Billings, the lady was waiting at the gate to pick him up. His entire staff was sequestered well out of cell phone contact, attending a trumped-up meeting to discuss medivac issues in the wilderness, and two guys were getting the video camera working and waiting at the rest area to record the deal for everyone's enjoyment.

The lady saw him coming and called the predetermined number and let it ring once to signal the video crew at the rest area that she had the victim in hand. There was a twenty-five-minute delay to ensure they were headed out of town and on the interstate headed toward the rest area. At that time she received a call on her cell that she said was her husband, but in fact, it was the rest area crew. The conversation was quite heated as she faked an argument with her husband, and this went on for several minutes with just the two of them in the car driving down the interstate, so he heard everything. The medical unit leader felt uncomfortable in the middle of the mess, but all he could do was sit there and listen.

When they approached the rest area, she pulled into it. She asked if she could have some privacy, which he gladly gave her as he had heard enough of the argument, so he got out of her vehicle. The video rolling, she got out of her car. Seemingly in deep distress, she said that her cell phone had died and that they were cut off before she could resolve the issue, and she pleaded with him to use his cell phone so that she could quickly call him back to let him know she didn't just hang up on him. Being a nice guy, he said she could, and he gave her his cell phone. She got back into the car, and he walked up toward the bathroom to give her some privacy and just get away from it all.

He was just hanging around and staying away from her car, giving her some space when the plot unfolded and she just drove off, leaving him without a ride, a cell phone, any friends, or anything at a rest area in the middle of Big Sky Country. The video caught him staring down the road, watching her drive off in utter disbelieve. The video was too far away to pick up any audio, which was probably a good thing, but one could tell that the reality of his situation was sinking in now.

He quickly understood the finality of the issue, but he was quick to resolve it. He found a pay phone there, so he walked over to it and placed a call to some of his medical unit collaborators, hoping they could come and rescue him. However, this proved futile as none of them answered their phones. We love it when a plan comes together.

The two guys taking the video were having the time of their lives documenting the events, and they were just about to spring the joke and go get him and give him a ride back to camp when the plot thickened. He walked up to a semitruck driver, produced his badge, declared himself as a federal agent, and demanded a ride. Everything is funny till someone gets their eye put out. The truck driver consented, and he jumped in the truck and headed west. The joke was over. The two video operators followed the truck to Columbus and pulled up as he was dropping off the pissed-off target of the prank. He wanted to kill the lady, and while we all felt we had gotten even, now we were forced to maintain vigilance for fear of reprisal.

Another experience happened on the Rodeo-Chediski Fire in Northern Arizona. The team had a rubber booter on as the structure protection specialist, and another served as a division supervisor. This fire was a huge and fast-moving one for the first couple of days, and it had burned down several homes. On the second day of the fire, the structure protection specialist and the division supervisor asked if they could get a recon flight in a helicopter to help make sense of things. The structure loss was a huge issue for the team, and of course, they were granted a flight. We'd try anything that would help them understand the big picture.

The flight was scheduled early the next day as that time would provide the best view of the fire before it started running again. One of the guys sat in the front seat next to the pilot since that was the best view, and the other sat in the back seat with me. We took off and started a recon flight over the fire. Helicopters generally don't experience the same rough air issues that a fixed wing aircraft does. Most flights are very smooth, and little turbulence is felt. This was one such flight—no bumps, no downdrafts, just a nice flight in the cool and calm air of the morning.

Our peaceful flight was interrupted when the guy in the front seat asked the pilot if he had a barf bag. The pilot said hell no. He told the guy that if he was going to throw up, he'd better do it in one of his flight gloves or his flight helmet but not in the aircraft. The other guy in the back with me started looking through a pocket on the back of the front seat and actually found a barf bag, and then he passed up to his buddy in the front seat.

The guy in the front seat fought off the air sickness as long as he could, but eventually, he lost it and started upchucking in the little barf bag. It didn't take long for the smell of the barf to spread throughout the helicopter. It was then that I noticed the other guy in the back with me starting to sweat. This was not good. It was just one of those things. The smell of barf could make some folks throw up too. It doesn't really bother me, probably since both my kids took turns barfing on me in their youth, making me more or less used to the smell.

In true fireman fashion, I started teasing him and laughing at him, telling him that he was next. Some things you just have to do. The guy in the back with me was a redhead, so he had a rather light complexion; however, his shoulders were wider than an ax handle, and he had the body of a middle linebacker along with a Fu Manchu mustache. The flight helmet he had on looked a few sizes too small, so his face was pushed out to some degree.

Well, he quit talking, and he started sweating even more. Beads of sweat were springing up all over his chubby face. His face started getting redder and redder as he started looking for another barf bag. He was successful in finding another one and held it at the ready. All the while, I was as amused as he was sinking like a rock. I'm sure if he didn't feel so bad, he would have liked to just open the door and throw my smart ass out of the helicopter, but he was fighting back barfing. If you have ever been airsick or seasick, you know that it's a losing battle, one which he soon lost.

He skillfully moved the barf bag into the proper positon and started barfing. He was holding the little white barf bag over his mouth and really letting go. As he barfed, tears started running from his eyes and down his chubby red cheeks. Beads of sweat ran off his forehead, and barf was shooting through his Fu Manchu mustache and running down his flight gloves. All the while I was laughing like a madman. It was one of the most pathetic and humorous things I had ever witnessed. While they did provide a lot of expertise to the fire team, they were not necessarily good aviators.

A rubber booter probably saved my life on the Cerro Grande Fire. The Cerro Grande Fire impacted Los Alamos, New Mexico, and the Los Alamos National Lab. While the impacts to the community of Los Alamos were tragic, the fire's impacts on the national lab were also complex. Security was paramount here. I don't want to expound on the intricacies of security within the lab, but it is still one of the most secure areas in our nation.

A security force wearing all black was tasked with the security of the area. They acted independently of the local law enforcement officers, and rumors were that they had the authority to shoot to kill if a security issue deemed that necessary. We knew from their mere appearance that they weren't just common law enforcement dudes. They looked like agents straight out of some spy movie. Obviously, these weren't people you wanted to screw around with.

While security on the lab was a huge deal, there were a few sites within the lab where security was raised to a much higher level. We had to leave a couple of these sites alone at all costs, and just about every security measure known man was put in place to protect the security of these sites.

One afternoon I was driving around with the deputy fire chief of Los Alamos when one of the division supervisors called me on the radio and asked if he could get a helicopter flight to help him make sense of the fire's progress. This was a common request, and of course, I agreed to the flight and contacted the helibase to schedule it.

I then called the division supervisor up and said that we had a helicopter headed his way and asked him where he wanted to be picked up. He informed me that he was in what he thought was a bank's parking lot and that it would serve as a great place for the helicopter to land and pick him up. He then asked if I wanted to go along on the flight, and I decided that I would accompany him. The helicopter left the helibase en route to pick us up, and the deputy fire chief and I headed to that area to hook up with the division supervisor. We located the division guy waiting in a parking lot, and just as we arrived, so did the helicopter.

As I said, this appeared to be a parking lot, and as the helicopter was coming in for a landing, we turned our attention toward it. I then turned around and saw this black hummer with three of these men in black approaching, all of them holding rifles at the ready. One stood in the hummer, manning the machine gun mounted on the roof. In a building behind them, they started rushing this guy in a suit into a black limousine, more men in black shielding him. They then rushed the limousine off with an escort of black hummers. The hummer headed our way, and two of these guys jumped out before it even stopped and ran up to us and ordered us to the ground. Of course, we hit the dirt, lying facedown in the parking lot. The two guys held us and the helicopter at gunpoint, and the machine gunner was trained on our position.

I wondered if these guys thought we were going to rob the bank, and I figured that it was just a mistake on their part. The deputy fire chief started yelling at them to not shoot us, that we were just firefighters. He was from Los Alamos, and he realized what we just did. The tone of his voice made us aware that this was a serious deal. But they did not flinch, they kept their aim on us and the helicopter locked and loaded. I was beginning to realize that we had done something we shouldn't have without knowing. The fire chief continued trying to tell these guys that we were just firefighters and not to shoot. We were just lying there on the asphalt, hoping that they listened to him. At last, they were given the order to hold on the radio, and they at least quit aiming their weapons at us and let us stand up.

The deputy fire chief finally had their ear, and he explained that we had just landed the helicopter to take a recon flight and hadn't known where we were landing. The security force made no expression. They stood at the ready until they were told to stand down, and they told us to just get in the helicopter and leave and not to return to this area. When we took off in the helicopter, we were relieved that we weren't dead. We started discussing our near miss with some relief and humor when the pilot, which had flown on fires for years, voiced his opinion. He informed both of us that if we ever asked him to land in an unsecure area again, he would kick our asses. His resolve in this communication left no wiggle room and showed his anger at our stupidity.

In discussions after the event, we found out that where we had landed the helicopter was one of the most secure places in the area. The guy who was whisked away was the secretary of energy, who happened to be at the facility at the time of the landing. There was usually a security net over the entire area to prevent any assault from above, but it was down for repairs. The landing of the helicopter had triggered the satellite security system, which constantly monitored air traffic in the area.

The only good thing about this whole deal was that I happened to be riding around with one of the top rubber booters from the area. We are still grateful to him.

CHAPTER 12
DEBRIEFING

The team debriefing takes on a much happier note and is usually accomplished after the official closeout. After the closeout and prior to heading home, the team will generally hole up at a motel and have a drink or two. I have gone on fires with many different teams, and this tradition is a common one. This is not to say that everyone gets sloshed, but it's always possible that some will. It is a good way to deal with the stress, and hell, it's just plain fun too. This is your last chance to get even with tricksters and just generally hash out all the stuff that happened on an assignment. This is also the last chance to spend time with all your teammates before your next assignment.

I'm sure that there are some that consider this kind of activity a sin, and no doubt, some feel it's breaking the rules. I reviewed a paper written by an up-and-coming human resource specialist who was appalled by this activity. He reported that he observed a firefighter doing a favor for another firefighter and the first saying, "Thanks. I'll buy you a beer after the fire." He went on to say that he was pretty sure that the team he was with was planning a party for after the assignment and that a hat was being passed around to collect money to buy alcohol. He went on for several pages, bringing these indiscretions to light, spilling the beans to anyone who was bored enough to read through his essay. This guy would have had a coronary arrest if he had attended some of our debriefings.

I don't mean to imply this other kind of closeout is a brawl or a bunch of offensive drunks getting together. We don't go out and trash motels like some acid rock band. For the most part, we are a mature crowd, just enjoying one another's company, and we make strong efforts to take care of our own. We always have a designated driver if we go anywhere, and we generally obey the laws wherever we are.

We had been on the Santiago Fire in Southern California, which was on the Cleveland National Forest, and multiple other jurisdictions. One of the major players on this fire was the Orange County Fire Authority. They had made a deal with a local restaurant to provide meals for the team as a way of showing thanks for our efforts on the fire.

After the official closeout, we checked into a room at the hotel and had a few beers prior to the scheduled dinner. Several of the ops guys got into a vehicle and drove over to the restaurant together. I usually have a cowboy hat on, and this evening was no different. As our group was entering the place, there was a lady sitting outside on a bench. While she was not a young thing, she was probably around our age and not a bad looker either. When I approached the door, she said, "Hello, cowboy. I think I really like you," and then she gave me a wink.

I then turned to my ops buddy and said, "It's the hat. Drives the ladies crazy."

He then said, "What makes you think that's a lady? I think it's a dude."

Of course, all the guys in our group heard the lady make a pass at me, and they also heard my buddy's comments. Boy, that was a funny deal to them. Like getting bucked off a horse, it provides quite a bit of entertainment—that is, unless you're the one getting bucked off. I became the laughingstock of the party. Then one of the guys noticed the lady had taken a seat at the bar. There was a little gap between the mirror at the bar and the room that was reserved for us. All the guys were lined up, peeping through that gap, looking at the lady in an attempt to identify gender. The unanimous decision was that it was a guy dressed up like a woman. It was something that few of us had any knowledge of or interest in—unless, of course, you needed someone to make fun of.

We had been on a few fires on the Lewis and Clark National Forest, and after the closeout, we headed to Helena, Montana, prior to heading home the next morning. We had all arrived and secured rooms by midafternoon, and we decided to head down to a brewpub and have a beer and eat lunch. This was a nice place in downtown Helena, and it was a beautiful day, so we sat outside, had lunch, and watched all the people do their thing.

Across the street our attention was directed at a cute lady who was walking around with a golden retriever. She was quite attractive, and she looked like an earthy or hippie kind of gal. Her dog was very well behaved like most of its breed, and it wore a red bandana for a collar. As we were watching, a young guy approached the lady and started a conversation. Eventually, they ended up crossing the street and joining our group at the brewpub. We sat close enough to hear the conversation between the two, and they kept us quite amused as the guy kept buying the gal beers and petting her dog. His intention was obviously amorous, and after a few beers, his flirting was more like pleading for her affection. This went on for quite a while and got more and more pronounced the more they drank.

After a while, we decided to leave, and so we left the guy, the gal, and the dog at the brewpub. Later that evening one of the team folks decided we could gather in his room and have a get-together. As folks started showing up, we were several people short, and someone knew that the rest of us were at a bar about a block away from the hotel. I said I would walk over there and let them know that the bulk of the team was headed to the room and tell them to head over as they wanted.

I walked over to the bar, and when I got there, I noticed that the golden retriever was tied up out front of the place. When I went in, I saw the two youngsters seated at the bar. The guy was still in hot pursuit of the gal, and while showing quite a bit of stamina, the gal's head was bobbing back and forth. The other team members were there, and I informed them that we were up at one of the rooms and that they could head over when they got tired of the bar. I visited them for a while and then left with a few of their party to walk back over to the hotel.

As we left the bar right outside the door, the young gal was on her hands and knees, puking on the sidewalk. Her suitor was still not giving up and was kneeling down beside her with his arm around her back, telling her that she would be all right. He still had hopes for the best. Her dog was standing beside her, lapping up the puke. Another date night was foiled, and I found another reason to not let dogs lick me on the face.

The team was kegged up in Ashville, North Carolina, after an assignment to a fire that had burned across the state line of North Carolina and Tennessee. It burned on the Pisgah and Cherokee National Forests. With the official closeout over and a Holiday Inn that offered a bar with a band, the folks gathered at the hotel. It was Thanksgiving weekend, and we were told that the forest service wanted to hold us through the weekend just in case another fire started. The prospect of another fire was dashed as it started raining hard, and the forecast called for additional moisture.

We were doing the regular thing and having a few beers together with the team and socializing. We were told that keeping us for another fire was futile; however, with the holiday, flights would be hard to book, so we stayed there the next day and started home the day after that.

An employee from one of the ranger districts knew that we planned to get together at the Holiday Inn, and he asked if we minded if he joined us. Of course, we didn't mind, and he showed up for our little shindig. After he had been there for a while, he told me he had some really good whiskey in his truck out in the parking lot. He asked if I wanted to go out there and try some. I didn't need my arm twisted too much before we went out to the parking lot.

When we got to his truck, he opened the door and produced a mason jar of whiskey. The fact that the whiskey was in a mason jar was a dead giveaway that it was moonshine. He confirmed my deductions and said that a friend of his had an old family recipe that produced some of the finest shine around. I had to agree with him as I had been introduced to shine earlier on some fires in Kentucky. I had purchased a quart just because it was offered by one of the locals we were dealing with there. It did prove to be a great purchase as the team kegged up after those fires in Clinton, Tennessee, and much to our dismay as we checked into the hotel, we discovered that Clinton was in a dry county. The quart that I had bought provided all the cheer that those who wanted to partake needed.

It was—and still is—the finest moonshine that I have ever experienced. His friend's family recipe was a good one, and he told me it had been around for decades. Making whiskey was one of the things that this area was famous for since people had moved there. We took another sip. Then he locked the jar in his truck, and we went back to the bar. Well, I started telling my teammates that I had just tried out some kick-ass moonshine, and before long, others wanted to try it out for themselves. However, they didn't feel comfortable asking the guy if they could go have a drink, and they asked if I minded asking him if they could try some.

I went up and asked him if he minded going outside with some of my friends. He had a good experience working with the team, and he told me that was why he and the moonshine were there. He really didn't want to take it home. We made another trip to the parking lot in the pouring rain, but after a few shots of shine, we didn't care if it was raining. We all went to the truck. He got the jar out, and we passed it around. Everyone had a sip or two, and then we headed back in. Everyone agreed that it was pretty good for shine, and generally, it was a hit.

Good news travels fast, and as other team folks learned of the availability and quality of the jar in the parking lot, they wanted to give it a try. They, too, felt weird asking the guy, so I ended up being the go-between for all those folks who wanted to go out and have a pull of shine. Unfortunately, every time anyone went outside, I went along, and every time I was out there, I took another sip. I think some folks wanted to go out more than once, but I lost count as the shine started to affect my judgment.

I'm not a very good drinker. In my younger days, I was better at it, but I lost my edge years ago. I was in the bar and hanging out with all the folks when I realized that I had drank way too much shine. It hit me in just a few minutes. I knew it was time for me to head to my room. I was pretty drunk. No, I was *very* drunk. I had a room at a nearby hotel that was well within walking distance, so I left and went outside. It was still raining, which was the least of my problems.

My hotel was only about three blocks away, but as I stood

outside—or tried to—I noticed that you could see the sign of my hotel across a vacant lot. I thought, *Why take the long way around?* So I decided that I could just cut through the vacant lot and close the distance by quite a bit. I got about halfway through the vacant lot and ran smack dab into a chain-link fence. The fence was about six feet tall, and while it did slow my progress, I thought, *Hey, not a problem. I'll just crawl over it.* I was almost there. I climbed up on the fence and noticed that all the wires at the top made an X and were not bent over. The tips of the wires were pretty sharp too. I was hanging on the fence, wondering if I would slice my guts out if I tried to go on over when all of the sudden, the whole world around me was lit up with a very bright light.

The bright light was followed by a voice on a loudspeaker ordering me to get off the fence. I looked around to see a police car with their spotlight on me. For the most part, I'm a law-abiding citizen, and so I complied with the order. Next, the officers ordered me to lie down and spread my arms and legs. I did as I was told and lay down in the mud. The officers then got out of their patrol car and approached me and asked who the hell I was and what the hell I thought I was doing.

I told the officers who I was and explained that I was a firefighter and had just got off a fire and had been drinking at a get-together over at the Holiday Inn and had had too much to drink, which was why I was headed to my hotel so that I could go to bed. They believed me and told me I could stand up. I was a muddy rat now and wet to the core. They asked me how much I had had to drink, and I told them about twice as much as I needed. There was no need to give me a sobriety test as it was pretty obvious that I was hammered. At this point, they were tickled to a degree and suggested that I not try and climb over the fence and offered me a ride back to the hotel in the squad car. I told them that if anyone on the team saw me delivered home in a squad car, I would never live it down. They offered me no sympathy, and they made me get in so that they could deliver me to my hotel. Thankfully, it was late, and no one witnessed my delivery.

As I have said, we had a day to spend prior to flying home, so most of the team had decided to take a few side trips rather than sit around all day. Some were headed to the Smokey Mountain National Park, some were going to Dollywood and some were headed to other places in the area. My ops buddy woke me up at five thirty in the morning. I had only been in bed for a few hours. We were part of the group headed to the Smokey Mountains, and he wanted to get an early start. I got up and went out to join our small group. They headed to a place for breakfast with me in tow.

I was in between being very drunk and very hung over, but I accompanied them into a place for breakfast. I wasn't doing very well, and eating was not on my radar screen. Some of the folks who had drank that poison with me the night before said that the supplier had said not to drink water in the morning but rather try tomato juice as the cure, so they ordered me a glass of tomato juice. Oh my, the thought of drinking that tomato juice was about to make me puke. Really, it was the shine from the night before, but the tomato juice put me over the edge. While the folks were enjoying breakfast and eagerly anticipating the trip to the Smokey Mountains, I was puking in the parking lot.

My friends told me they weren't sure if they wanted me along unless I could ensure that I wouldn't puke in the rental car. There was no way I could make that promise as I was just sick as hell. They took me back to my room and abandoned me, which was fine with me.

The whole affair gave the team something to rub in my face, and they did a great job of doing just that. I would have done the same if it had been someone else. At the team meeting the next spring, I was awarded a team shirt with "moonshine madness" in bold letters on the back just to keep the embarrassing story going. I felt like they should have thanked me for being the guinea pig in the shine-drinking quest. I demonstrated to the team that too much moonshine was not a good thing, and that should mean something. I tell everyone that I won a blue ribbon in the moonshine-drinking contest in Ashville, North Carolina, but to this day, no one has been too impressed.

The team had been assigned to the Aspen Fire, which burned on Mount Lemon north of Tucson, Arizona. This fire was a bad one and had resulted in the loss of several structures and radio towers. There was also damage to the ski lifts for the ski area on top of the mountain. The team had not contained the fire at the end of fourteen days, and we were forced to transition with another IMT from the Southwest. After the transition occurred, we all checked into a local hotel to spend the night prior to heading home the next day. As was the custom, the team got together that evening to have a few beers and decompress.

The hotel we had checked into provided a nice pool area, and after we all got cleaned up and had dinner, most of the team came to the pool area, where we socialized and shared a beer or two. I have always felt that these debriefing meetings were one of the best ways to build team unity, and most of the members developed friendships within the teams. Having a drink together was a great way to spend the last night together. Not all the team members participated in these debriefings, and it was not a requirement; however, we did have a good turnout for this one.

I don't want to make it sound like these get-togethers were like drunken fraternity parties. We were all grown-ups, and besides, we represented the team even when we were not working. We all knew that. The pool area of the hotel was a great place as no one had to drive or really be out in public. We could just hang around the pool and visit and have a libation. We grabbed what ice chests we had, secured some beer, and just hung out at the pool, splashing around and generally enjoying a relaxing evening.

After a few hours of this fun, I'd had enough to drink, and I started getting sleepy. So I said my good nights and headed up to my room. When I got to my room, I didn't hesitate. I just jumped into bed and quickly went to sleep. Sometime around two thirty in the morning, I was awakened by a knock on my door. This was out of place as it was pretty late, and I immediately thought that something had happened and that someone needed some help.

Wearing only my boxers, I got up out of bed and answered the door. To my surprise, a very attractive black lady was standing there, and she wore a scanty outfit. I was taken aback to say the least, and I then told her that I thought she had the wrong room. She looked at a matchbook that she had written a room number on and looked at the number on my door. Then she informed me that she did have the right one and walked right past me into my room. I had just woken up from a sound sleep and may have still been under the effect of the evening's libations. I was both embarrassed and somewhat in shock, standing there in my boxers. It soon became apparent that she was a lady of the evening and ready to fulfill any needs that I may have had. The first thing that I told her was that I didn't have any money and that I really thought she was in the wrong place. I really wanted her to leave as I was feeling very uncomfortable about the entire deal. She asked if she could go to the bathroom, and in my stupor, I said that she could. She then walked into the bathroom and removed her blouse and exposed her bare breasts. She turned to me and asked if I liked what I saw. She informed me she had just spent $5,000 on a breast enhancement and was giving me a glimpse of what $5,000 would get you. I must admit that she really got her money's worth, but I really felt weird now. I didn't really feel she wanted to leave. When I finally woke up, I pretty much ordered her out of my room.

This entire deal made it a little hard to go back to sleep, and as I lay there, I realized that I had been had by someone on the team. I must admit that it was a great joke, and as I tried to go back to sleep, I started wondering who had done this to me. I spent quite a while trying to figure who knew my room number as that was one of the key bits of information I needed to solve the mystery. I only remember telling one guy my room number, so of course, I suspected he was the culprit. The next morning as I was checking out, I ran into this guy, and I interrogated him about my visitor the night before. He claimed he knew nothing of the incident, and his wife, who had joined him for the debriefing, upheld his story. I did want to figure out who had done this. After all, it was an unwritten rule that a retaliatory strike should follow such a great prank. I had played out my only lead in the investigation and decided that if I just remained patient, the culprit would have to reveal himself. He would have to if he wanted to find out what had actually happened. Patience was my best bet if I wanted to learn who the prankster was.

Several years later I was at a gas station in Flagstaff when one of the division supervisors on the team came walking in. It is always great to run into a team member, and I was surprised to see him as he lived in another town. We were visiting for quite a while when his wife came into the gas station. She knew me from a fire that had threatened the community they lived in a few years before, so she walked in and said hello. She then said, "Hey, isn't this the guy you called the prostitute for down in Tucson?"

Her husband turned quite pale, and he started backing out of the door of the gas station. He immediately said, "That wasn't me who did that."

Then she said, "Look at him. That's his lying face." Finally, after several years the truth came out. I was amused at my buddy's behavior at the time and the comments by his wife. A cold case had been solved, not in a timely manner but solved nonetheless.

I have not made any efforts to get even; however, if he reads this account, he should be forewarned that I am just waiting for the right opportunity. So watch your back, amigo. My revenge is still in the works.

CHAPTER 13
DEBUNKING

After any team assignment, there is a closeout. Actually, there are two separate closeouts. During the first, the team members gather together along with any and all jurisdictions impacted by the fire. Generally, the team is reviewed for their performance by each jurisdiction's representative if they choose to attend. The team also has the ability to offer advice to the local area about ways to polish their efforts working together for future events. The fire team usually meets prior to the official closeout to have a candid discussion about how things went and discuss any other important items at the main closeout meeting.

At the closeouts the incident objectives are reviewed, and a final report is submitted by the team for the host agency. Depending on how many folks show up and want to discuss something, the closeout can be a quick or a lengthy meeting. I have attended quite a few closeouts, and usually, the team has done a great job. People give out thanks and pats on the back for a job well done. Most of the operations people feel that the meetings are just a waste of time, and quite frankly, they could do without the pats on the back. That's not why we do what we do.

I always thought it would be kind of cool to attend one where the host agency was pissed off, and the thanks and pats on the back were replaced with a general ass-chewing. I wondered about them until that actually happened. It wasn't nearly as much fun as the pats on the back.

My first major ass-chewing came after the Cerro Grande Fire at the team closeout. We met prior to the full closeout. This was usually just a candid discussion about how we did. The Cerro Grande Fire was a challenge, and even with the complexities of the incident, the team did a good job managing it. As with all issues, there are two sides to every story, so I will attempt to cover both.

From my point of view, the apparent bad decision that led to my ass-chewing started one windy afternoon. Fire camp was set up in an old burn scar that was several years old, and while the pine trees had not regenerated as often occurred in fire scars, the trees that had been killed were all fallen. The entire area had a continuous grass cover, and a huge number of fallen trees too. The fire became active with the wind, and bone dry conditions and started moving pretty well through the old scar, and while not directly headed toward camp, the location of our fire camp was definitely not out of harm's way.

Fire camp was set up on a gravel road, and everything in camp was positioned on one side of the road. The road provided a line that could be ignited if the fire kept heading that way. It was very windy, and the fire started to build, and with the increase in activity became more and more of a threat to burning down fire camp. In my humble opinion, it started lining up on camp. This was not a huge deal as I did have a hotshot crew, a dozer, and a strike team of engines handy. They, too, thought the fire was headed to our camp. They were at the ready and briefed on burning the road out, and it would be a quick and pretty easy process, the wind being the only real challenge.

Within a few hours it was obvious that now the fire was headed toward camp and there was no doubt it would be impacted. I was concerned that all the folks in camp who didn't have experience with fires would freak out when we burned out around camp on the adjacent road. I made the call that we needed to burn the road, briefing everyone that we would just burn the road and let the fire burn past camp, making the fire camp safe again. I then went to camp and informed everyone that we needed to burn around camp and that they needed to leave immediately. They would have to pull back to a safe distance on the highway and wait for us to give them the all clear to reenter camp. This would only take about an hour or so. I just needed everyone to leave as a precaution.

I attempted to do the evacuation without causing alarm, especially since there were several people in camp had no fire experience. We wanted them is a safe place as soon as possible.

All things considered, I felt the evacuation of fire camp went well, and it was an orderly exodus. The camp crews were told to drive down the highway with our escort while we burned the road. We would have someone come and get them when it was safe to come back.

The burnout went quick and as planned, but the down and dead trees did produce a huge amount of smoke, which impacted camp for a little longer that an hour. The wind made holding this little burn a nasty deal, and all the resources left except me and the hotshot crew. But it was a success in the end. Fire camp was smoky but safe, and we sent a runner to bring back all the folks on the highway. At this time I thought we really kicked ass and pulled it off with no injuries. We didn't even burn up the caterer. While we had snot dripping off our chins, it was a safe and successful operation.

Now let's here the other side of the story. The incident commander knew that the fire had been pretty complex and that it was just zoned, which meant a second incident management team had been assigned to manage the north half of the fire. He was out meeting with the new team to discuss coordination with their team in our collective efforts. While the fire had been active during the past days, he was unaware of any emergencies, and so he briefed the incoming team and headed back to our fire camp.

As he was driving down the highway, he noticed a large column of smoke building up on the fire camp side of the fire. He wasn't too concerned because he was confident that his sage operations guys would have contacted him if there was anything happening on the fire. He figured that something interior was going up and there were no issues. Then he drove up on all these vehicles parked on the highway and wondered what was going on. As he approached, he realized that the vehicles were all from his fire camp, and when he asked why they were all there, he found out that they had be ordered to evacuate by the operations dipshit.

If you're a kid at Christmas, surprises are really cool. This obviously doesn't hold true if you're an incident commander. While I assumed we kicked ass, it would have probably been a vastly more acceptable success if I would have contacted the incident commander and let him know what we were doing.

I remained unaware of my stupidity until the team closeout, and then I found out that I had genuinely pissed off the incident commander. He didn't think my actions that day were nearly as cool as I did, and he informed me that if I ever did anything that stupid again, he would cut a part of my body off. I'll leave that part to your imagination, but there have been a few times since then that I've felt it may have helped my judgment if I had actually undergone that surgery.

Another bad closeout happened when the team went to the McNally Fire, which was burning in the Sequoia National Forest in California. This fire was a big fire and quite active. For several reasons, this fire was a difficult assignment to all the various parts of the team. The incident command post was established in Kernville, California, and we had several spike camps. Most of the firefighters were in a huge spike camp several miles up the Kern River's drainage area at Johnsondale. Because we were spread out so much, the team had quite a bit of extra work. We needed multiple briefings. There were feeding issues, and we had plans and maps to deliver too. A narrow two-lane highway connected most of the camps, adding issues of slow travel times and safety, and a forest service supervisor was out on the fire daily.

I've been on quite a few fires, and having the forest service supervisor, which was also the agency administrator, out on the fire on such a regular basis is quite uncommon, and a pain in the ass. This is a good lesson for anyone who is still active in fire suppression. While the team gets their direction from the agency administrator, having one on the actual fire directing resources to take actions that he has deemed worthy becomes a no-win situation.

One afternoon I received a call from one of the division supervisors. He told me he had been directed to abandon the portion of the fire line he was working on, load up all his resources, and head over to a Boy Scout camp several miles away from the fire. Upon arrival, his instructions were to burn out around the camp. I asked him just who the hell told him to do that, and he said the order came from the agency administrator. I instructed him to hold tight and do what we had planned. I said I would find the guy and explain how that order was not going to happen.

I drove out to the fire, looking for the agency administrator. When I found him and told him that I had scraped his plans to burn out around the Boy Scout camp, I also explained that he should run any future ideas through the ops guys. This didn't go over well, and he chewed me out a bit. He informed me that this was his, that he was the forest supervisor and that I worked for him. As a part of the chewing-out, he informed me that his son was working at the Boy Scout camp for the summer and that he was on the board of directors. While this made him feel better about his actions, it made me more resolute in not letting it happen. I informed him that when and if the fire threatened the camp, we would take appropriate actions. I didn't make any friends that day.

A few days later, the agency administrator cornered me and told me to send home—or "demob"—a strike team of California Division of Forestry (CDF) engines. I asked him why he wanted them sent home, and he informed me that as he was driving back from the fire that day, an engine of this strike team had swerved over a double yellow line, almost hitting his vehicle. They were unsafe and needed to be released from the fire. He also told me that this wasn't my choice and that I needed to do as I was told.

Having already been a party to some of this guy's ideas, I asked that the leader for the CDF strike team see me after the morning briefing. I wanted to find out what their take on the infraction was. The guy readily remembered the incident and informed me that when they were driving on the highway, some dirt and rocks had fallen on the road and that he had driven over the yellow line to avoid the debris. This was a common occurrence as the narrow road followed the bottom of a steep canyon that had burned on the uphill side of the road.

With that information, I decided that the strike team should not be sent home. I had driven the highway daily. It was indeed a common and ongoing thing. I looked up the agency administrator to let him know that I had talked to the guilty party and that after hearing his side of the story, I had decided to not demob the group. While this was not my first error in judgment, it ended up being one of the most remembered. I again received a public ass-chewing from the guy, and to make a sad story short, I demobbed the entire strike team that afternoon. You win some, and you lose some.

One good thing about this deal was that the agency administrator didn't want to talk to me or even really look my way. I had been a bad boy, and I needed to be shunned for my rebellious attitude. I must admit that I didn't mind his avoidance. In the few days since he wasn't talking to me, the incident commander approached me, and gave me a description of a vehicle, and ordered me to demob the driver. The agency administrator had ordered this. I was informed that there was no wiggle room and to just get rid of the guy for unsafe driving.

It wasn't a hard task to find the guilty individual because the vehicle was a Crown Victoria and there weren't many on the fire. When I found it, I discovered that the driver was a high-ranking individual from the California Department of Emergency Services. When I told him that he had been reported for unsafe driving, he said, "I was following all these engines down the canyon forever. There are no passing zones for miles, and when I saw a little straightaway, I punched it and passed all five of the engines." He went on to explain that the vehicle he was driving was a California Highway Patrol car and that it had a lot of guts. He also told me that he never went more than seventy miles per hour when he passed the line of vehicles. The speed limit on the highway was thirty five and this speed was too fast for some of the turns. When I told him the agency administrator had given direction to demob him, he just laughed and said, "Go ahead. I don't give a shit." So he went home that afternoon.

Hell, if I would have seen this guy pass the group of vehicles like he did, I would have sent him home too. I hate to admit the agency administrator had actually made a good decision, but even a blind pig finds a acorn every now and then. A few days later, the rascal hit again. I got a call from one of the divisions, and he asked if I was aware that there was a group from the local forest service that was going to burn out around a grove of redwood trees that were a few miles away from the fire. This grove of redwoods was not even in the direction the fire was headed but off to the flank of the fire by a few miles. Needless to say, I headed up there to find out what was going on. I felt I knew who had ordered the action.

When I got there, there were indeed quite a few guys from the forest service, and they had received direction from my buddy to ignite a perimeter around the grove of redwoods to protect them. The grove did have some truly ancient redwoods; however, they were growing out of an overstocked stand of mixed conifer, and they were on a pretty steep hillside. The site offered many challenges, the biggest being the extreme burning conditions of the fuel bed. This was easy to determine by glancing at the column of smoke the fire was putting up a few miles away.

The group that was sent by the forest supervisor did have fire experience, and upon seeing firsthand what they were supposed to do, they thought it was as stupid an idea as I did and scrapped the plan. They did have concerns that they had been given pretty direct orders to burn and save the redwoods. I explained that I had burned my bridges with the guy several days ago and that they could put the blame on me for the decision not to ignite any burn, and they did.

One evening well into the fire, the smoke column, which had been capped, or had a pryocumulus cloud over the smoke column daily, could not be seen any longer from Kernville. The local agency folks were giddy that we were gaining control of it as indicated by the lack of smoke. I couldn't believe they thought the fire was waning. I had to explain that the curvature of the earth just didn't allow them to see the fire's smoke column and that it was getting farther and farther away. They perceived this as a smart-ass remark and added a few more arrows to my back.

The seed had been planted as to the interactions with me and the agency administrator, but he also spread his charm on other functions of the fire team. I have just shared mine. The team had reached the fourteenth day of the assignment and was timing out on the fire. Another team was ordered to move in behind us. While we had made progress with the fire, it was still active and making daily runs headed toward the Inyo National Forest as the other team arrived. Being relieved of command by the other team, it was time for the closeout.

As already mentioned, most closeouts mean a pat on the back and a safe trip home; however, this one wasn't going to play out that way. The agency administrator was the first to speak. He informed us that he was a world-class jazz musician and runner. He went on to explain that since he was so skilled that his rating of the team, which was just an average rating, that really meant that the average person would consider it as excellent. Additionally, he added that he held himself above the average person because he excelled at whatever he did, and he maintained that his excellence would not allow him to rate us as excellent because we weren't in his class.

After the explanation about why he was superior to the rest of us peons, he wanted to give us an award for working on the Sequoia National Forest. He produced some Sequoia National Forest pins and went on to tell us how much these pins meant. He didn't just pass them out to anyone but saved that honor for those individuals who had helped "save the redwoods." So with deep compassion, he handed out the pins and took a seat.

The next guy who got up was the director of fire and aviation from the regional office. We were glad the agency administrator was done, and we figured at least this guy knew fire and would be more appreciative of our efforts on their fire.

Our fire team was made up of folks from most government agencies that dealt with fire. We were a diverse group, and traditionally, we would wear team apparel to the closeout meeting. Each team member purchased their own shirts and clothing with the team logo, and we wore these to the briefings and closeout meetings. We thought this was professional and showed team cohesiveness. We had done it for years.

When the director got up, he informed us that we looked very unprofessional. He went on to add that we looked like a band of hobos and that he was unable to tell what agency we all worked for and that this was unacceptable. I looked over at our boss, the incident commander. He was sitting there, wearing a weathered team T-shirt with a hole in the belly. He had his index finger through the hole, playing with his belly, obviously trying to keep his mouth shut. The director then told the team that if we ever wanted to come back to California and work on a fire, we would have to wear our agency uniform, or else we weren't welcome ever again.

As I stated, this fire was a tough one, not only for the operations guys but for everyone. The team had pretty much all been beat up for a variety of reason, and the closeout ass-chewing was the icing on the cake. We were asked if the team had anything to say, but we declined. They sure as hell didn't want to hear anything we were thinking. So we were given our special pins and dismissed. As I walked out of the building with my cherished Sequoia National Forest pin, I noticed that just about everyone on the team had tossed their pins on the ground just outside the door. The ground was littered with them, and I proudly tossed mine on the ground too. That was our parting message.

If getting into trouble is bad, at least getting into trouble with your friends makes it somewhat better. There is a strong bond that a good fire team produces, one that is strengthened by a host of different situations and issues. Just like a group of kids getting into trouble together can strengthen bonds, this closeout had the same effect on the team. While we were sure it was a spanking, it had the opposite effect on the team and made us stronger. It was obvious we didn't want one of their pins, and none of us gave a damn if we ever went to California on a fire again.

Not all fire stuff is funny ... or fun. One of the biggest stories I've been involved with started on the Cerro Grande Fire, which was in Los Alamos, New Mexico. This fire had many *stories,* many of which were as inaccurate as they possibly could be. This fire burned hundreds of homes in Los Alamos, and it was a true tragedy. The fire was started by the park service on top of one of the mountains. It was a prescribed fire, which was ignited without any control lines, and weather forecasting windy conditions. The forecast predicted high winds that would impact the area of the prescribed burn. They lost control of the burn, and it grew into the Cerro Grande Fire. While there was little discussion about why the burn was conducted at the time, when we arrived at the fire, officials blamed two forest hotshot crews that were unable to catch the fire when it escaped. It was not very accurate and just plain wrong to blame the escape on the hotshots, as they did their best considering the shit show they were assigned to.

This was one of those times when the weather forecast was correct, and after the fire was lost, the winds did blow very hard and ended up driving the fire into the community of Los Alamos. This was one of the first fires in the Southwest that burned multiple homes and became a national news item. After the fire one of the forest service research scientists from Montana came to the scene of the tragedy to study what had happened. He determined that the loss of all the homes resulted in a backing fire with flame lengths of twelve inches. He published his findings, and the word went out nationally that people should create a defensible space around their homes to prevent such losses in the event of a wildfire. His supposed research indicated that if homeowners were to clear an area thirty feet wide, their homes would be safe from burning down. Across the nation this information was shared and taken as a factual research item and adopted by most communities.

I was one of the operations section chiefs on this fire, and the deputy fire chief at Los Alamos, the other operations section chief assigned to the fire, and I were all there when the fire burned into Los Alamos. We witnessed the fire firsthand as it burned into town. We were humbled by the intensity of the fire. In truth, the fire that burned into town was a sustained crown run in heavy timber that was driven by a fifty-mile-per-hour wind with stronger gusts. The flame lengths were around 150 feet, but they could have easily exceeded that with the stronger gusts. The research study couldn't have been any more inaccurate, and at first, I thought it was a joke. If it was a joke, it was a bad one, and I couldn't believe it was not challenged by the wildfire community. If every home that was consumed by fire at Los Alamos had the thirty-foot defensible space at the time the fire ran into town, not one home would have been saved. The thirty-foot defensible space when the flame lengths easily exceeded 150 feet would have had absolutely no benefits.

A few years later, the Aspen Fire, which was on Mount Lemon just north of Tucson, Arizona, also burned down multiple homes. I was also operations section chief on this fire. The communities on top of the mountain that were impacted by the fire included Loma Linda and Summerhaven. The bulk of the homes that were lost were in the Summerhaven subdivision. This fire was started south of the community on a very steep slope, and it had a heavy fuel source. The fire built into a sustained crown and headed toward Summerhaven, and everyone withdrew from the community as it was obvious that the fire was going to run right into them. The fire lined up on Summerhaven, and many of the firefighters and I watched from a viewpoint as the fire burned through the subdivision. We could feel the radiant heat from more than a mile away as the fire made a sustained crown run in heavy timber.

While the fire impacted Summerhaven, it flanked past the Loma Linda subdivision, and after the fire made its push, we reentered Summerhaven in an attempt to save any structures that had not been consumed by the initial run. While there was still a lot of fire in the area, Loma Linda had pretty much been spared. It was decided to burn around the homes in the Loma Linda subdivision that first night as fire conditions lowered to prevent another uncontrollable run burning additional homes the following day. This burn was done throughout the night, and it resulted in no additional home losses in Loma Linda and blackened the area, thus preventing a high-intensity fire.

The fire that burned into Summerhaven was a sustained crown fire with flames up to and no doubt exceeding 150 feet. Again, after the fire the same researcher from Montana visited the area and used this fire to confirm that a backing ground fire had burned all the homes to the ground and that if a thirty-foot defensible space was provided, the loss would have not occurred. In his defense, which makes me want to rinse my mouth out with soap, if he looked at the fire's effects in the Loma Linda subdivision, which was burned with as low of an intensity as the crews could achieve during the night, his conclusion may have made sense. However, looking into Summerhaven, where there was an obvious stand replacement burn, the information did little to support his theory.

I objected to this research as it was obvious to me and anyone else who was actually there when these fires burned that it was worthless and that he had spread a horrible mistruth. This researcher never made contact with anyone who was actually on either fire, and as operations on both these fires, I felt that he should have contacted me or someone else who was an eyewitness to the actual events in order to aid in his research. This was one of the hard lessons of my career. There are those who write about fire and may have several degrees in fire science. They publish their research, which may include no actual knowledge or experience with fire. Those of us who have had snot dripping from our noses in the smoke have little worthwhile knowledge.

I just viewed a video that was produced by the same guy. It has been more than a decade since his great discovery of the home-burning backing flames. A home was constructed in the lab and exposed to fire to see how and why the home would catch fire and burn. It was determined that fire brands landing on litter like pine needles in the rain gutters or debris laying around the house would start a spot fire and would lead to the home burning down. He could have asked just about any wildland firefighter and found out this information as it is pretty basic stuff, and then he could have saved his valuable research budget for some other study.

Casinos are great places for closeouts as they often offer cheap room for the team and conference rooms for the actual closeouts. I have attended many closeouts at casinos. After the Mistake Peak Fire on the Tonto National Forest in Arizona, the team retreated to a local casino. The official closeout was scheduled for the next morning, and after we all checked into our rooms, cleaned up, and ate dinner, we met at the bar, which was a wing off the casino floor.

I was visiting with one of the ladies on the team sitting at the bar when a guy approached her and called her a very despicable name. The term would usually get you slapped in the face by any self-respecting lady. The lady started saying that she was not the term the guy called her, and she did this with some volume in her voice, which attracted some attention. She was pretty upset and kept repeating that she was not the term this guy had used. It did start quite a stir, and pretty soon there was a guy dressed up in a black suit with an earbud in his ear. This guy looked like one of the secret service guys who hang around the president.

Another lady on the team was attempting to calm the situation when more of these guys in black suits and earbuds started entering the fray. Pretty soon five security folks were on the scene, and they were starting to grab the ladies and getting physical with them. From my place at the bar, I had a ringside seat as more and more of these guys in suits approached and started grabbing the ladies. I noticed several of the ops guys watching from a nearby location. As they started getting physical with the ladies from the team, the ops guys got into the deal and told them to leave the ladies alone.

The fray rapidly escalated, and in the drop of a hat, the security force told the ladies they were thrown out of the bar and started to physically toss them out of the bar area. The ops guys didn't like the rough treatment of the girls and got involved, which immediately attracted more security folks. I was sitting at the bar, and one of the security guys approached me. I told him in rather tough terms that he was full of shit. He asked me what I had said, so I repeated my statement. As soon as I said that, it dawned on me that this was how old farts like me got their ass kicked, but it was too late to withdraw my words. He immediately grabbed me and threw me out of the bar.

By kicking us out of the bar area, we were just all on the casino floor now. Because of the treatment of the ladies, most of us were pissed off. We didn't think any of us should be treated that way. The whole incident left the bar, which was somewhat secluded, and poured into the casino, where everyone could witness the infraction. Several of these security goons were arguing with multiple team folks and telling us that we were to leave the casino as we'd been expelled from the entire place. They must have thought that they were in jeopardy because one of them close to me instructed someone through his earbud to call the cops.

It goes without saying that hearing someone talking into a hidden microphone in their sleeve and ordering up the cops tends to stop the old party spirit. However, in my wisdom I tried to stave off the need for the cops by telling everyone that they needed to shut up and go to my room. My intention was just to calm the situation, and I figured if we went to my room, the goons would have accomplished their objectives of getting us out of there and could return to just letting all the old retired folks spend their annuities on the slot machines. We could go to my room and continue our little closeout debriefing without a problem. Some folks asked what room I was in, so I told them all, "Room 308," an easy one to remember if you're a cop or a security goon.

The goons must have thought this was a good idea too as they started backing off, and we fled the casino floor and all headed up to my room. We were all worked up about the rough treatment by the security force of the casino. We felt we were all in trouble, and the guy who had started it all escaped without even a word or one of the goons grabbing him. We had been in my room for about sixty seconds when there was a hard knock at the door. I opened the door, and I wasn't surprised when I saw three security goons. They informed me that there had been complaints about the loud party in my room. They said that we had to shut up, or else we were going to be expelled from the hotel. I told them that we had just got there and doubted if anyone had time to even dial the front desk and complain about anything.

However, we were the team, and they damn well knew it, so I assured them we would quiet down and apologized for the group and shut the door. Being there with the team changes things. We just wanted to have some fun, and we sure didn't want anything bad to come down on the team because of some misunderstanding. If I was there without the team or wasn't worried about reflecting poorly on the team, I probably would have told these jerks to pound sand, and they would have kicked my ass and tossed me out. We decided that we should move to someone else's room and continue with the festivities. We did that, and there were no additional assaults from the goons.

The official closeout was the next morning, so I got up, showered, packed my stuff, and headed down to the main desk to check out. When I approached the main desk, there was a lady working behind the desk and one of the security goons standing there with a very stoic look on his face. I informed the lady that I was checking out of room 308. Then she cast a glance toward the security goon. He immediately started talking into his sleeve. The lady behind the desk then informed me that I was not welcome in the casino anymore and was not to return for the rest of my life. I was then surrounded by three additional goons, and they told me they had been informed that I had trashed my room during the party the night before and that they had witnessed the damage when they came to the door the night before.

This was a fairy tale as we had only been in my room for a few minutes before we got busted again by the goons and moved the party to another room to escape prosecution. I had only slept and showered in the room. I started worrying that these guys had plans to damage the room on their own and blame it on me. Being accused again of wrongdoing by these goons was starting to piss me off. I told them that there was no damage to my room and that the report was false. All four of them just stared at me.

I still had the key to my room, so I said that I was going up to photograph my room. I got a camera out of my briefcase and started out of the lobby. One of the goons got into my way and blocked me from leaving, so I grabbed my cell phone and informed him that I was calling the police if he didn't allow me to return to my room to take photos and ensure that it was undamaged. He stepped aside and let me head back to my room.

I took a bunch of photos of my room and headed back down to the lobby. I entered the lobby, and now there were five security goons waiting for me. They all surrounded me as I entered. They were all within grabbing distance from me as I walked up and gave the lady my key. Then I grabbed my bags and walked out the door. All five of these guys walked me out the door and a ways into the parking lot. Then they blocked my way again. One of them said that I was never to return to the casino and that I was not welcome there if I didn't already get the message from the lady behind the desk.

I told them that it would be a cold day in hell before I ever went back to their damn casino. I was mad as hell as I pulled out of the parking lot. Then I started thinking. It took five of those security goons to toss me, an over-the-hill firefighter, out. Maybe I looked pretty tough. Hell, I hadn't been thrown out of a place since I was in my twenties. I started thinking it was pretty cool. How many old farts like me actually got tossed out of a place? This was the first and hopefully the last time a debriefing ended with ejection.

In the past, one of the best resources for fire crews was the Southwest Fire Fighter Program (SWFF). This program enlisted several hand crews from throughout the Southwest area. Several forests around the region maintained these crews. In the Coconino National Forest, the crews that were sponsored were from the Navajo reservation. These crews were gathered and dispatched from the Rock Point Trading Post, which is in the northern portion of the Navajo reservation. These crews varied greatly for each assignment. The crew boss may be the same, but the crews were filled with the first guys to get on the bus. The bus is one of the mainstays of this story. These Navajo SWFF crews were always transported by an old blue and white school bus that had definitely seen better days.

As these crews were dispatched, a forest service employee was sent to accompany them for the fire assignment. The position was called the crew liaison officer (CLO). The CLO was to go with the crew to ensure their safety, keep their time, and just generally do whatever needed to be done to make sure they were successful on the assignment. I served as the CLO on multiple fires and obtained quite a bit of experience and had a lot of fun on assignments with the SWFF crews.

On one of these assignments, a crew was ordered to several fires that were burning in the Kingman BLM area. I was contacted by our dispatcher, and then I headed into Flagstaff to await the arrival of the crew from Rock Point. When they arrived in their vintage bus, we had a quick briefing and loaded up and headed to Kingman, Arizona. I asked the bus driver if he was filled up with gas and ready to go, and he said he was, so we pulled out. I was driving my forest service truck, and as always, I fell in behind the bus as our journey started.

As I said, this bus had seen better days, and it would slow to forty-five miles per hour on any hill and speed up to fifty-five miles per hour on the downhill portions of the highway. I soon became tired of following it and decided to pass it and head on into Kingman. I could get there first, head to the BLM office, and get briefed up on our assignment while the crew in the old bus was chugging along. I passed the bus and did make it to Kingman. I got a briefing on what they wanted us to do, but afterward, the bus had still not arrived. I went out to the first off-ramp of the new freeway to await their arrival. I waited and waited but still no bus. So I parked at a gas station and watched cars coming off the freeway and asked them as they stopped at the gas station if they had seen a blue and white bus along the highway.

This went on for a few hours, but there was still no bus. Then one lady said that she remembered a bus full of prisoners that was parked along the freeway over by Seligman, which was probably ninety miles from Kingman. It had to be the right bus as the firefighters were wearing fire gear and could easily be misunderstood for inmates. I headed back that way to look for the bus, and the lady said that the bus was just a few miles west of Seligman and parked on the shoulder of the road and that the crew was sitting next to it in the shade. Luckily, I found the bus.

I turned around, and when I asked what the problem had been, the driver said that he had run out of gas. This was kind of good news because this bus had a reputation for the worst breakdowns, and this one was easy to fix. I headed into Seligman and grabbed a gas can and some gas and returned to the scene of the breakdown. We put some gas in the old girl and tried to start it up; however, it didn't want to start, and the battery was starting to fade. We decided to prime the carburetor with some gas and see if it took hold then. We had already put all the gas from the gas can in the bus, but we were able to get a little out still and put that into a Coke can that we found along the highway.

We popped the hood, and one of the guys on the crew climbed into the engine compartment with his Coke can of gas. We took off the air filter, and we were ready to prime the carburetor. Then we got the go-ahead. The guy in the engine compartment sat at the ready with his can of gas. The bus driver gave him the signal and tried to start it again. The driver hit the starter, the guy with the Coke can poured some gas in the carburetor, and then all hell broke loose. The old bus backfired, shooting flames a good two feet in the air, which immediately caught the Coke can and the guy's arm on fire. He immediately tossed the Coke can as far as he could. The fire didn't burn the guy's arm because he patted it out quickly, but the Coke can landed in the deep and dry grass along the freeway, which quickly started the grass on fire. At first, the crew burst out laughing. Then it became apparent that the fire was spreading at a pretty good clip. The crew would usually get fire tools when they arrived at a fire, so we had this fire, a fire crew, but no tools to fight the fire. This quickly turned into a serious deal and quite a mess as we were all trying to stop the fire by stomping on it and using our shirts to beat it out.

As we watched the fire approach the right-of-way fence along the freeway, we saw that the other side of the fence had been grazed. Thank God! After that, we were able to catch our fire before it got really big. We were hanging around to ensure the fire was out when a highway patrolman arrived on scene and thanked us for stopping and taking immediate action to stop the fire before it got big. We all just stood there with guilty looks on our faces and let him go on his way. He never knew that we were the guilty ones who had started the fire. One of the best things about SWFF crews was they could keep their mouths shut.

It can pretty easy to get into trouble on a fire. Sometimes it happens even when you're trying to do good. While on the Moose Fire which, was in the Flathead National Forest and Glacier National Park, a few of us got into a little issue while we were trying to do our best. On the first day that we took over the management of the fire, a couple of us drove out to the fire to see what was going on. We followed the road, which went along the north fork of the Flathead River, and headed north as the fire threatened the road. This was our last chance to stop it before it crossed the river and burned into the park.

As we left camp the fire became pretty active, and it was obviously making a pretty good run toward the park. We went north until we were about where the fire wanted to cross the road. This was in the vicinity of the Glacier Institute. As the afternoon progressed, so did the intensity of the fire until it had developed a sustained crown fire with a front probably three miles in width. It was headed into the park with a vengeance, and there was little anyone could do about that. I had a camera with me, and I took a photo as the head of the fire was well within our view and burning with just about as much energy as possible. I snapped a few pictures of the fire from the road and managed to capture a few of us onlookers standing on the road, looking up at the approaching fire. We pulled back to the flank of the fire and gathered at the Glacier Institute.

The Glacier Institute was an old ranger station that was in the Flathead National Forest; however, it was no longer the forest service station. It had been renamed the Glacier Institute and had become a joint venture with the forest and the park services. As we were regrouping there, we all knew that the fire would burn it to the ground, probably within the next few hours. In our little group of spectators, we had the team safety officer, a team division supervisor, both operations chiefs, and a smoke jumper from Grangeville, Idaho. We decided that rather than just leave the fire to destroy the institute, we should attempt to burn out around it and maybe save all the buildings. The head of the fire was crossing the north part of the road when we made our retreat, so we determined that one of us needed to go back and close the road as it was impassable because of the fire. The other four of us hauled ass and burned around the institute. Then we ran away before the fire, which was now really cooking now, got there.

The four of us lined out four deep and started burning around the institute to try to get as much depth in our burn out as we could. We didn't have much time, but we did manage to complete the burn just as the fire got there. Our burn sucked back into the approaching fire and actually kept the Glacier Institute from going up in smoke. We did lose the old gas house, but it was old wood that was soaked with years of oil and grease. We probably saved quite a bit of hazmat cost by burning that up.

I did have my camera with me, and I photographed the place prior to the burnout. I did this to provide a photo of what was there and to show the approaching fire in case our decision failed and we got blamed for burning a place with historic value to the ground. As I said, the fire was really boiling now, so we lit the burnout and immediately got in our vehicles and pulled back until the flaming front passed. The fire did jump the north fork of the Flathead, which put it into the park in just a few minutes. After it had cooled off, we went back in to see if our burnout was a success, and much to our amazement, it was. I had a few pictures left, so I took the rest of them, and we all felt great that our little burnout saved the place.

We were stretched on time to get back for the planning meeting, so we jumped into our trucks and headed in to fire camp. When we arrived, both the forest supervisor and the park superintendent were in camp. They were very sad that the fire had burned up the Glacier Institute, and they even explained to us the historic value of the place. We gladly informed them that whatever they had heard was false and explained our actions and their success. Not only did we save the place, but I had photos of the before and after on my roll of film. They were very happy that we had managed to save the place, and the forest supervisor asked if I would give her the roll of film so that she could have it developed. It meant a lot to them, so of course, I gave her the roll of film, and all was good.

We were going along fat and happy for a few days, and then we found out, much to our dismay, that the forest supervisor had posted the pictures from my roll of film online. This in itself wasn't a big deal; however, several of the pictures showed the safety guy, the operations guys, and our division standing on the road and looking up at the approaching fire without much of the personal protective equipment that was an absolute requirement for being on the fire line. There we were no fire shelters, and all of us were wearing ball caps, standing there and staring at the fire. We all looked like we were in harm's way. We really couldn't say that it wasn't as bad as it looked. The saving of the Glacier Institute took a back seat to us standing there and setting such a poor example for the rest of the troops. I got calls for months giving me static about this, and I really wished I would have kept my photos to myself. So did the guys I was with.

CHAPTER 14
STRIPPERS AND REEFERS

Several years ago I went to a fire on the Dixie National Forest in southern Utah. This was the Oak Grove Fire, which was burning on the east side of Pine Valley Mountain. I was a strike team leader for a team of engines from several different forests in Arizona. We were sent to Oak Grove Campground, where fire camp was set up. Oak Grove Campground is located on the eastern side of Pine Valley Mountain and lies at the end of the road. When we turned off the interstate and headed up the road to fire camp, we were stopped by incident personnel. It turned out that the fire was developing and making a pretty good downhill run. They didn't feel going up the road to fire camp was very safe, so we were told to hold our location for the time being.

As we were holding, the fire continued to build to the point that it developed into a sustained run and headed downhill toward the road. It was very apparent that the road was going to be impacted. The fuel was seven foot tall brush and burning with a building intensity. We were concerned that if the fire burned across the road, it would put the fire camp in pretty severe danger. The road was the only way out because it dead-ended at the campground. If the fire crossed the road it would cut off any escape route for the folks in the fire camp.We approached the guy who was in charge and voiced our concerns about fire camp. We had the personnel and equipment to ignite the road and attempt to stop the run and hold the road. We offered our services, but the guy did not want us to apply any fire. The run kept increasing in intensity, and our requests to ignite the road were continuously denied. In pretty short order, it was obvious that the fire would burn across the road, and finally, we were given the green light to ignite the road. This decision was put off until the last minute, and the successful burning of the road had to happen quickly.

We had already prepared to ignite the road, and we were ready once we were given the approval. The run was getting very close, and when we started igniting the road, we had to haul ass to get ahead of the run, which we did. This completely freaked out the guy in charge, and once we started at a brisk pace, he immediately told us to stop. I told him I didn't think I could catch the guys putting fire on the ground, which really pissed him off, and he drove off. We were successful, which was somewhat a surprise to us as we really thought we had waited too long. We kicked ass that afternoon, but we also pissed off our hosts. This resulted in two things. The fire camp was moved to a safer location, and our strike team of engines was spiked out at a gravel pit and not allowed to go to camp.

I don't know if they thought this was punishment, but it suited us just fine. We were confined to the stretch of road we had burned out for our entire stay on the fire, returning to our gravel pit each night and getting supplied meals from fire camp. The stretch of road we had burned out had burned extremely hot and was totally moonscaped, a fire term meaning that the fuels had all burned. There was absolutely nothing left, not even a single blade of grass. Because of this, we became bored as there was just nothing left to do on our portion of the fire.

With nothing to do, we naturally started screwing around. One day I was standing around and put my hand into my pants pocket and felt something that was weird. So I grabbed it and pulled it out to see what the hell it was. To my shock, it was the cardboard tube part of a used tampon that some idiot had snuck into my pocket. All the guys got a great chuckle out of it. I didn't know who the culprit was. The next day I was standing around again when I had this weird sensation that I had just peed my pants. I put my hand into my pocket again to find out that I hadn't peed my pants, but the toad that someone had snuck in my pocket had. Again, quite a funny deal, and everyone got a good laugh out of it. However, this time I found out who the little trickster was.

The next day I came walking down the road and saw this guy and a few more of his trickster buddies hiding something. Upon my investigation, I found they had captured about a five-foot-long bull snake. I dashed their plans and made them release the little animal as snake jokes sometimes become violent. They were a little upset when I rained on their parade, but I didn't care. Boredom and revenge got the best of me that afternoon, and as we were sitting around, a lizard wandered by and checked us out. I wasn't doing anything, but then I got the idea to capture the lizard and stuff it into the trickster's bedroll.

Well, now we had something to do, namely catch the lizard. Lizards can really haul ass when they know you're after them. They're fast little critters. It made us wonder. If a little lizard could run that fast, how fast could a dinosaur run? Boredom makes you think way too much. The chase was on, and since all the lizard's hiding cover had been moonscaped by our burnout, there was little other than a few rocks for the little speedster to hide behind. After a chase of several furlongs, the lizard tired, and we grabbed him and relocated him into the trickster's bedroll.

That afternoon I got a call on the radio, and we were told that they were tired of supporting us at our gravel pit and ordered us to come into camp. I think they figured we were having too much fun and wanted us under their thumb. We loaded up at the end of the shift and moved to the new fire camp, which was set up just off the interstate. We rolled in, found a place to bed down, and went over to the caterer for dinner. Everyone but the trickster was aware of the surprise awaiting him in his bedroll. We ate, and then we headed back to go to sleep so that the trick could be sprung.

The trickster was a lady's man, at least in his own mind. While we all ate and went back to our bedding area, the trickster was filling a few girls who were working for the caterer in on how cool and good-looking he was. This delayed him getting back to camp. We all were lying around on the ground and talking when someone saw him headed our way in the darkness. It had taken a long while for him to convey his coolness, but he was finally headed back. We immediately quit talking, and we all acted like we were asleep when he got there.

I was lying there, watching him as he got his pack out, pulled his bedroll out, unrolled it, and gave it a few hard shakes. I thought, *Shit. Goodbye, lizard.* I was sure the little guy had made his escape with the shaking. The trickster then started undressing and stripped down to his undies. He started flexing and rubbing his muscles before he lay down and slipped into his bedroll. As he slipped in, the lizard saw his opening and made a dash for freedom. The lizard ran right across the trickster's bare chest. The reptile scratched him a little with his claws and frankly scared the hell out of him. He let out a womanly scream, which was exactly what we were all waiting for. At the same time, everyone burst into laughter, and the guy knew he'd been pranked.

This freaked the trickster out, but it must have also freaked out the lizard too because unknown to anyone, he quickly retreated back into the bedroll. After the laughter had died down, the guy crawled back in his bedroll, and the lizard followed that same path across the guy's bare chest and made a successful escape. The trickster let out another scream, and we all had one more laugh.

While I was serving as a division supervisor on the team, we went to the Thunderbolt Fire, which was on the Boise National Forest in Idaho. We arrived and got a briefing and moved out to where we were supposed to establish fire camp. Upon arrival, we all set up our camp, and after a few shifts, we decided that I would take a couple hotshot crews and construct a line up a ridge starting at the road that followed the south fork of the Salmon River and another ridge to the top of Shell Rock Mountain several miles to our east. This fire line was several miles indirect, meaning that it was quite a distance from the actual fire, hopefully giving us the time to construct the line and burn it out in order to create a break in the fuel sources and stop the progress of the fire. We were supposed to meet another division that was constructing a line from Johnson Creek on the east flank of the fire to tie in with us at Shell Rock Mountain.

Cutting lines in timber is a slow process, and the steepness and remoteness of the chosen ridge only complicated things. This undertaking took several days, with each day of work, we were farther away from the road. As a result, we started employing coyote tactics. This consisted of our group digging a line up the ridge daily, and as the day ended, we would locate a place for a helicopter to drop off the needed supplies by a sling net. The supplies we received each day were hot canned dinners, cold breakfasts, and sack lunches for the next day. Other needed items that were provided included saw gas, chain oil, and batteries. We didn't have bedrolls or any personal item that we didn't carry in our line packs. Each night we would grab a bite to eat and lie down on the ground like coyotes in an attempt to get some rest.

The first night we worked up the ridge, it got pretty damn cold when the sun went down, and we all spent a restless night at camp because of the drop in temperature. The Boise National Forest was very dry, and they had started enforcing smoking and campfire restrictions because of this drought. As a result, everyone had to gain the forest supervisor's approval to start a campfire. After that first freezing night, I radioed into operations and asked if we could get approval for a warming fire as we had frozen our asses off the night before. This request was passed up the channels for approval.

Two more nights passed, and we didn't hear anything about our request for a warming fire. Both of these nights were miserable, and we couldn't get much rest. On the third night with still no response about a warming fire, I made a decision that we were not going to go through another night of below freezing temperatures without a warming fire. I figured we were way out in the middle of nowhere. Who the hell would ever find out we were violating the forest closure anyway? As we grouped up after getting our daily supplies from the helicopters and eating dinner, I gave the approval for warming fires. This was a hit among the crews. At least they could huddle around a heat source and get some rest now.

Bright and early the next morning, I got a call from one of the operations guys. He informed me that the infrared flight over the fire the night before had detected a few spot fires that were really close to where we had been resupplied by the helicopter. They were concerned because we were several miles away from the actual fire. I acted concerned and said we would locate these spots and extinguish them. I know damn well the operations guys were very aware of what was going on, but they just went along with it. I had been on several fires with both of them when they were division supervisors, and they would have done the same thing. Over the next several days, the infrared flights picked up similar spot fires that seemed to follow us up the ridge. We never did get approval.

We finally reached Shell Rock Mountain after eight days of digging the line. I tied in with the division supervisor who was leading the group from Johnson Creek, and now it was time to initiate the backfire. He was headed back down to Johnson Creek, and my group was to burn our line back down to the road on the south fork of the Salmon River. The guys heading back to Johnson Creek started their burn before we were in place, and they immediately lost their burnout. It rapidly produced a cap or pyrocumulus cloud over the smoke column and hauled ass. Their burnout soon jumped Johnson Creek and burned well into the Frank Church River of No Return Wilderness.

We had spent many days building the line up our ridge, and as we sat there and watched the cloud develop over our partner's burnout, we decided to hold up on applying any fire. Burning out with this fuel type was a very tricky business. The mixed conifer and subalpine fir lichen grow like Spanish moss on all the trees. This often causes multiple spot fires, and easily you could lose everything. The operations guys called me on the radio and asked if we were going to ignite our line because they were worried. Looking at what was going on in the other division, I told them it didn't look like a good time to do any burning. We wanted to wait for the conditions to change, mainly the wind direction, and this ended up with us sitting there for a few days as conditions remained the same.

We waited to ignite our line much to everyone's fear as each day the main fire gained more ground. If unburned, it would not even make the main fire pulse. After two days the weather finally changed, and we got a breeze at our backs, meaning it would blow all the hot material that causes spotting back into the fire side of the line. So late in the afternoon, we set sail, and throughout the night we successfully burned our line all the way down to the river. This was the kind of night we all live for in the wildfire community. We kicked ass that night.

The next morning I got the daily call from operations. They were wondering if we had ignited our line as each day it was getting more critical. I told them that we had gotten it done throughout the night and that we were all back down at the river now. This was a huge relief to everyone, and I was instructed to come on back into camp. I hadn't been there for thirteen days. A truck was parked on the river road, and I was told it was waiting for me. So I headed into camp. The other division called and asked if I would swing by and pick him up, which I agreed to do. After a long day, I still managed to retrieve him and make it back into camp but well after dark. We found it pretty much deserted as most of the folks had bedded down already.

I wanted to take a shower and change my clothes as I had been wearing the same outfit and hadn't bathed for our entire time on the fire. This may sound gross, and admittedly, it is. The other division supervisor and I headed to the showers, and after we got out, we started prowling around camp. We then noticed that there were goodies on all the tables in the chow tent. I'm talking M&M'S, candy bars, smoked almonds, jerky, soda pop, and a treasure trove of goodies that our crews had not received on our coyote tactics assignment.

We felt kind of left out from a logistics standpoint. There were all these goodies in camp, and we had been living on hot cans and sack lunches. A logistics guy came up to us and visited for a while, and when we brought up all the candy and sodas, he informed us that the reefer truck by the caterers was loaded with boxes of all the goodies. Times were changing, and we decided to raid the icebox for all our crews. We walked over to the reefer truck, and the three of us went in. The reefer truck consisted of a semitruck trailer with a refrigeration unit and some wood stairs leading up to the back of the trailer. We had hit the mother lode. The guy wasn't lying. We saw box after box of all these goodies, and we immediately loaded up three big cardboard boxes of goodies to steal for our guys.

All was going well until we tried to get back out of the reefer truck. The door latch had slipped down between the makeshift stairs, and we were trapped inside now. Remember, the other division guy and I had just gotten out of the shower. We both had wet hair, and we were just wearing T-shirts. We were freezing. It was a growing concern, especially because it was late and the camp was pretty much deserted. There was no one walking around to hear our shouts and the pounding on the door. After an hour or so, we quit yelling and pounding on the door because it wasn't doing any good. We started wondering if we could stave off hypothermia by eating candy bars until someone was up in the morning and could rescue us.

Finally, after about an hour and a half of bearing the dark and freezing reefer, the logistics guy thought he heard someone outside, so we started pounding and yelling again. Thank God there was a guy who had to get up to pee in the middle of the night and came to our rescue. He was surprised when he opened the door and found the three of us. He asked us what the hell we were doing, and we just said that we were getting some stuff for our guys. We started dragging our boxes of goodies out of the reefer, not willing to give them up after our ordeal. The rescue guy thought we were stealing the stuff and said we couldn't take it. He asked us who the hell we were, and we explained we were division supervisors on the team. He thought that was bullshit because he had been here for two weeks and he hadn't seen us on the fire at all. He went to wake up security as we loaded up our stuff and hauled ass back to our crews with all our hard-earned goodies, thinking we had gotten away with it.

Of course, everyone found out about our plight, and we were the laughingstock of the fire. We even made the cover of the incident action plan, which displayed the three of us locked in that dark reefer truck.

The fire team was assigned one year to a complex of fires in Florida. A complex or what's commonly called a "fire complex" is a term that many folks and news stations misunderstand and rarely get right. A fire complex doesn't necessarily mean that the fire is complex but rather means that the team is managing more than one fire. At any rate, the team was assigned to the Flagler-St. Johns Complex, which consisted of several fires burning on the east coast of Florida between the cities of Daytona Beach and St. Augustine. The Flagler-St. Johns Complex consisted of fifteen different fires that ranged in size from a few hundred acres to some that were more than a hundred thousand acres. The complex was spread out over several miles and had impacted multiple communities and counties. It was one of the absolute worst fire years that Florida had ever experienced. At our briefing, we were told to not feed alligators and not to mess with them for any reason.

Florida is as wet as Arizona is dry. In the arid Southwest, there are not very many streams, creeks, or water holes. Arizona (from the reference "arid zone") has that name for a reason, or so we were taught in grammar school. Many of the so-called creeks in Arizona may only have water in them after a thunderstorm, but otherwise, they remain dry washes throughout most of the year. When I first came to Florida, I thought, *How can this all be burning? It's as green as it can be, and there is water in every depression.* All the wildland firefighters were schooled in two triangles. The fire triangle teaches that in order for a fire to burn, it needs fuel, heat, and oxygen. Each of these fill one leg of the fire triangle. The fire behavior triangle, which is another training aid, teaches that fire behavior is also dependent on three things—fuel, weather, and topography—each representing a side of the fire behavior triangle. In Florida, you can toss out the topography side of the triangle as the state is as flat as a pancake compared to the western states. For example, consider Interstate 75, which runs from Fort Lauderdale on the Atlantic Coast west to Naples on the Gulf Coast. The route is as straight as a string, and I think I'm taller than any land mass across the entire state. All this water is home to many different species, and one of them is the alligator.

In the management of these fires, we were required to travel around quite a bit to keep things headed in the right direction. One day as the other operations section chief and I were driving around, we drove past a fire engine that was attempting to draft water out of an irrigation ditch. They had parked the engine where a culvert pipe crossed the ditch, and all three of the guys were actively in the process of drafting a load of water. As we approached them, they suddenly took off running and screaming. We narrowly missed one of the guys as he ran across the roadway we were driving down. After slamming on the breaks to avoid running this guy over, we stopped to see what the hell was going on.

The engine crew informed us that when they were placing the draft line into the ditch, an alligator came rushing out of the culvert and that was what had scared them. The alligator then retreated back into the culvert, but they were a little scared to continue with the drafting operation. My fellow operations section chief was also raised in Northern Arizona, and his family had a ranch, which meant that he followed the cowboy way. He suggested that we rope the gator and get it out of the way so these guys could draft a load of water. I immediately thought it was a stupid idea. Then he informed me that he had roped gators on other fires and that it wasn't that big of a deal.

We didn't have a rope; however, there was a clothesline in a nearby yard, so we went over to the yard and stole a length of clothesline and fashioned it into a lariat to rope the gator. This gator wasn't really that big. He was only about four feet long, and he was hiding inside the culvert. I had to go and splash around at one end of the culvert while my buddy waited at the other end to rope the dude as he made his escape. I got a shovel off the engine and went to my end of the culvert and started making as much noise as I could. The gator headed for the other end where my buddy was waiting at the ready with our makeshift lariat.

It worked great, and as the gator made its escape and headed out the other side of the culvert, my buddy dropped a loop on it. The gator started thrashing then. Gators don't like to be roped. That was pretty obvious, and they could make quite a fuss about it even if they are only four feet long. This caused quite a flurry of excitement for all the folks who witnessed it, and we dragged the fighting gator across the road and decided to turn it loose. If you ever rope a gator, you will find out that roping it is the easy part. Trying to get your rope off the gator is where the real challenge comes into play.

In the cowboy world, sometimes you're forced to deal with animals that want no part in whatever the situation is. You can choke these animals down to deal with them. This sounds pretty cruel, and I suppose that if that was happening to you, there would be no doubt about how cruel it really is. However, it was the only way we could figure to get the rope off the gator and let it go. So we choked it down until it quit raising hell and then quickly took the rope off and set it free. The gator wasn't impacted too much as it ran into the woods to get away from us as fast as it could.

After it was all finished, we felt pretty damn cool about what we had done. Not every Arizona boy has roped a gator and lived to tell about it. In Florida, most of the ponds, canals, ditches, or even swimming pools have gators in them. The fire camp was set up at a county fairground, which had several ponds on the property. Word got out that we were gator ropers, and one of the ladies who worked in finance didn't believe that the roping had really happened. We figured there were gators in all the ponds located on the property, so we took the lady and headed down to a pond with our clothesline lariat to prove that we knew what we were doing.

As we approached one of the ponds, we saw a fire crew that had been sent from Russia standing around and watching several gators that had taken up in a pond. We saw at least twenty Russians, and they couldn't understand English any more that we understood Russian. The alligators they were watching and taking pictures of moved out to the middle of the pond as we walked up with our rope. They were way too far off the shore for our makeshift rope; however, one of the Russian guys had tossed a rice crispy treat into the pond, and the gators quickly swim over to eat it. The rice crispy treat floated really well, and after they had fed several to the gators, it was obvious that the animals really liked them.

With sign language, we finally parlayed a rice crispy treat from the Russian crew and tossed it in the pond close to the bank within easy roping distance, and then we waited for the gators to head into our trap. Just like clockwork, one of the gators swam in our direction to eat the floating rice crispy treat, and as it got close enough, my buddy threw a loop and caught it and quickly dragged the gator out of the pond and up on the bank. This freaked the finance lady out, and she took off running and screaming at the top of her lungs. The Russians quickly came over to snap a few pictures, and they watched the gator rolling around and raising hell, trying to get away. Even if we had no verbal contact with the Russian fire crew, we all did share a good laugh and some excitement that afternoon.

The next day we were approached by some of the guys in the planning section of the team. They had heard that we had actually roped a gator, but they didn't believe the rumor. They wanted proof, and they informed us they knew where there was a gator if we wanted to prove ourselves to them. Maybe it's human nature to feel you have to prove yourself if someone thinks you're spinning a yarn and you aren't. With that frame of mind, we informed them that we were indeed gator ropers and that if they showed us their gator, we would damn sure rope it.

They said they would take us to a place one of them had found that was a little secluded and had some gators to rope. As I said earlier, the locals we worked for had informed us that in no way were we to screw around with or feed the gators as it could cause a dangerous situation if they started begging food, making them less afraid of humans. We all loaded up in our vehicles and followed several of the guys to their secret gator pond. On the way there, we started to doubt our gator knowledge, and we had to admit that the only thing we knew about gators was what we had learned watching the Discovery Channel. Two Arizona boys were still headed to a gator-roping.

When we got to this secret pond, we discovered it was actually a slough that had a bridge over it. The guys had been feeding the gators from the bridge, and a few of the gators had taken up residence underneath it. When we got there, the first gator we saw looked like a monster. He was ten feet long and a good two feet wide. We scared it off, and then we acted like our feelings were hurt that we missed roping that monster. In reality, though, we were glad it swam off. We grabbed our rope and headed out on the bridge. We tossed a rice crispy treat into the water and waited with rope in hand for a gator to come out and eat the treat. All the nonbeliever guys were standing about a hundred feet away at a safe distance to witness the act. We thought they were acting like a bunch of little girls by staying so far away.

In short order, a gator noticed the rice crispy treat floating by his bridge and swam out to eat it. My buddy, now pretty skilled at gator-roping, quickly dropped a loop over its head and jerked the slack out of the rope. This gator was about seven feet long and may have been a little on the big side for our skimpy rope. It started rolling and raising hell in the water and just about pulled my buddy off the bridge into the water. I grabbed him by the belt to keep him from going in, and he pulled the gator right up onto the little bridge with the both of us. The gator was going crazy, rolling and hissing, just genuinely pissed that it had been roped and dragged onto the bridge.

Things went to hell very quickly. We were on the small bridge with a pissed gator, trying to stay away from it and not fall or get knocked into the water by the gator's tail, which was whipping around in a frenzy. All the spectators were laughing their heads off from their distant viewing spot, not offering any sort of help. Eventually, we dragged the gator to the end of the bridge away from the water, and after we had successfully proved our skills, it was time to retrieve the rope from the gator. Some of the spectators had gotten a little braver and approached us to take a picture or two of the gator as we went into the choking process. This gator was bigger and proved to be harder to choke down than the others. All we seemed to be doing was making it mad as hell about being captured. I thought that we could tie its mouth shut and then get our rope back, so I moved in and attempted to take several dallies around its snout; however, when I tried to pull the dallies tight, they just slipped off the gators nose, and the battle went on. Some of the guys started worrying about us choking the gator to death and voiced their concern, but I kept telling my buddy to keep choking as the gator still had a lot of fight in him. One of the brave spectators eventually said that he would get the rope as the gator was calming down, and then he approached the gator very cautiously to remove the rope. As he reached in to take the rope off, another guy reached in and grabbed him on the inside of his thigh. As his friend grabbed him, this guy let out a scream like a little girl. We got the rope back and laughed at the scream the dude let out for several minutes. This situation ended up being a little more than we had bargained for, so that was the end of the gator-roping for that trip.

Florida is one of the states that does experience quite a few wildfires and after a few years, the team was headed to another fire in the Sunshine State. This time we were headed to the Jarhead Fire, which was burning in the Big Cypress Reserve, which lies adjacent to and north of the Everglades National Park. This is also a gator-rich environment, and we were given the same gator policies we had received before. Some members on the team remembered the gator-roping acts, and some of the operations folks discussed the issue. My buddy who had demonstrated his gator-roping skills was not on the team anymore, and that left me as the expert. Several members of the team didn't think it really happened, and after a few days, they kept bringing up the fact that no one had roped any gators on this trip.

One of our friends and teammates had suffered a horrible accident while rafting the middle fork of the Salmon River in Idaho, which had resulted in him losing one of his eyes. This guy is everyone's friend, and he himself is quite a trickster too. He has scared the hell out of me with his hijinks more than once. One day while out on the fire, the gator-roping deal resurfaced, and rather than lose face with my teammates, a gator was targeted and roped. We wondered about what we could do with the gator, which was a rather small one that was probably only three feet long. We decided to play a trick on the guy who had lost his eye, so we tied the gator's mouth shut with several wraps of electrician's tape. We all flew to the fire in Florida and rented small SUVs to use on the job. We tossed the gator we had caught and wrapped into the back of our SUV, and we headed back to fire camp. This gator was thrashing around in the back of the SUV, which made me nervous as hell. I could imagine it slipping out of its tape and attacking us while we drove back into camp. Luckily, it didn't escape, and we made it back to camp safely.

When we got back, we put the gator into an empty ice chest in the back of a pickup truck. Several of us were standing around, trying to lure the victim over to the truck. Eventually, this guy came over and started visiting with us without any clue about the trick we had in store for him. After a few minutes, one of the guys standing around asked him to get a bottle of water for him out of the icebox. When he opened up the icebox, the gator saw his chance for escape and lunged out, which scared the hell out of our one-eyed buddy. He screamed very loud as the gator made a dash for freedom, and we all got a good laugh out of it.

Two days later the victim of our joke came up to me and wanted me to go with him because he had something he wanted to show me. He wanted me to go look in a five-gallon pail that he had in a reefer truck. I knew that he was up to no good, so I refused to go with him. I later wanted to see what was up, so by myself, I went into the reefer truck to look in the pail. I popped the lid and looked inside only to find the biggest diamond back rattlesnake I have ever seen. It did scare the hell out of me, but thank God there weren't any witnesses.

You can learn something on every assignment you take if you really want to. One of the lessons we all learned about gators ran somewhat contrary the cautions we received. Feeding the gators will make them less scared of people and no doubt somewhat more of a hazard. But if you feed these rascals, rope them, drag them out of the water, and choke them till near death, they won't want anything to do with humans. They may not be the smartest animal in Florida, but they are really hard to rope twice.

I have already mentioned that many of the guys enjoyed fishing. Another gator issue started up on an innocent fishing trip. Again, we were in Florida on another fire. As we caught the fire and business slowed down, a few of us were lured out by all the fishing opportunities.

We purchased a very cheap rod and reel from a local store, bought a few lures, and headed out. We also purchased a fishing permit for a few days. In order to gain one, you had to call an 800 number and provide your credit card, and after you paid up, they would assign a number to you. If you were checked by any game and fish officers, they could run the number to verify your permit, so it was important to keep the number on you while you were fishing.

Armed with a cheap rod and reel as well as a permit, we headed out to one of the many canals that are beside almost every roadway in the area. Fish were everywhere, and they were easy to catch; however, we soon found out that as you hooked a fish, one if not all the resident gators viewed this as an easy snack. While you could hook at least a small brim on most every cast, the race was on to get it in before one of the gators ate it. The small struggle offered by the brim was soon replaced by a gator that had eaten the brim. We freaked out the first time this happened, but then we found it to be great sport.

We had some great battles as the gators obviously had played this game before. I am not exaggerating. In some areas as you hooked a fish and started reeling it in, up to five gators would be in on the chase to grab it for a snack. Once they did grab the fish, the real fight was on. Even a gator on the small side can offer quite a battle, and hooking a sizeable one on our cheap little fishing rods was quite a hoot. We pursued this until we burned the drag up on our cheap little reels, which didn't take but a few gators.

One afternoon while we were fishing in a canal—though we were practicing the gator game in reality—a family in a pickup truck pulled in a few hundred yards down the canal from us and started fishing. This group consisted of four adults and probably a half dozen small kids. They all got out of the truck and produced several fishing poles and started fishing. It was only a few minutes when they all were screaming like crazy all of the sudden. One of them had hooked a fish, and as they were reeling it in, the same gator behavior we had noticed occurred. When we looked to see what the screaming was about, we saw all the adults tossing kids in the back of the truck and jumping in themselves, causing quite a racket. As one of them had reeled in a fish and the gators started chasing it, they just reeled faster in order to keep the gators from eating their catch. This resulted in the gator running out of the water onto the canal bank and chasing the fish.

As the gator came out of the water, it was then among their group, which was what caused the excitement. They were all unharmed, and we laughed our asses off as we saw a gator swim by, dragging one of their fishing poles behind.

One position that was not on incident management teams in the past was the human resources specialist. I was golfing with a longtime friend I first met when he as was working on hotshot crews. He was a hotshot on a few of the first hotshot crews established on the Coconino National Forest. These crews were established in the early '70s, and that was the era that my friend obtained his experience fighting fires.

As we were golfing, the human resource specialist position on fire teams came up for some reason. He said he had no recollection of being on a fire that had that position. I explained that the position was a relative newcomer to the teams. So he asked what the position was supposed to do for the fire. I explained that they were there to help ensure fair treatment of everyone and to assist in mitigation of issues if they occurred. He just stared at me in disbelief with a wry smile on his lips.

Then he said, "If someone gets their feathers ruffled, they go and cry on this guy's shoulder?" I explained that it was more complex than that and tried to explain the challenges of the position. Remember, this guy is an ex hotshot from the '70s. I then explained the depths of issues with equal employment, gender and racial discrimination, hazing, and sexual harassment. Additionally, there were union issues and other agreements that could not be compromised.

He responded, "You have got to be shitting me." He went on to explain that the only right he felt he had as a hotshot was to shut up and dig. If you offered an objection in his era, you were told to shut the hell up and get to work. He couldn't think of anyone who really gave a damn if your feelings were hurt, and if you really felt the need to raise the bullshit flag, you were sent home or made fun of. Basically, there were two choices—gut it out or quit.

The team was on a fire within the Cleveland National Forest in Orange County and the host of jurisdictions that come along with Southern California. I was one of the operations dudes. One of the other operations guys was a dear friend of mine who happens to be Hispanic. (I hope that is the right term.) We had been busy, but as always, we never missed a chance to zing each other. This was a great way of dealing with stress. We had been on the fire for several days, and for some unknown reason, I was approached by the human resources specialist. He asked if my operations partner and I were getting along, as it seemed to him that we may be mad at each other. He went on the say that this would have dramatic and harmful effects on the team if they knew we were not getting along. His concern was such that he felt the need to counsel me if I thought that would help or to even get the two of us together so that we could safely resolve our disagreement.

This was a great opening, so I asked if there was somewhere private where we could talk about the issue. We went to his little office and closed the door. Then we sat down and started our chat. I went on to explain that I had a huge issue working with Mexicans. I said that they had kicked my ass daily when I was growing up, and I damn sure was sick of taking orders from my ops buddy. I was tired of working with his "Pancho Villa attitude," and I didn't know who had made him my boss. I said all this with a nasty sneer to make it seem as bad as I could.

The guy's face was pale. What he thought may be a little problem had just exploded. In a heartbeat he went from thinking I was a good guy to thinking I was a racist, bigot, and just a general asshole. I then said that I didn't want to talk about it anymore, acted as mad as I could, and stormed out of his office, slamming the door on my way out.

After leaving my counseling session, I found my buddy to let him know what had happened. I located him and filled him in about my session. We laughed our asses off as the human resources guy had swallowed the worm. We parted ways and went about the normal business, waiting to hear what was next. I ran into two different people who asked if I knew where my operations buddy was as the HR guy was looking for him. They were concerned and wanted to make sure that everything was all right. It could mean bad things if the HR guy was looking for you.

Later that afternoon the HR guy ran down the other ops to guy to resolve our dispute. He took the same route I had. He said that I was a stupid cracker, and he basically recited the same line of bitching that I did but from a Mexican's standpoint. Then he acted mad and stormed away. This session worked a little too well as the HR guy must have decided he was in over his head. That was when he went to the incident commander and filled him in. The IC knew both of us well and also knew that neither of us actually felt the way we made out and told the HR guy that he thought he had been had. We acted mad at each other for a few days just to push the joke as much as we could, and then we let him know we were just pulling his leg.

Another close HR call occurred on the Wallow Fire in Northern Arizona. One day while walking through fire camp, I was approached by one of the logistics guys. He informed me that they were planning on playing a prank on the food unit leader. They wanted me to isolate him and keep him busy while they set up a little joke. Of course, I'd do anything to help out a fellow teammate, so I agreed to keep him busy so that they could do whatever it was they had planned.

I walked through camp and looked for him. When I found him, I noticed that the pranksters saw I had him, and they all scurried off. I started talking about something with the food dude and asked why their spike camp had a better caterer than we did. I kept him in the conversation for ten or fifteen minutes though, allowing the pranksters the time to play their little trick.

As it turned out, the prank was to put a plastic blow-up doll in his bedroll, which was in his tent at the edge of camp. This blow-up doll was of the pornographic variety, and it wore a cute little sexy outfit. Plus it had all the correct anatomical attachments. The food dude was a busy guy, and he usually didn't hit the sack until after everyone had been fed and turned in for the night. That is what happened that night. As he went into his tent, he turned on a flashlight and sat on his cot. He noticed a bump on his cot, but he thought it was his pillow and dismissed it. As he started getting ready for bed, he noticed that his pillow was lying on the floor of his tent. This made him wonder what the bump was in his bedroll, so in the gloom of the tent, he looked behind him and saw the doll. He immediately thought it was a dead person in his bedroll. He then responded as most of us would if we found a dead person in our bedroll. He let out a scream.

What good is a great prank if you can't talk about it, and as the word got out about what had happened, we all found out that not everyone on the team thought it was so funny. The IC sure didn't think it was too funny. He was worried that the HR slant of the joke could be a disaster and chewed out the guys and told them in some choice words to put the damn thing away. I must admit that after I viewed her firsthand, I could see how some could find her offensive. She was deflated and put away, but she would not be forgotten.

Rumor has it that one of the logistics guys rolled up a bottle of whiskey in her deflated state and hid her in one of the logistics guy's bags after the fire but before we headed home. Unfortunately, this guy had a trip planned at the time he returned home and didn't check his bags very well and set off for a vacation with his wife and mother-in-law. As he was going through the inspection at the airport, the security folks identified the bottle of whiskey in his bag, and as they opened his bag in front of his wife and mother-in-law, they discovered that the bottle was rolled up in the blow-up doll. The security guy said that he would have to take the whiskey but that the guy could keep the doll, which he had unfurled in all her glory. Some things are hard to explain. You have to keep your eyes on those logistics guys.

The Bullock Fire burned pretty much the entire north side of Mount Lemon by Tucson, Arizona. The fire camp was set up north of the mountain in a large field. One day while I was walking around in camp, I noticed a very attractive lady and another guy walking through camp. It was obvious that they didn't belong there. The lady was wearing a nice purple dress and high heels, and she was all dolled up. The guy with her was wearing civilian clothes, and he had a camera and a tape recorder. I thought they were from one of the television stations that was covering the fire. I fell in behind them as they walked through camp as it seemed they were headed the same direction I was.

I was headed to the logistics tent because we hadn't been getting certain supplies to the troops on the fire, and I was trying to find out where the breakdown was. The lady and the man she was with walked up to the logistics guy I was looking for and started talking with him. I needed to talk to the same guy, so I stood back and let them have their discussion. The more they talked, the more amused the logistics guy looked. It looked like he was about to start laughing. Their conversation came to an end, and the lady and her guy headed off. Then I walked up to talk with the logistics guy.

When I approached, it was obvious that he was tickled, and he was having a hard time hiding it. I asked him what was going on as he watched the two walk away. He just said, "You've got to see this." He went on to tell me that the lady was a stripper from a place in Tucson and that she was looking for the incident commander. This guy knew that the incident commander had gone to take a shower at the shower unit and had instructed the stripper and her friend where his truck was and where they could wait for him. He said she was going to take her dress off as a joke on the IC. As the two got to the IC's truck, they just stood there for a minute. Then the IC emerged from the shower unit and headed to his truck.

As he walked up on his truck, he saw the two standing there and started talking with them. Then out of the blue, the lady just removed her pretty purple dress, which I'm sure shocked the hell out of the IC. It blew my mind from where I was watching too. She wasn't totally nude. She had what appeared to be a skimpy bikini. She walked over to the IC and gave him a big hug. The IC was trying to get away from her, and then she posed a few times by him before she put her dress back on. In the logistics guy's mind, this was one of the best pranks on the IC he could imagine. However, the other shoe was yet to drop.

While it was true that the lady was a stripper from Tucson, what we didn't know at the time was her companion was a disc jockey from one of the local radio stations. Another thing that we didn't know then but soon found out was that the lady had a website. In reality, they had come into our fire camp to do a radio show on the firefighters, and they had taken several pictures that they later posted on the lady's website. Of course, when we learned that there was a website, we logged on to see what it was all about. There were a few pictures of the lady in her bikini standing by our freaked-out IC. They had raided the helibase, and there were pictures of the lady with some of the heliattack crew there. Then there were some pictures of the lady just standing alone in the desert, and in them she was completely nude. To the uninformed viewer, it appeared that the stripper lady had paraded around nude.

The next morning after the briefing, several hotshot crews were sent around the mountain to the road up to the top of Mount Lemon. Fire camp was located north of the mountain and the drive around to the top took a few hours. The hotshots loaded up into their vehicles and started around. As it turned out, they heard the radio show about firefighters. The crews started calling into the radio program and talking with the stripper that had been there the day before. She instructed everyone on the air to go to her website to view her visit to fire camp the day before. I'm sure quite a few folks logged onto her website, and we soon found out that some of those people got really mad at what they saw. The pictures of the stripper and the IC fell into enemy hands, and he was called out.

The radio show asked the hotshots they had on the phone if they had everything they needed, and she said that the listeners could provide anything they didn't have. One of the hotshots said that they were chaffing a lot because of the heat and that Gold Bond powder worked great to resolve this issue. The listeners were asked to mail some gold Bond Powder to the local forest service office for the hotshots. This came at a time just after powder-filled letters had been mailed to federal offices, and powders looked like potential sources of anthrax. This was probably the icing on the cake, and the message caused a huge issue. Powder-filled letters arrived at the local office and played into the anthrax scare that was already in the national news. The radio program most certainly disclosed the website, and our IC ended up in the crosshairs for the entire ordeal. He got dragged through the coals for this, and all he did was get out of the shower and wander over to his truck. This was a funny prank for about the first two or three hours, but it ended up looking pretty ugly.

I also worked on the Fish Fire on the Sequoia National Forest in California. The actual fire was well inside the Golden Trout Wilderness, and fire camp was established in a vacant field near the community of Springdale. A large spike camp was established inside the wilderness, and one could only access it by pack trains or helicopters.

While the bulk of the actual firefighters were up at the spike camp, the other team stayed in the fire camp. Most of the ops folks who get stuck in camp find a quiet place not in camp but close by to bed down each night. We mostly just bed down in the beds of our pickup trucks, and if it doesn't rain or snow, this makes for some great sleeping arrangements. We followed this common practice during this fire too, and there were a few of us who parked on the far fringes of camp to sleep each night.

Really early one morning as the eastern horizon was just showing a little light from the rising sun, we were awakened by the most horrible screaming that I have ever heard. One of my buddies was sleeping in his truck parked close to mine, and we were still tucked into our bedrolls, enjoying a good night's sleep. There is no way to describe how loud and horrid this screaming was, and as the first wave hit us, he sat up in bed and asked if I had heard it. I immediately said, "Hell yes."

Of course I had heard it. The sound would have wakened the dead. We were spooked by what the hell was making this horrible screaming. As we sat up in our bedrolls, a great horned owl took off, trying to gain altitude. It almost hit my buddy's truck though, just clearing it by only a few feet. Its wings were flapping hard as it took off, and in its talons was a large house cat, which was the source of the horrible screams.

The owl flew off into the rising sun with the house cat still making these loud and scary screams. The sound actually woke up quite a few folks in the fire camp even though they were a long way off. It did spook some of the folks on the fire team as they couldn't figure out what was making the bloodcurdling noise. As we gathered for the morning briefing, the big question was if we had heard the alarming noise. We admitted that we had. In fact, we'd had a ringside seat for the entire deal.

When we told the story to the concerned folks, our rendition alarmed the cat lovers on the team. We didn't subscribe to the cat lover group, and while it was a brutal way for a cat to meet its maker, it did provide us with a bone-chilling wakeup call.

CHAPTER 15
CAN-DO GUYS

One of the benefits of my career is that I have had the pleasure of working with a lot of great and hardworking people. Because many of these guys worked for the forest service at a ranger station that was quite a ways from town, they were often ranchers, sheepherders, cowboys, loggers, and generally guys who made their living out in the country. I have had the pleasure of being humbled, teased, cussed, and trained by many such men. It amazes me the way they can adapt and use whatever they have on hand to solve pretty much any dilemma that halts progress. I cannot think of one of these guys who acts or in any way comes across as a know it all. Most would not help if someone expected them to do it; however, if you were trying to figure it out or stumbling along, they would offer advice and often give the solution to whatever the issue was. Seldom if ever did someone say, "I told you so." They just basked in the moment and seemed amused that they helped.

One day the task at hand for the day was to install a gravity flow pipeline to be used for livestock. This waterline would be buried, and it would be a couple of miles long. The plan was to rip the pipeline using a D7 dozer while at the same time laying plastic pipe that came in five-hundred-foot rolls. A guy from Payson had made an attachment for a dozer that would feed the pipe off a spool and down the back of a ripper tooth through a curved pipe. This allowed you to lay the pipe and rip the line at the same time. It was really a slick deal. After the pipe was ripped in, a road grader covered it up and dressed up the mess the dozer had made, and then the person made cutouts to prevent water from running down the new line.

The water pipeline was for one of the ranches that had the grazing permit in the area, and while the dozer was a government one, the rest of the equipment plus the two guys helping me with the pipe and the one guy driving the road blade were from the ranch. I had known the folks from the ranch for most of my life, and I was looking forward to a productive day working my friends.

The two guys from the ranch who were assigned to help me with the pipe and I were the first to arrive that morning. We said our hellos and fired up the dozer and started getting things ready. The attachment consisted of a huge spool probably five to six feet in diameter to hold the five-hundred-foot rolls of plastic pipe and a huge ripper tooth with an attachment off the back to feed the pipe through. Both these deals attached to a tool bar on the back of the dozer. The tool bar on the dozer could be raised and lowered with hydraulics. The spool went on without a hitch, and then progress stopped. We could not get the ripper tooth into the tool bar on the dozer, and this turned into quite a mess.

We had to stand up the ripper tooth, which was huge, and stick it into the tool bar. It took all three of us just to stand it up and two of us to hold it while we tried again and again to get the darn thing stuck into the hole on the tool bar of the dozer. The problem was that I could only raise the tool bar on the dozer so high, but that was not enough to slide the ripper tooth through the tool bar. Progress was halted as we tried to think of what we could do to get it attached so that we could get started. This went on for about an hour and a half.

The other guy from the ranch was driving the road blade up from the lower country. He was father to one of the dummies on the scene with me. He had been the foreman on this ranch for decades, and he is one of the finest men I have ever met. As stated before, he was one of the guys who knew how to get stuff done.

When he arrived at the dozer, I'm sure he was thinking, *What the hell? What is the problem, and why aren't these guys working?* He didn't know that we had been mentally taxed, trying to stab the ripper tooth in the tool bar for the last hour and a half. He stopped the blade, got out, walked over, and ask what was going on. We explained that getting the ripper tooth stuck up in the tool bar was slightly more complicated than solving the Rubik's Cube. He looked at it for between five and ten seconds and said, "Why don't you push up a little berm of dirt and back the dozer up on it so the tool bar will be high enough?"

You would have to have been there to experience the humbling effect this had on the three of us. No wonder the older generation thinks we are a bunch of dummies. They're right! Well, after ensuring we were online, he got back on the blade and let us start laying some pipe. He never did bring it up and tell us were a band of idiots. He didn't need to.

I was assigned to a fire up on the Arizona Strip. The Arizona Strip is the land that is generally north of the Grand Canyon in the northwest corner of Arizona wedged against Nevada and Utah. I was a crew liaison officer for one of the Southwest's Navajo fire crews. The crew came from Rock Point Trading Post and consisted of twenty men who were always transported by the old blue and white school bus. This was same bus they used most of the time whenever the crew went out, and it was always suffering from mechanical issues.

The Arizona Strip is isolated from the rest of Arizona by the Grand Canyon. While some of the Arizona Strip may be inviting, much of it is in the Mojave Desert, and this was the portion we were headed for. The fire was just north of Lake Mead, and the route to the fire led us through Mesquite, Nevada. If you have ever been there in the summer, you know that it gets hotter than a firecracker there. So too, the strip is one of the least traveled areas around the country. It is a vast and lonely place. Our directions to the fire from Mesquite consisted of the following: "Turn on the gravel road, and follow it for about thirty miles. You will hit a junction. Turn right, and stay on that road for about fifty miles. You will hit another junction. Take another right, and the fire is only around twenty more miles. You'll see the smoke."

Several hours into our drive, the bus broke down. I was not very surprised as it had happened before a few times. Now we were sitting out there on the Mojave Desert on a fine July afternoon, no shade to the horizon, basking in the scorching heat. We tried everything we knew to do to get the bus going, but we were failing horribly. Nothing we did mattered. Everything was unsuccessful. We had no communications with the outside world. We had no radios, and this was before cell phones were a thing. However, I would be quite surprised if there was any cell service out where we were then. We were running out of water, and clearly, we were in quite a pickle. The tracks on the road looked like there hadn't been anyone on it for a few weeks or so. Hopefully, someone on the fire would notice in a few days that we hadn't shown up and would send out a search party.

Then off in the distance, we saw a little dust cloud. Someone was actually on the road, and through the heat waves, it looked like they were headed our way. It was probably someone from the fire. Now our rescue was looking good. The vehicle that pulled up was a beat-up old jeep. Inside was a very old and weathered cowboy guy. He stopped and asked if everything was all right. We explained that we had broken down and that we were at our wit's end trying to figure out what was wrong. It was hot, and we're running out of water. We couldn't call anyone either. He just sat there, staring at me, and then he asked if we had any water. I told him that we had a little left but that we were on the verge of rationing it so that we all wouldn't die. "I don't need much," he said. So we grabbed a canteen and gave it to the old guy. He climbed up on the hood and poured a little water on the fuel pump and hollered at the driver to give it a try. The bus rumbled to life like it just came off the assembly line. The old cowboy guy gave us a wry smile and informed us the bus had vapor locked and to save a little water in case it happened again. We thanked him, and he headed on his way. We continued to the fire without another issue.

One of my buddies and I took a fire assignment to Nevada. We were flown to Winnemucca, Nevada, and given a ride from the airport to the Bureau of Land Management offices. When we checked in, we were informed that they had suffered a large lightning storm the day before and that it had ignited several fires in the area that they were in charge of. The area that the BLM offices oversee is a huge area, and fires had started all over the place, many of which didn't have a soul on them. This was several years ago, before the days of programmable radios. It fell upon the local unit to provide you with a radio that really only had two channels that were programed to the local frequencies. Today everyone takes a programmable radio and punches in whatever frequencies the team on the fire is using. We also didn't have many vehicles as rental vehicles were not used much if at all on fires in those days. The place was very busy, but because we had no radios and no vehicles, we were just standing around, waiting for an assignment.

Finally, a guy approached us and told us he had a vehicle with a radio. He wanted us to go and check on a new start that was seen by an airplane about fifty miles northeast of Winnemucca. We loaded our stuff into the truck and took off with a small map of the general area.

Nevada—at least in this area—is huge country, mile upon mile of sagebrush and ridges to the horizon. The population density is very low, and most of the rural residents are cattlemen, sheepherders, or miners. To say that the federal government is not well thought of may be an understatement. We were unaware of any issues. We were just two guys from Arizona up here to help with the fires. Most of the folks we dealt with at home didn't bring up their issues with the government, and in general, we all got along great.

We could see the fire that we were headed to from quite a ways off, but we were having difficulty finding a road that came somewhat close to it. Finally, we got on the right road and drove up to the fire. It wasn't very windy, and the fire was pretty active but not running very hard. It looked like it was about a thousand acres and burning in sagebrush and cheat grass. As we drove up, so did a crusty old man in an ancient road grader He didn't stop to say anything. He just came by us, lowered his blade, and started digging a fire line around the fire. The land was pretty flat and not too rocky, and this old guy was actively engaged and hauling ass on his old blade.

He was really getting after it. He stayed as close as he could to the fire but left a small strip of unburned sagebrush between his line and the edge of the fire. We dug through the toolbox of the truck we were in and found a case of fusees, so we were off to the races. The old dude was just hauling ass and punching a line with the blade, and the two of us were burning out the edge. His line was good enough to drive on.

When it came to the firing, one of us sat on the tailgate burning while the other drove the truck down the line. Maybe we weren't following the best safety practices in our tactics, but it was effective. In a few hours we had gone around the head of the fire and stopped the forward progress. What was left would be a cakewalk to finish up.

This was one of the times when everything came together and we kicked ass on this fire. My buddy and I were having the time of our lives, hardly breaking a sweat. When they heard about this back in Winnemucca, we would be heroes. That was about to come to an end.

The old guy on the blade stopped and climbed off and waved us forward. He didn't seem to have the same feeling of success we did, and he was kind of pissed off. He walked up to us and said, "This is the first time I've seen any of you sons of bitches do anything." We thanked him for lining the fire and told him that he really did a great job. He said, "This is the first time any of you sons of bitches ever said thank you." In an effort to not let this guy rain on our parade, we tried to change the subject. We told him that maybe he could get paid for using his blade to help stop the fire. This got his attention, and he asked what office we worked in. We told him we were from Arizona and didn't work around here. He said, "I figured that. The only time I see any of these sons of bitches they just come out and tell me what I can't do."

We visited a while, and I think he kind of liked us. After a few minutes, he asked if he could use the radio in the truck to call in. We were young and stupid, but we said, "Sure. Go ahead. You can use the radio." So he got on the radio and said, "Winnemucca? Winnemucca? You sons of bitches, answer your goddamn radio." We about shit and told him that wasn't the protocol used on radios. He just stared at us and repeated, "Winnemucca? Winnemucca? You sons of bitches, answer your goddamn radio." We were trying to wrestle the radio from him when Winnemucca answered, "Unit using profanity on the radio, please identify yourself." We tried to signal the old guy to shut up, but he told them who he was and informed them that he was with two boys from Arizona. After this transmission he gave me the radio and stomped off in disgust. I got on the radio and apologized for the outburst, and I was ordered to return to the office immediately.

We knew we were in deep shit, so we retraced our steps across the vastness of Nevada and returned to Winnemucca, but at a slower rate than we had used heading to the fire. Upon our arrival, we got a pretty good chewing-out, and we were told that they were going to send us home because of the infraction. We were instructed to go outside and await transportation to the airport.

We were sitting out front of the office, waiting for instruction about how and when they were going to send us home. Then out of the office came the old blade guy. He had followed our advice and attempted to get paid for using his blade on the fire. He had failed in his effort, and they weren't going to pay him anything, which didn't help his attitude toward the local BLM office. He asked what we were up to, and we told him we were in trouble and being sent home. He said that if he had anything to do with it, he was sorry and told us "They don't want anyone up here that works because it makes the rest of the sons of bitches look bad."

A family on summer vacation had stopped in the BLM office for information. The family consisted of a man, his wife, and two little girls, probably four and six years old. As they approached the office, they must have thought we worked there. They informed us they were on vacation from Vermont, and they were wondering where they could go look for arrowheads. The old blade guy looked at them for a minute and said, "Arrowheads, arrowheads. If you would have been here a hundred years ago, you would be picking them out of your ass." The old guy's pronunciation of arrowheads sounded more like "airheads." We both thought that was funny. So did the blade guy. But the husband and father didn't, and he went inside and finished cooking our goose for good measure.

A good ass-chewing cuts deeper if you're guilty, and while we got another one, we really didn't feel we'd done much wrong. We knew we needed to pick our friends better, but this old dude was one hell of a blade operator, just one with a sailor's mouth.

There was a grazing permittee on the Coconino National Forest who was quite a remarkable man. He still ran the family ranch pretty much by himself well into his nineties. I considered him a friend, and I spent quite some time visiting with him about his long history in the area. He once told me he cowboyed through the war because he was too young to go. It occurred to me later that he was talking about World War I.

Another amazing thing about this gentleman was his ability to remember things. He could remember who married who and who did whatever for decades past. His long life in the area was recorded in his mind, and he often shared his memories for those who took the time to visit. The area of the Coconino National Forest was subjected to a spectacular ponderosa pine seed crop along with stellar growing conditions in the years 1918 and 1919. This resulted in a crop of ponderosas that we have been thinning, burning, and cussing ever since. I asked the rancher one afternoon when if at all he remembered seeing any wolves. He said that there were wolves when he was as kid, and then he tried to remember the last time he'd seen one. He couldn't come up with a date, but he said it was when all the trees were "this high." Then he drew a line halfway between his knee and boot. There are only few folks around who can measure time by how much the trees have grown. I got a kick out of it.

He didn't have a huge grazing allotment. It consisted of about sixty head of cows and calves on a small allotment divided into three main pastures. One hot and breezy afternoon, a fire started on his allotment and quickly spread into the crowns of the trees and started moving around pretty good. There was a threat that it would burn up all his pastures that afternoon, and the fire even threatened the welfare of his cattle.

He showed up on the fire, and while I was leading a dozer around and trying to catch the fire, he tied in with the incident commander. He was pretty worked up and concerned that we weren't doing enough. He gave the incident commander hell, as things were not looking so good. The incident commander knew that I got along well with him and that I had also administered the grazing permit that he had, so he called me on the radio and asked if I could come over and attempt to calm him down.

I went to their location, and when I got there, he was already pretty worked up about what was going on. When he saw me, his face lightened up, and he immediately quit talking with the incident commander and walked over to me. He was concerned, but after I talked with him and assured him that all his cattle were all right, he started calming down. He was also concerned about where he could graze his cattle for the remainder of the summer because the fire was burning up all the grass at a pretty good clip. He would be forced to move them in the next few days, and he didn't have anywhere to put them.

I told him that I would head into town and talk it over with the district ranger and decide what options we had to relocate his cattle for the remainder of the summer. I also agreed to come out to his ranch really early the next morning to let him know what they had decided. He wanted to get an early start moving his cattle, which was the norm, and I didn't want to inconvenience him any more than the fire already had. I left the fire and went into town to meet with the district ranger so that we could decide and get approval on what to do about the problem. We made a decision that day, so I woke up early the next morning and headed out to his ranch to let him know what was going to happen.

Now, I need to discuss the hanta virus. Northern Arizona had just determined that the hanta virus had caused many deaths in the region. Like almost everyone else, I had never heard of the hanta virus. But it had been on the news a lot lately because doctors had determined that it was the cause of many deaths and sicknesses across Northern Arizona. The virus was spread by the deer mouse and was impacting many people who lived in rural environments and shared their houses with these cute little animals. Further studies had determined that it was spread because deer mice were urinating on stuff. These cute little critters would pee on a food item in order to prevent other deer mice from packing it off for their own use. Officials also cautioned people to avoid their droppings, as that could also serve as a vehicle for the virus.

So I knew where we could move this man's cows, but I had a limited knowledge about the upstart virus impacting Northern Arizona. In any case, I headed out to the ranch. I got there about five in the morning and went up to the ranch house. The rancher had been born in this house around 1905, so it was an old house. He was waiting for me when I arrived, and he was very happy to see me. He was all dressed, with the exception of his house slippers, which he still had on. When I went inside, being the hospitable man he was, he immediately offered me a cup of coffee.

I am not a good housekeeper and have no room at all to talk trash, but neither was the rancher. The counter by the sink had a few days of dishes piled up, and quite a few mouse turds were lying around. But I had said I would have a cup before I had looked around much. He picked up a dirty coffee cup, spit in it, rubbed it out with his shirttail, and poured me a cup of joe. There was no way I was going to drink the coffee, but he acted like there was no problem. He said he needed to put his boots on, so he went into the bedroom to do that. As soon as he left, I poured out the coffee. He came in, ready to go to work. He immediately saw my empty cup and offered me another, but I dodged this offer by saying that I knew he wanted to get an early start on the day. I paid more attention to the news the next few days, hoping to hear that a hanta vaccine had been developed, but I never heard about one.

The same gentleman came into the district office to discuss something one afternoon. He talked really loudly, probably because his ninety-year-old ears were giving out, and the receptionists always wanted me to grab him and quickly take him back to my office. The receptionist called me on the phone one day and told me he was up in the reception area and asked if I would come get him. Of course, I headed up to the front desk.

The reception area at the front desk was pretty busy that day, full of people looking for hiking trails or complaining or whatever they were doing. As I walked up, my old buddy said in a rather loud voice, "Look at that lady. She ain't wearing a brazier." I immediately tried to downplay his words and whisk him away, but he said, "Hell, she doesn't care. If she did, she would be wearing a brazier." Of course, I looked at the lady and then at the receptionists. Everyone had a red face, and I knew I needed to get him back to my office quickly. After he left that day, I got a good talking-to by the ladies at the front desk. They instructed me to come up and get him much quicker next time to avoid embarrassing the visitors when he came in. I don't think they said anything to the lady without a brazier.

Another friend of mine who was a rancher and a novelist had some publisher folks out to his ranch from New York City to discuss publishing his new novel. There is a huge difference between Northern Arizona ranch life and New York City. The publishers were definitely city dwellers and were quite critical about the isolation of the place and the rustic accommodations it offered. They were way out of their element, and they had never been in such a remote location. The whole basis for their trip was to get his book published, so even with their highbrow behavior, everyone was nice and hospitable.

The rancher's wife was a wonderful lady and an excellent housekeeper and cook. She had actually performed on Broadway in her younger years. She ran her house with proper manners and no cussing, and she was the model of a proper and well-educated woman.

Every week when the television show *Little House on the Prairie* came on, no one was allowed to even talk until the program was over. She had dealt with city folks more than my buddy had, and she was holding things together rather well.

The visit from the publishers ended with a great dinner that his wife had prepared. The disapproval and highbrow activities continued through dinner, and finally, it got the best of my friend. Like anyone, he was ready and willing to defend his loving wife, but he knew he couldn't cuss them out. After all, his wife didn't allow such behavior in her house. As they finished dinner and while they were still all seated, he calmly cleared the table of all their dishes. He placed all the dinner plates on the floor and let his dog lick them all clean. Then he calmly stacked them up and put them back into the cupboard, acting like it was an everyday occurrence. They went back to New York City after that, and that dog cleaning the dishes was the last thing they remembered. This got him in some serious trouble with his wife, but he thought the trick was well worth it. I think it was a great joke, and I will do the same thing if the opportunity ever presented itself.

I had a friend who was also raised on a ranch and fancied himself quite a trickster. This was a fun-loving guy, but he had a devilish streak, as he was always ready to pull a prank on people who let their guard down. One day I was lamenting about how it must have been tough raising him, and he informed me that he had knowledge of some of his dad's major screwups and that should cut him some slack. I asked for an example, and he told me that when his dad was a kid out on the ranch, he caught a toad and rubbed some rubber cement on it and then set it on fire. This immediately caught my attention. I had also played with rubber cement and fire as a child. He informed me that when his dad set the rubber cement on fire, the toad hopped under the barn and burned it to the ground.

With this I will end my stories of my involvement and my experiences both with the forest service and fighting wildfires. I feel that I have forgotten more stories than are captured in this book, and since this writing I have recalled other stories. I guess it is a product of getting old that you just can't remember everything that has happened. I hope I have captured some interesting stories and have entertained those that took the time to read my book. I also hope that in reading these stories that I have planted a seed to make somebody decide to get involved in wildland fire suppression. It has provided me with great friendships, exposed me to many of our nations beautiful places, and a sense that I have helped both people and our forested lands.

Lightning Source UK Ltd.
Milton Keynes UK
UKHW011533011020
370854UK00001B/218